द्राम् – *Drām*

Śrī Dattātreya Sahasranāma Bhāşyam

*

Kamalātmānanda Nāthaḥ @ **Dr. Ramamurthy N.**

M.Sc., B.G.L., CAIIB, CCP, DSADP, CISA, PMP, CGBL, Ph.D.

*

*

Name: *Śrī Dattātreya Sahasranāma Bhāṣyam*

First Edition: 2025

Author: *Kamalātmānanda Nāthaḥ* @
Dr. Ramamurthy N,
http://ramamurthy.jaagruti.co.in/

ISBN (13): 978-93-343-9565-5

Number of pages: 309

Price: ₹ 400.00

Printed at:

Published by:

*****

Table of Contents

*****

Dedication

Oṃ Dattātreya Hare Kṛṣṇa Unmattānanda Dāyakā |
Digaṃbara Mune Bāla Piśāca Jñāna Sāgara ॥

ॐ दत्तात्रेय हरे कृष्ण उन्मत्तानन्ददायका |
दिगंबर मुने बाल पिशाच ज्ञानसागर॥

This book is dedicated with devotion to all Swamijis who follow the *Avadhoota* Sanyasa system known as *Turiyatītam*. Especially to my *Srividya Guru, Parama Pūjya Paramahamsa Parivrājakāccārya Śrī Śrī Śrīmad Swāmiji Praṇavāṇunda Brahmēndra Sarasvati Avadhūta Yati Varēṇya Mahāsvāmi* and to that lineage of Gurus. There is no doubt that they will bestow their blessings upon all of us.

Kamalātmānanda Nāthaḥ @ Dr. Ramamurthy N

Parāpara Guru
Śrī Śrī Judge Swamiji

Parameṣṭi Guru
Śrī Śrī Swayamprakashananda Swamiji

Parama Guru
Śrī Śrī Śāntānanda Swamiji

Guru
Śrī Śrī Pranavānunda Swamiji

*****

உ

ப்ரஹ்மைவ ஸத்யம்

SRI SWAYAMPRAKASA AVADHUTHA SADASIVA TRUST

Sri Sri Judge Swamigal Adhishtanam, East 7th Street,
PUDUKKOTTAI-622 001
Phone: 04322-221440, 222128
Email: sribhuvaneshwari@gmail.com

Śrī Mukham

Āṉandam Śupam Maṅgaḷam I *Jay Buvaṉēśvari* I

Śrī Buvaṉēśvari Pīṭam,
2025

Śrī Praṇavānanta Svāmiṉaḥ
Pudukkottai

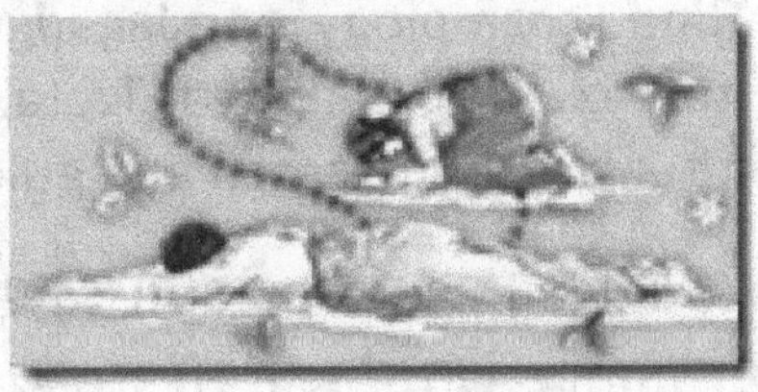

*****

Introduction

Oṃ Śrī Gurubhyo Namaḥ ॥ ॐ श्री गुरुभ्यो नमः ॥

Oṃ Āṃ Hrīṃ Kroṃ Ehi Dattātreya Svāhā ॥

ॐ आं ह्रीं क्रों एहि दत्तात्रेय स्वाहा ॥

The force of *Parabrahmam*, without any image, qualities and undefined, which includes a number of morphological, incomprehensible and inexhaustible materials, seems to be limited. The absolute philosophical paradigm is not amorphous.

However, we are not yet mature enough to realise the formless *Parabrahmam* (no need of writing/ reading this book, if we are that much mature). Someone has to hold back or attach side wheels until one learns to drive a bicycle. Once he becomes expert these are not needed. We need a boat to cross a river. Once we have reached the other shore, what is the need of a boat.

Therefore, until we mature, we will try to learn about a God.

In Hindu cosmology, one Jagadguru is born and associated with each of the four *yugas* (Satya, Treta, Dvapara, and Kali) as a prominent spiritual leader to teach and guide us in a proper path;

ॐ कृते तु भगवान् सत्यः, त्रेतायां दत्त एव च,
द्वापरे भगवान् व्यासः, कलौ श्री शङ्कर स्वयम् ।

Oṃ Kṛtetu Bhagavān Satyaḥ, Tretāyāṃ Datta Eva Ca,
Dvāpare Bhagavān Vyāsaḥ, Kalau Śrī Śaṅkara Svayam ।

1. Lord Satyadev (Lord Brahma or Dakshina Murthi) for Satya Yuga
2. Lord Dattatreya for Treta Yuga,
3. Veda Vyasa for Dvapara Yuga, and
4. Adi Shankaracharya for Kali Yuga.

- Satya Yuga – This is also called as Kruta Yuga – This is the golden age, characterized by truth and righteousness. The associated Jagadguru is Lord Satyadev, representing the embodiment of divine knowledge and wisdom. Lord Brahma or Dakshina Murthy is called Satyadev.

Krutayuga Jagadguru Sri Satyadev	Tretayuga Jagadguru Sri Dattatreyar

Dvapara Yuga Jagadguru Sri Veda Vyasa	Kaliyuga Jagadguru Sri Adi Shanara

- Treta Yuga – This yuga is marked by a decline in spiritual purity compared to Satya Yuga. The Jagadguru is Lord Dattatreya, known for his role in guiding humanity towards spiritual progress.
- Dvapara Yuga – This is the age of duality and conflict, where dharma (righteousness) is fading. The Jagadguru is Veda Vyasa, who is credited with compiling all the Vedas and writing other important scriptures.

- Kali Yuga – This is the current age, characterized by decline and materialism. The Jagadguru is Adi Shankaracharya, whose teachings and philosophy are seen as a guide for spiritual seekers in this era.

Śrī Ādi Śaṅkara Bhagwat Pādar, the greatest philosopher and thinker, in a short life span of 32 years, has created a collection of art-essays of Indian culture and the intellectual and emotional integration of this sub-continent.

The supreme beauty of his teachings is that they apply to all human beings irrespective of religion or race, caste or creed or nationality. That is why he is undoubtedly *'Jagadguru'*.

The four ashramas, or stages of life in Hinduism, are *Brahmacharya* (student), *Grihastha* (house holder), *Vanaprastha* (forest dweller/ hermit) and *Sannyasa* (renunciate).

- Brahmacarya (Student Stage) – This stage focuses on learning and spiritual discipline, often involving celibacy and studying under a guru.
- Gruhastha (Householder Stage) – This stage is characterised by establishing a family, pursuing a livelihood and fulfilling societal duties. It is the moral duty of Grihastha's to feed the Brahmacaries and Sannyasins.
- Vanaprastha (Hermit Stage) – As individuals age, they transition to this stage, often involving a move to the forest or a more secluded life, focusing on spiritual contemplation and detachment from worldly affairs.
- Sannyasa (Renunciate Stage) – In this final stage, individuals renounce worldly attachments and dedicate themselves entirely to spiritual pursuits and seeking liberation (moksha).

These general divisions are represented by various subdivisions, different philosophies, philosophical schools and traditions. The philosophy is a necessity as far as the Bharat Sanatana Dharma is concerned. For others, it is an entertainment (philosophy is a pastime).

Within the above Sannyasa Ashram[1], there are four stages or kinds *Kuţīcaka, Bahūdaka, Haṃsa* and *Parama-Haṃsa*.

Above all these, there is one highest level called *Turīyātītam* or *Avadhūtam* to attain *Aatmānubhava* (Soul Experience). Such type of Sanyasis renunciate even their clothes and move as *Digambaras*. The foremost (Adi Guru) among such Sanyasis is Sri Dattatreya.

One book was written about Sri Dattatreya alongwith yantra, various stotras, etc. Earlier the Bhashyam by Sri Bhaskararaya on Sri *Lalitā Sahasranāma* was translated into English. Then Bhashyam on Sri Gayatri *Sahasranāma* and Sri Sūrya *Sahasranāma* were written English and Tamil. There were requests by close friends to write Bhashyam on Sri Dattatreya *Sahasranāma* and hence this attempt. Wherever possible comparisons have been provided from Lalitā, Śiva, Vishnu, Gayatri *Sahasranāmam*s and other Vedas.

Writing meanings and comments for Samskruta verses is not an easy task. The meaning and beauty of the source should not be fragmented but the clarity of the words should captivate the mind of the readers. The readers should dissolve and melt in the mind of the author of the source. The comments should be written in such a way that the readers can enjoy the sweet juice in it.

Conventions – Wherever **She** is used, it indicates *Sri Devi.* The transliterated Samskrutam or other language words are written in *italics*. When Samskruta words are transliterated in English diacritical marks are used for proper pronunciation like;

ā – as in Rama *ḍ* – as in mud
ḍh – as in godhood *ḥ* – visarga in as in *Rāmaḥ*
ī – as in peel *ṇ* – as in pun
ṛ – as in strewn *ś* – as in Shankar
ş – as in fish *ţ* – as in cut
ţh – as in anthill *ū* – as in root

Humble pranams to HH *ŚrīŚrī* ***Pranavānanda Swamiji***, who has blessed me and the readers with his nice introduction and some

[1] A separate book explaining the Hindu Sanyasa methods, stages, etc., has been written by the same author in English and Tamil.

pleasantries. I am fortunate to have association with people like ***Swamijis***, who are my *Gurus*. Sincere thanks are due to all who helped me in bringing this book so nicely. It is only because of the blessings of such gurus that I am able to continue my efforts to write books. It is because of their kindness that this 109th book has been written. I pray at the feet of the gurus to continue such efforts.

Appreciation and acknowledgements are due to all those who supported in this noble cause. The readers are requested to feel free in providing feedback. Let all the readers be blessed with glory of Gods.

With the splendid blessings of our forefathers, priests and Sri Devi, this 109th book has been completed. My humble salutations to all of them. May their blessings continue.

This book is also being written by the same author in Tamil simultaneously.

Om Tat Sat

Chennai
2025 **Dr. *Ramamurthy N***

*****

Śrī Dattatreya – 1,000 Divine Names

This *Sahasranāma* Stotram on *Shrimad Dattātreya* is from Brahmanda Puranam as a dialogue between Sage Narada and Sages Sanat kumaras. One Thousand divine names on *Shrimad Dattātreya* have been culminated from 142 shlokas of this Stotram, which are given in the next chapter.

There is one other *Sahasranāma* on *Śrī Dattātreya* written by *Śrī Parama Pūjya Paramahaṃsa Parivrājakācārya Śrī Śrī Paramahamsa Shrimad Vāsudevānanda Sarasvati Yati Vareṇya* Swamiji. The beauty of this *Sahasranāma* is that all the 1,000 names start only with the letter *'D'* and its family. Hence, it is called as *Dakārādi Datta Sahasranāmam*. Since the *Sahasranāma* given below is an older one from a Purana, it has been followed by most and we also.

Let us try to understand the inner meanings of the 1,000 divine names so that the fruits will be multifold when used in pujas. These divine names on *Dattatreya Deva* culminated from 142 shlokas of *Śrī Dattātreya Sahasranāma Stotram* given in another chapter;

1. *Śrī Dattātreyāya* – श्री दत्तात्रेयाय ।

One who has been offered to Atri (sage).

Datta = to give. *Atreyāya* = to Atri. Trimurtis offered themselves to Sage Atri and *Dattātreyāya*.

Shrimad Bhagavatam (1.3.11) says Lord Vishnu had his sixth incarnation[2] as Dattatreya to the sage Atri and his wife Anasuya. He is considered as a partial representation of Lord Vishnu and a combined form of the trinity Gods, Brahma, Vishnu, and Shiva. Dattatreya is said to have descended to Earth on the Purnima (Full Moon) day in the Margashirsha month (December-January) of the Hindu calendar. That day every year is celebrated as Dattatreya Jayanthi by all.

---

[2] Normally we are aware of 10 main incarnations of Lord Vishnu. But Bhagavatam describes 24 incarnations of Lord Vishnu.

2. *Mahāyogine* – महायोगिने ।

He is a great Yogi.

Yoga means union. It means one has breached the boundaries of the physical. A Yogi is a practitioner of Yoga, including a sannyasi or practitioner of meditation. To be a Yogi means to live without the coffins that people build around themselves. The feminine form, of Yogi is Yogini. Dattatreya is a great Yogi.

When the word 'Maha' is prefixed with any other name, it makes it very great. For instance, Prabandhak means Manager and Maha Prabandhak means General Manager. That is the word 'Maha' indicates.

The *yoga* bestowed by him is the route to reach him.

Yoga is the assumption of union. Since he is in that form and since he bestows that to the devotees, he is in the form known by the same.

Yoga has four parts – *Mantra, Laya, Hata* and *Rāja*. *Rājayoga* has three parts – *Sānkya, Tāraka* and *Amanska*. These details are to be learnt from *Yoga sastras* from an appropriate guru.

Similarly in Astronomy also there are *devatas* starting from *Mangala* till *Sankata*. Since he is in all these forms, he is *Yogi*.

In *Śiva Sahasranāmam* – 79th and 782nd names – *Yogiḥ* – He in a great Yogi.

In *Sūrya Sahasranāmam* – 33rd name and in *Viṣṇu Sahasranāmam* – 849th name – *Yogine* – He is a Yogi.

In *Sri Lalitā Sahasranāmam* – 653rd name – *Yoginī* – One who can be reached through *Yoga*.

Again, in *Sri Lalitā Sahasranāmam* – 654th name – *Yogadā* – She is the bestower of *Yoga* to her devotees.

It is said that there are a total of 64 crore Yogini deities and that Sri *Lalitā Sahasranāmam* was composed by the Yogini deities on the orders of Sri *Lalitā* Devi.

645th name below may also be referred.

3. *Yogeśāya* – योगेशाय |

He is the lord of all the Yogis.

The definition of Yogi is mentioned in the above 2nd name. He is the Lord of all such Yogis including Yoginis.

4. *Amara Prabhave* – अमर प्रभवे |

He is the lord of all the Devas.

Amara = not dying = Devas, since they drank Amrut they will not die. He is the lord of all such Devas.

In *Viṣṇu Sahasranāmam* – 49th name – *Amara Prabhuḥ* – he is the Lord of immortals.

5. *Munaye* – मुनये |

He is a great Muni.

Muni is a sage, ascetic, or monk known for their spiritual wisdom and practices, particularly silence and contemplation. They are individuals who have renounced worldly attachments and dedicated themselves to spiritual realization through practices like penance (tapas) and meditation. For example – Valmiki Muni, Vyasa Muni and so on.

He is in-charge of Ursa Major. Ursa Major, also known as the Great Bear, is a constellation in the northern sky that includes the Big Dipper asterism. It is the third largest constellation in the sky and the largest in the Northern Hemisphere.

In *Śiva Sahasranāmam* – 320th name – *Muniḥ* and 495th name – *Mahāmuniḥ* – He himself is a Muni. He is a very great sage who is silent and devout.

In *Sri Lalitā Sahasranāmam* – 816th name – *Munimānasa Hamsikā* – She swims like a swan in the rivulets of minds of the saints.

In *Sūrya Sahasranāmam* – 774th name – *Munaye* – He is a Muni.

491st name below may also be referred.

6. *Digambarāya* – दिगम्बराय |

He moves in a sky-clad manner.

He is a naked mendicant.

Fifteenth incarnation of Sri Dattatreya is Sri Digambarar. In this incarnation he established *vairagya.*

7. *Bālāya* – बालाय |

He is seen as a boy.

8. *Māyā Muktāya* – माया मुक्ताय |

He is free from illusion and hence he frees his devotees from illusion.

Unless the darkness called illusion from the mind is removed, the knowledge cannot be obtained.

One of the 16 main incarnations of Sri Dattatreya is *Maya Mukta Avadhootar*. This incarnation was taken just to free his devotees from illusion.

The energy which obscures, what is plain, is *maya* or illusion. Or to make plain what is not available. Both these are the acts of *maya*. In addition, the acts of dream or supernatural powers are all due to *maya*.

- The *Devi Purana* says, "It is called *maya* because it is the instrument of marvelous actions, producing unheard of results, like dreams or jugglery".
- In *Shrimad Bhagavad Geeta* (VII-14) also it is mentioned that the divine illusion is made up of qualities, is hard to surmount; but those who take refuge in *Sri Krishna* alone, can cross over it.

- The *Shandilya Sutra* (86) says, "His (the Lord's) energy is *maya*".
- The power of *maya* has been explained in *Saptashatee* also.
- *Sri Muthuswami Deekshatar* also has sung addressing *Sri Devi* as '*Māye*'.
- The *Shakta Pranava*, also called as *Bhuvaneswari Beeja* or *Hrīm*, is called as *Māyā Beeja*. **She** is in that form.
- In the *Mahāshoḍa Nyāsa*, illusion is being appropriated in three places – in *Prapancha Nyāsa* as *Dvīparūpā* and *Guhārūpa* and in *Devata Nyāsa* as *Sahasra Koṭigaṇeshwara Kulasevita*. **She** is in these forms.
- It is being reiterated here that the secret initiations have to done only through appropriate teachers. Only with the advice of the teacher the illusion is to be reached (according the *Shakta* method) and the illusion is to be crossed (according to non-duality philosophy).
- According to the non-duality advised by *Sri Adi Shankara*, only when the illusion is removed the knowledge of *Brahmam* can be obtained. According to *Sri Vidya* practice illusion is the energy (*shakti*) of *Brahmam* only.
- *Sree Kanchi Kamakoti Paramacharya*'s talk in this regard is (The book – Voice of God, 6th Volume) - The question, that why and how the illusion happened, does not arise according to non-duality principle. *Shakta Sastra* says that *Chit Shakti* only plays a game by reflecting the illusion in many forms. The soul, in the as is form – having the senses as tools, has to unite with the eternal *Brahmam*.
- The combined form of *Ichā*, *Gnāna* and *Kriyā shaktis* is called illusion. Further details in this regard may be seen in the explanation given in *Soota Samhita*.
- 716th name of Sri *Lalitā Sahasranāma* is also the same *Māyā*.
- 170th and 302nd names of Sri Vishnu *Sahasranāma* – *Mahāmāya* and *Naikamāyaḥ* – he is the Maya and he creates various Mayas.
- Many Puranas, Sri *Lalitā Sahasranāmam*, Shrimad Bhagavat Gita, Sri Devi Bhagavatam, Sri Vishnu Bhagavatam, Saptashatee and all talk in detail about illusion.

The *Brahmam* only seems as soul due to illusion. The non-duality principle says that, if the illusion is removed through knowledge, then the soul will become the *Brahmam*. Basically, the soul and *Shiva* are one and the same. Again, it is same at the end of salvation also. This has been clearly accepted in *Shakta* more particularly in *Sri Vidya Tantra*. The difference between the two is the creative duality. No difference about salvation. It has to be simply ignored that it is only illusion which seem to be dual. *Shakta* says that *Sri Devi* created it. All this duality enters into that *Sri Devi* and **She** plays a game. This illusion can be overcome by worshipping and praying to **Her**. Overcome this illusion and merge with the root cause. Again, merge with that *Brahmam*, wherein this root cause itself has merged, as a single entity.

In *Sri Gāyatri Sahasranāmam* – 773rd name – *Māyāyai* – One who is in the form of illusion.

9. *Madā Pahāya* – मदा पहाय |

He is the destroyer of arrogance.

Madam (arrogance) is one of the six internal negative qualities. He removes it for his devotees.

The fundamental six enemies of the mind are – Lust (*Kama*), Anger (*Krodha*), Greed (*Lobha*), Want/ desire (*Moha*), Ego (*Mada*) and Envy or Jealousy (*Matsarya*).

The above 9 names were taken from the 1st shloka of the *Sahasranāma* Stotram.

10. *Avadhūtāya* – अवधूताय |

He is free himself from worldly feelings and obligations.

The term Avadhoota refers to a realised soul who has transcended worldly attachments and lives beyond the limitations of the body and mind.

Colloquially, *Avadhūtā* is meant to indicate naked sanyasi. But real meaning is renunciant.

There is one text called Avadhoota Gita attributed to the Lord Dattatreya, considered a profound treatise on Advaita Vedanta, the philosophy of non-duality (Advaita), expressing the experience of Brahman, the ultimate reality.

In spirituality, in general, Dattatreya is revered as an Avadhoota sanyasi and while he is known to have many incarnations, the 16 most significant are considered the "*Shodasha Avatars*".

11. *Mahā Nāthāya* – महा नाथाय ।

He is the great master/ leader.

About the prefix *Mahā* it has been discussed in one of the earlier names.

12. *Śaṅkarāya* – शङ्कराय ।

He arranges to give the pleasure including happiness and peace, to this world being.

In Raghuvamsa (1.10) Kalidasa, says that Parvati Parameshvara is in the form of mother and father *Pitarau* (parent) to this world.

Vāgarthāviva Sampruktau Vāgarthapratipattaye I
Jagataḥ Pitarau Vande Pārvatīparameśvarau II

Bhagavan Krishna, declares Himself to be "Among the *Rudras*, I am *Śaṅkara* – (*Gīta* X-23). According to *purāṇas* there are 11 *Rudras*; the fourth '*Rudra*' is called as *Śaṅkaraḥ – Sam Karoti Iti = Śaṅkaraḥ* – One who blesses all with Auspiciousness (*Sam*) is *Śaṅkara*.

Nagendrakanyāvṛṣaketanābhyām Namo Namaḥ Śaṅkara Pārvatībhyām II

I bow to Lord Shiva and Goddess Parvati (*Shivā*).

116th name below may also be referred.

13. *Amara Vallabhāya* – अमर वल्लभाय ।

He is beloved by all the Devas. He loves all the Devas.

In the 4th name above, it was mentioned as he is the head of all the Devas. Here it is mentioned as he is beloved by all the Devas.

14. *Mahā Devāya* – महा देवाय |

He is the greatest among the Devas.

Generally, the term *Mahā Deva* will denote Lord Shiva. Here it denotes Lord Dattatreya. This implies both are one and the same.

Among the 11 *Rudras*, the first *'Rudra'* is *Mahā Deva* Rudran.

In *Śiva Sahasranāmam* – 599th name – *Mahādevaḥ* – the greatest god.

In *Vişņu Sahasranāmam* – 491st name – *Mahādevaḥ* – the great Lord.

15. *Ādi Devāya* – आदि देवाय |

He is the primordial deity.

In *Vişņu Sahasranāmam* – 334th and 490th names – *Mahādevaḥ* – the first deity. He is the first through whom all the beings came to exist.

960th name below may also be referred.

16. *Purāņa Prabhave* – पुराण प्रभवे |

He is the ancient Lord. He transcends time.
He is the most ancient being. He is primordial.

He was there even before creation of all other beings. He only created all. Hence *Purātana*. It can be compared to the poem in Tamil – *Thiruvempavai* (9th song) by *Mānickavachagar*;

"Munnai Pazham Porutkum Pazham Porule".

Since he has ancient qualities, he is *Purātana*.

Lord Vishnu's incarnation as Dattatreya and his story, have been mentioned in Shrimad Vishnu Bhagavata Maha Purana (1.3.11). Hence, he is Purana Prabhu.

In *Viṣŋu Sahasranāmam* – 498th name – *Purātanaḥ* – He is the ancient.

In *Lalitā Sahasranāmam* – 802nd name – *Purātanā* – She is the ancient.

In *Sūrya Sahasranāmam* – 643rd name – *Purāṇa Puruṣottamā* – He is the greatest among those mentioned in Puranas.

17. *Īśvarāya* – ईश्वराय ।

He is the Supreme ruler.

He pervades in everything. He enjoys/ experiences everything.

In *Viṣŋu Sahasranāmam* – 74th name – *Īśvaraḥ* – He is omnipotent.

Usually, Lord Shiva is called as *Īśvara* and Sri Devi is called as *Īśvari*. But here Lord Dattatreya and Lord Vishnu are also called as *Īṣvara*. This clearly means that all the Gods are one and the same.

If Brahmam is Ishvara, then she who is in two aspects mixed with that Ishvara is Ishvari. Can flowers and fragrance be separated? Can milk and whiteness be separated? Saguna-Brahmam, itself is called Ishvara in Advaita texts. Five activities viz., the creation, preservation, destruction, annihilation and re-emergence of the universe by Brahma, Vishnu, Rudra, Ishvara and Paramasiva.

The above 8 names were taken from the 2nd shloka of the *Sahasranāma* Stotram.

18. *Sattva Kṛte* – सत्त्व कृते ।

He does good activities only. He generates goodness.

19. *Sattva Bhṛte* – सत्त्व भृते ।

He is the sustainer of truth.

20. *Bhāvāya* – भावाय ।

He exists always – he has no origin neither end as well.

He expands himself as the Universe or remains, he alone as pure existence.

In *Viṣṇu Sahasranāmam* – 7th name – *Bhāvaḥ* – He is the absolute existence.

In *Śiva Sahasranāmam* – 521st name – *Bhāvaḥ* – He absolutely exists. 32nd name below may also be referred.

21. *Sattvātmane* – सत्त्वात्मने ।

He is the essence of reality.

22. *Sattva Sāgarāya* – सत्त्व सागराय ।

He is the ocean of truth.

23. *Sattva Vide* – सत्त्व विदे ।

He is the knower of ultimate truth.

24. *Sattva Sākṣiṇe* – सत्त्व साक्षिणे ।

He is the witness of essences.

25. *Sattva Sādhyāya* – सत्त्व साध्याय ।

He propitiates the truth and truth alone.

26. *Amarādhipāya* – अमराधिपाय ।

He is the head of all Devas.

Since, Devas drank Amruta, they cannot dye and hence they are called Amaras. He is their lord or Adipati.

The above 9 names were taken from the 3rd shloka of the *Sahasranāma* Stotram.

27. *Bhūtakṛte* – भूतकृते ।

He is the creator of existence.

He creates all beings, assuming the quality of Rajas in the form of Brahma.

Kṛt also means to destroy – he destroys the beings in his Tamasa aspect in the form of Rudra.

20th name above can be compared here.

In *Vişŋu Sahasranāmam* – 5th name – *Bhūtakṛt* – He is the evolver of all beings.

28. *Bhūtabhṛte* – भूतभृते ।

He sustains all beings.

Bhṛt means support – he supports or protects all beings in his Satvika quality.

In *Vişŋu Sahasranāmam* – 6th name – *Bhūtabhṛt* – The sustainer of all beings.

29. *Bhūtātmane* – भूतात्मने ।

He is the atman inside all beings.

The Brahadaranyaka Upanishad (5.7.4) says – this is thy Self, the inner Ruler and immortal Being.

In *Vişŋu Sahasranāmam* – 8th name – *Bhūtātmā* – He is the self of all beings.

39th name below may also be referred.

30. *Bhūtasambhavāya* – भूतसम्भवाय ।

He is the existence of all beings.

31. *Bhūtabhavāya* – भूतभवाय ।

He supports/ nourishes all beings.

In *Vişŋu Sahasranāmam* – 9th name – *Bhūtabhāvanaḥ* – He generates or nourishes all beings.

32. *Bhāvāya* – भावाय ।

20th name above may be referred.

33. *Bhūtavide* – भूतविदे ।

He only has knowledge about all the beings.

54th name below may also be referred.

34. *Bhūtakāraṇāya* – भूतकारणाय ।

He is the cause of existence of all beings.

The above 8 names were taken from the 4th shloka of the *Sahasranāma* Stotram.

35. *Bhūtasākṣiṇe* – भूतसाक्षिणे ।

He is the witness of all activities of all beings.

Because he cognises by his own wisdom (Bodha) everything is directly visible with no veil between.

According to Panini Sutras, the word *'Sākṣī'* is derived from *Sa* + *akṣī* – meaning the direct cogniser.

In *Viṣṇu Sahasranāmam* – 15th name – *Sākṣīḥ* – He is the witness.

52nd name below may also be referred.

36. *Prabhūtaye* – प्रभूतये ।

He is the origin of the entire universe. That is, he only created the entire universe. But he has no origin.

37. *Bhūtānāṃ Paramaṃ Gataye* – भूतानां परमं गतये।

The highest resort of all beings.

38. *Bhūtasaṅgavihīnātmane* – भूतसङ्गविहीनात्मने ।

His mind is unattached to other beings/ things in the world.

39. *Bhūtātmane* – भूतात्मने ।

29th name above may be referred.

40. *Bhūtaśaṅkarāya* – भूतशङ्कराय ।

He only confers happiness to all beings.

The above 6 names were taken from the 5th shloka of the *Sahasranāma* Stotram.

41. *Bhūtanāthāya* – भूतनाथाय ।

He is the master of all beings.

42. *Bhūtamahānāthāya* – भूतमहानाथाय ।

He is the greatest Lord.

43. *Bhūtādināthāya* – भूतादिनाथाय ।

He is primordial master of all beings.

15th name above and 960th name below may also be referred.

44. *Maheśvarāya* – महेश्वराय ।

He is the highest deity.

The Trimurtis *Brahma*, *Vişŋu* and *Rudra* do three main functions of creation, protection and destruction. *Maheshvara* is above these three and is transcending the three characteristics (*Guŋas – Rajas*, *Tamas* and *Satva*) in equal proportion.

As per below verse of *Veda*, *Maheshvara* is devoid of the three *guŋās* (*nirguŋa*);

Yovedādhou Svaraḥ Prokto Vedāntecapratishtitaḥ I
Tasya Prakruti Leenasya Yaḥ Paraḥ Sa Maheshvaraḥ II

The word *Maheshvara* means – one who is the head of all the *Bhūta Gaŋas* or by all the great practicing celibacies. *Linga Purāŋā* says;

Tamasā Kālardrākyo Rajasā Kanakāŋṭa Jaḥ I
Satvena Sarvako Vişŋuḥ Nairguŋyena Maheshwaraḥ II

In *Viṣṇu Sahasranāmam* – 181st name – *Maheśvāraḥ* – He owns the mighty bow and arrows.

In *Lalitā Sahasranāmam* – 208th name – *Maheśvarī* and 750th name – *Māheśvarī* – She is the greatest.

In *Gāyatri Sahasranāmam* – 798th name – *Maheśvaryai* – conveying the same meaning.

In *Śiva Sahasranāmam* – 164th name – *Maheśvaraḥ* – conveying the same sense.

45. *Sarvabhūtanivāsātmane* – सर्वभूतनिवासात्मने ।

He resides in all beings.

46. *Bhūtasantāpanāśanāya* – भूतसन्तापनाशनाय ।

He destroys the entire afflictions of all beings.

The above 6 names were taken from the 6th shloka of the *Sahasranāma* Stotram.

47. *Sarvātmane* – सर्वात्मने ।

He is the soul of all.

In *Śiva Sahasranāmam* – 4th name – *Sarvātmaḥ* – conveying the same sense.

48. *Sarvabhṛte* – सर्वभृते ।

He is the sustainer of all beings.

19th and 28th names above may also be referred.

49. *Sarvāya* – सर्वाय ।

He is the everything in this world.

375th name below may also be referred.

50. *Sarvajñāya* – सर्वज्ञाय ।

He is omniscient.

Muṇḍako Upanishad (I–1–9) says – one who perceives all and knows all – *"Yaḥ Sarvagnaḥ Sarva Vid"*

In *Viṣṇu Sahasranāmam* – 453rd and 815th names – *Sarvagnaḥ* – conveying the same meaning.

In *Lalitā Sahasranāmam* – 196th name – *Sarvajnā* – She is omniscient.

In *Śiva Sahasranāmam* – 85th name – *Sarvagnaḥ* – conveying the same meaning.

51. *Sarvanirṇayāya* – सर्वनिर्णयाय ।

He only ascertains everything.

52. *Sarvasākṣiṇe* – सर्वसाक्षिणे ।

He is the witness for every action of all beings.

35th name above may also be referred.

53. *Bṛhadbhānave* – बृहद्भानवे ।

He is the great giver of enlightenment. He is greater than greatest.

794th name below may also be referred.

54. *Sarvavide* – सर्वविदे ।

He is the knower of all.

33rd name above may also be referred.

55. *Sarvamaṅgalāya* – सर्वमङ्गलाय ।

He is the source of all that is auspicious. He is the root of all those. He gives all good fortune to those who satisfy him through meditation, praising through songs and worshipping through *poojas* (even if they are stupid).

This can be compared with *Mangalānām Mangalam* in *Vişŋu Sahasranāma*, first part.

In *Lalitā Sahasranāmam* – 200th name – *Sarvamangalā* – All that are auspicious is she herself. *Sarvamangala* is one of the 16 *Thiti Nityā Devīs*.

In *Lalitā Triśatī* – 124th name –*Sarvamangalā* – *Śrī Devī* is the *Chit* energy nothing different from *Brahmam*.

The above 9 names were taken from the 7th shloka of the *Sahasranāma* Stotram.

56. *Śāntāya* – शान्ताय ।

He is the most peaceful Lord. One who does not have any vehemence on devotees.

In *Lalitā Sahasranāmam* – 131st name – *Śāntimatī* – 141st name – *Shantā*, 447th name – *Shānti* and 963rd name – Shamātmika – One who has controlled mind.

In *Gāyatri Sahasranāmam* – 935th name – *Śāntāyai* – A peaceful Devi.

489th and 727th names below may also be referred.

57. *Satyāya* – सत्याय ।

He is a very truthful Lord. Being Paramatma, he is the reverse of the unreal.

Taitreeya Upanishad (2-1) says, Brahmam is existence, knowledge and infinite.

Again Taitreeya Upanishad (2-6) says He is endowed with form and devoid of form (*Saroopa* or *Niroopa*).

Or *Sat* – Prana, *ti* – food or matter and *yam* – the Sun. He is Satya because his form is made up of Prana, matter and the Sun or he is virtue in the holy men.

In *Vişŋu Sahasranāmam* – 106th, 212th and 869th names – *Satyaḥ* – he is the real truth.

In *Śiva Sahasranāmam* – 998th name – *Satyavrataḥ* – he has taken truth as a vow.

225th and 372nd names below may also be referred.

58. *Śamāya* – शमाय ।

He is very much in Tranquil state. The same was explained in 56th name above.

59. *Samāya* – समाय ।

He is unchanging, not wavering.

He has no one equal or above him. He is incomparable/ unequal/ peerless. There is nothing to compare with him. We cannot weigh him comparing with anything else.

60. *Ekākine* – एकाकिने ।

He is solitary without equal or superior.

Being devoid of any distinction pertaining to same species or different species or different parts of the same thing.

Chandokya Upanishat (6-2-1) says – there is only one without a second.

Brahma Tanmangalam Viduḥ – *Brahmam* is the only one, says *Vişŋu Purāŋa*.

In *Vişŋu Sahasranāmam* – 725th name – *Ekaḥ* – The one.

61. *Kamalāpataye* – कमलापतये ।

He is the consort of Kamala, the Lakshmi.

Lord Vishnu is the consort of Goddess Lakshmi. Lord Dattatreya is an incarnation of Lord Vishnu and hence he is the consort of Lakshmi Devi.

159th name below may also be referred.

62. *Rāmāya* – रामाय ।

He is *Rāmā*, in whom yogis get delight.

He is an incarnation of Lord Vishnu. Lord Rama is also an incarnation of Lord Vishnu. Hence, he is Rama.

The Padma Purana says, the name 'Rama' stands for the supreme Brahmam being the ternal Bliss and absolute consciousness in which Yogi's revel.

Lord Vishnu took the incarnation as son Dasaratha, because he assumed the handsome form of Rama, by his wish.

In *Vişŋu Sahasranāmam* – 394th name – *Rāmaḥ* – In him, who is always blissful, Yogis take get delight on him.

63. *Rāmapriyāya* – रामप्रियाय ।

He is the beloved of Lord Rama.
In the previous name it was mentioned that he is Lord Rama. Here it is mentioned that he is beloved of Lord Rama.

64. *Virāmāya* – विरामाय ।

He is the cessation of delusory activities. Brahma and others take rest on him.

In *Vişŋu Sahasranāmam* – 395th name – *Virāmaḥ* – The abode for all beings to take rest.

65. *Rāmakāraṇāya* – रामकारणाय ।

He is the cause of joy for all beings.

The above 10 names were taken from the 8th shloka of the *Sahasranāma* Stotram.

66. *Śuddhātmane* – शुद्धात्मने ।

He is the pure soul, i.e., the Paramatma with which all the Jeevatmas merge.

67. *Pavanāya* – पवनाय ।

The purifier – solely by his remembrance.

His story, if repeated, purifies the tellers and the hearers like his foot-water – river Ganga, which has her sources at Lord Vishnu's feet and Lord Shiva's head.

It can be noted for this reason, to repeat his stories, Ramayana, Bhagavata, etc., are being chant for 7 days, 9 days and so on continuously even today, after thousands of years.

Varuna, the god of purifying water, has a name called *Pavana*. The *Punyakavasana mantra* recited for purification is called *Pavamana Sookta*.

In *Vişŋu Sahasranāmam* – 291st name – *Pavanaḥ*, and *292*nd & 811th names – *Pāvanaḥ* – The purifier.

In Shrimad Bhagavad Gita (10.31), Lord Krishna says, of purifiers, I am the wind, the mover.

68. *Anantāya* – अनन्ताय ।

He is infinite and eternal. He is eternal, all-pervading and unlimited by space and time.

He is in the form of serpent Anantan.

In *Vişŋu Sahasranāmam* – 886th name – *Anantaḥ* – The endless.

388th name below may also be referred

69. *Pratītāya* – प्रतीताय ।

He is very much resolute, (on account of creation and protection of this universe).

In *Vişŋu Sahasranāmam* – 319th name – *Pratitaḥ* – He is very famous.

70. *Paramārthabhṛte* – परमार्थभृते |

He is the sustainer of the highest quest.

71. *Haṃsasākṣiṇe* – हंससाक्षिणे |

He is the witness without discrimination.

He removes the fear of Samsara of those meditate upon Him with the sense, "I am He".

The root 'Han' means to go or to move. Hence, he is moving in all bodies.

Katopanishat (5.2) says, He is Hamsa dwelling in Heaven.

Earlier also, it was mentioned that he is the witness to all activities of all beings without omission or bias.

72. *Vibhave* – विभवे |

He is all-pervading. Though he is formless (Niroopa), he has multiple forms.

Mundaka Upanishat (1.6) says, He is eternal and multiform.

In *Vişŋu Sahasranāmam* – 240th & 880th names – *Vibhuḥ* – He is multi-formed.

73. *Prabhave* – प्रभवे |

He is the most powerful, showing it forth in all his actions.

In *Vişŋu Sahasranāmam* – 35th & 299th names – *Prabhuḥ* – The really existent. He specially drags the eyes and mind of all by the beauty of his form.

74. *Pralayāya* – प्रलयाय |

He only performs the final dissolution at the end of each yuga and also at the end of chatur (all the 4) yugas.

The above 9 names were taken from the 9th shloka of the *Sahasranāma* Stotram.

75. *Siddhātmane* – सिद्धात्मने |

He is the realised soul, the Paramatma.

76. *Paramātmane* – परमात्मने |

He is the supreme soul.

He is beyond cause and effect, eternal, pure, absolute consciousness and free.

In *Viṣṇu Sahasranāmam* – 11th name – *Paramātmā* – The supreme self.

In *Śiva Sahasranāmam* – 888th name – *Paramātmaḥ* – The soul above all and above everything.

77. *Siddhānāṃ Paramagataye* – सिद्धानां परमगतये |

He is the highest refuge of the self-realised (*Siddhas*).

He is perfect without depending on others. The good ones attain perfection of their penance, salvation, etc., by serving him.

In *Viṣṇu Sahasranāmam* – 97th and 819th names – *Siddhaḥ* – He is eternally perfect.

78. *Siddhisiddhaye* – सिद्धिसिद्धये |

He only enables Siddhas to achieve self-realisation.

79. *Sādhyāya* – साध्याय |

He is the only tool/ route for salvation/ liberation.

569th name below may also be referred.

80. *Sādhanāya* – साधनाय |

He is the guiding tool to attain the goal i.e., liberation.

81. *Uttamāya* – उत्तमाय ।

He is the ultimate refuge.

The above 6 names were taken from the 10th shloka of the *Sahasranāma* Stotram.

82. *Sulakṣaṇāya* – सुलक्षणाय ।

He is endowed with all the auspicious qualities.

Samudrika Shastra has defined the proportions of each organ of the body for males and females separately. He is a perfect example in this regard.

83. *Sumedhāvine* – सुमेधाविने ।

He is very intelligent.

Agni Purāṇa says *Medhā* is remembrance.

In *Viṣṇu Sahasranāmam* – 752nd name – *Sumedhā* – He is of bright intelligence.

In *Lalitā Sahasranāmam* – 538th name – *Medhā* – She is in the form of special knowledge.

According to the *Padma Purāṇa*, the deity called *Medhā* is in Kashmir.

84. *Vidyavate* – विद्यवते ।

He is full of knowledge.

Vidyā, a certain kind of art, which is in the light (*tejas*) and its nature are described in the *Saiva Tantra* – By the discrimination of the products of *māyā*, one recognises the state of wisdom, that supreme art is known as *Vidyā*, consisting of knowledge and action.

Vidyā (knowledge) means self realisation. *Isāvasya Upanishad* (11th verse) – one who simultaneously knows both knowledge and ignorance having crossed over the death by ignorance attains immortality by knowledge.

Linga Purāṇa says *Shiva* has three forms, *Bhrānti*, *Vidyā* and *Para*. The knowledge of different objects is called *Bharānti* (confused) by the learned. Knowledge in the form of self, is called *vidya*. Knowledge concerning *Brahmam* without ambiguity is called *parā* (supreme);

In *Lalitā Sahasranāmam* – 402nd name – *Vidhyā'vidhyāsvarūpiṇī* – 549th name – *Vidyā* – She is in the form of both knowledge and ignorance. She is the *vidyā* conferring salvation.

85. *Vigatāntarāya* – विगतान्तराय ।

His attention is turned inside. Inward looking person.

In *Śrīmad Bhagavad Geeta* (IV chapter) *Śrī Krişhṇa* clearly advises the inward-looking powers.

Sri Adi Shankarar, has authored a text called "Mantra Matruka Pushpamala". This clearly explains inward looking aspects, imaging the Brahmam internally and doing puja by mind.

In *Lalitā Sahasranāmam* – 870th name – *Antarmukhasamārādhyā* – One who is well adored by those who are inward looking.

608th name below may also be referred.

86. *Vijvarāya* – विज्वराय ।

He is free from any kind of passion.

303rd name below may also be referred.

87. *Mahābāhave* – महाबाहवे ।

He is broad and expansive shoulders. For all the warriors, the shoulders should be broad, so that they can correctly, pull the string well and shoot the arrow.

Again, referring to Samudrika Shastra, males should have broad shoulders.

In Valmiki Ramayana, Sita addresses Sri Rama as *Mahābāhu* in lot many areas.

Similarly, in *Śrīmad Bhagavad Geeta, Śrī Krişhŋa* addresses Arjuna as *Mahābāhu* in many an area.

88. *Bahulānandavardhanāya* – बहुलानन्दवर्धनाय |

He promotes all kinds of bliss.

Annamaya, Prāŋamaya, Manomaya, Viññāŋamaya and *Ānandamaya* – five kinds of bliss according to *Taitreeya Upanishat*. The above 7 names were taken from the 11th shloka of the *Sahasranāma* Stotram.

89. *Avyaktapuruşāya* – अव्यक्तपुरुषाय |

He is an imperishable supreme being.

When the Brahmam (*Vichikeershā*) feels to create, the form taken by it on account of *māyā* (illusion) is called *Avyaktam*.

By the word *Avyakta* the *Brahmam* is indicated. In *Brahma Sūtra* (III–2–23) it is said, that *Brahmam* is *Avyakta* for the scriptures say so – *Tadavyaktamāha Hi.*

Śrī Ādi Śaŋkara explains this with the following *Veda* statements – *Muŋḍaka Upanishad* (III–1–8), He is not to be felt by the eyes, nor by the speech, nor by the other senses, nor by penance, nor by actions; *Nachakshushā Gruhyate Nāpi Vāchā Nanyaidevais Tapasā Karmanā Va.*

Further this has been evidenced through *Brahādaraŋya Upanishad* (III–9–26), *Muŋḍaka Upanishad* (II–1–6) and *Taitreeya Upanishad* (II–7–1).

In *Śrīmad Bhagavat Geeta* (II–25)– this *ātman* is said to be unmanifested, unthinkable and immutable.

The *Linga Purāŋa* says that *avyakta* means *Vişŋu*. The names of *Vişŋu*, who is ever capable of creation, are *Pradhāna, Avyaya, Yoni* [origin], *Avyakta, Prakruti* and *Tamas*.

In *Viṣŋu Sahasranāmam* – 305th name – *Vyaktarūpaḥ* – *Śrī Ādi Śaṇkara* in his commentary – his gross form as universe can be clearly perceived. (It need not be mentioned that this is opposite to the meaning of *Avyakta*).

In *Lalitā Sahasranāmam* – 398th name – *Avyaktā* – she cannot be visibly seen – She is in an un–manifested state.

90. *Prajñāya* – प्रज्ञाय ।

He is so wise, incomparable to anybody else.

91. *Parajñāya* – परज्ञाय ।

He is the knower of the supreme. He enables his devotees to realise the supreme.

92. *Paramārthadṛśe* – परमार्थदृशे ।

He is the seer of the most sublime truth.

914th name below may also be referred.

93. *Parāparavinirmuktāya* – परापरविनिर्मुक्ताय ।

He is free from high and low esteems.

He is beyond the very great *Trimoortis* – *Brahma*, *Viṣŋu* and *Rudra*. There is no one equal to or above **him.**

According to *Kāli Purāŋa* – one day (one day and night) of *Brahma* is called as *Para*. His day and night are of equal duration and they are called *Parārdham* – (it can be reminded that during any *Sankalpa* [declaring the desire to do *pooja*, etc.] this is being used). But, for the person, who is subtler than the subtle and minute than the minutest there is no bindings like day, night, year, etc., because he only creates the time and he is not controlled by time;

In *Lalitā Sahasranāmam* – 809th name – *Parātparā* – she is the most supreme of the supreme.

94. *Yuktāya* – युक्ताय ।

He only possesses the truth.

In *Śiva Sahasranāmam* – 740th name – *Yuktaḥ* – He is with everything.

170th name below may also be referred.

95. *Tattvaprakāśavate* – तत्त्वप्रकाशवते ।

He is endowed with bright lights.

The above 7 names were taken from the 12th shloka of the *Sahasranāma* Stotram.

96. *Dayāvate* – दयावते ।

He is so merciful, that he bestows more that his devotees ask for.

505th name below may also be referred.

97. *Bhagavate* – भगवते ।

He possesses all the divine qualities.

The Vishnu Puranam (6.5.74) says, the word Bhaga means full dominion, Dharma, fame, wealth, dispassion and salvation. He who possesses these six attributes is called Bhagavan.

Again, Vishnu Puranam (6.5.78) says, he who knows the origin and end, the coming and going, of beings and also Vidya and Avidya, is called Bhagavan.

In *Vişņu Sahasranāmam* – 558th name – *Bhagavān* – He is the goal to wisdom, truth, wealth, etc.

98. *Bhāvine* – भाविने ।

He is endowed with super-human powers.

99. *Bhāvātmane* – भावात्मने ।

He is the embodiment of affection.

He expands himself as the universe. Remains as pure existence.

In *Viṣṇu Sahasranāmam* – 7th name – *Bhāvaḥ* – He is the absolute existence.

100. *Bhāvakāraṇāya* – भावकारणाय ।

He is the cause of this entire universe.

The word *Bhava* has three meanings – Lord *Mahadeva*, the human life cycle and Cupid. He gives life to all these three and hence *Bhāvakāraṇā*.

Since Lord *Paramashiva* creates all the living things his name is *Bhava*. Lord Dattatreya and Lord Shiva are one and same and hence, he is *Bhava*.

Out of the eight forms of Lord *Paramashiva*, the form of water is called *Bhava*. One who gives life to all the living beings.

Thus ends 100 divine names on Lord *Dattātreya* from 1 to 100.

*****

101. *Bhavasantāpanāśanāya* – भवसन्तापनाशनाय ||

He destroys the afflictions of his devotees. The bondage of samsara can be relived only by him.

In *Gāyatri Sahasranāmam* – 764th name – *Bhavabandhavimocinyai* – She is unique in smashing the tough and harsh bonds of Samsara.

102. *Puṣpavate* – पुष्पवते |

He is like a blooming flower.

103. *Paṇḍitāya* – पण्डिताय |

He is very much learned.

104. *Buddhāya* – बुद्धाय |

He is an enlighted God. He is always in an awakened state.

275th name below may also be referred.

The above 9 names were taken from the 13th shloka of the *Sahasranāma* Stotram.

105. *Pratyakṣavastave* – प्रत्यक्षवस्तवे |

He is a perceivable reality.

106. *Viśvātmane* – विश्वात्मने |

He is the atma of this universe.

Viśva = Universe. *Ātmane* = soul. He is the soul of this entire universe.

In *Vişŋu Sahasranāmam* – 225th name – *Viśvātmā* – He is the absolute the universal soul. He spreads energy to the Universe.

Purusha Sooktam says "He covers the Earth, etc.".

107. *Pratyagbrahmasanātanāya* – प्रत्यग्ब्रह्मसनातनाय |

He is the eternal inner-most soul.

108. *Pramāṇavigatāya* – प्रमाणविगताय |

He is beyond the means of knowledge. He can be realised only through focused meditation.

109. *Pratyāhāraṇī Yojakāya* – प्रत्याहारणी योजकाय |

He is the Practicing restraint of the senses.

The above 5 names were taken from the 14th shloka of the *Sahasranāma* Stotram.

110. *Praṇavāya* – प्रणवाय |

He is the Primordial Reverberation *Oṃ* – the Pranava mantra.

The monosyllable *Oṃ* denotes Paramatma. He is indicated by this.

Sanatkumara says – as the Vedas salute Him, he is Pranava.

Vedas say – therefore (the worshipper) praises or salutes (Him) by '*Oṃ*'.

In *Viṣṇu Sahasranāmam* – 409th and 957th names – *Praṇavaḥ* – He is the Lord praised by all.

In *Gāyatri Sahasranāmam* – 109th name – *Oṅkārāyai* – and 671st name – *Praṇavāyai* – She is the Pranava mantra *Oṃ* – there is no difference between them.

111. *Praṇavātītāya* – प्रणवातीताय |

He is the one who has transcended (beyond) the *Oṃ* Pranava mantra.

In the previous name, he was referred to as *Oṃkara* Pranava mantra. Here, he is said to have transcended that too.

112. *Pramukhāya* – प्रमुखाय |

He is the Foremost Guide taking his devotees in the path of liberation.

905th name below may also be referred.

113. *Pralayātmakāya* – प्रलयात्मकाय ।

He is the Spirit of dissolution of worldly illusions.

Illusion is the darkness of ignorance. Only when that is dispelled through the light of wisdom can be obtained.

114. *Mṛtyuñjayāya* – मृत्युञ्जयाय ।

He helps his devotees to overcome the death.

Shukla Yajurveda (16.41), contains the *Mahā Mrutyunjaya Mantra*. It is chant alongwith Sri Rudra Namakam.

Lord Shiva, killed Yama (the Lord of death) to protect Markandeya and hence he is usually called as *Mṛtyuñjayā*. Here Lord Dattatreya is called so, confirming that there is no difference between Lord Shiva and Lord Dattatreya.

Again, Yama was given life by Lord Shiva. This can be seen in the temple at Thirukkadayur.

115. *Viviktātmane* – विविक्तात्मने ।

He is the solitary soul, i.e. Paramatma.

426th name below may also be referred.

116. *Śaṅkarātmane* – शङ्करात्मने ।

He is the very soul of Lord Shiva.

Lord Shiva is called *Śaṅkarā*. Again and again it is being emphasised that Lord Shiva and Lord Dattatreya are one and the same Lord.

12th name above may also be referred.

117. *Parasmaivapuṣe* – परस्मैवपुषे ।

He is surpassingly beautiful.

He is the Supreme. There is no one above or equal to him.

In *Sūrya Sahasranāmam* – 844th name – *Parasmai* – He is the supreme.

The above 13 names were taken from the 15th shloka of the *Sahasranāma* Stotram.

118. *Paramāya* – परमाय ।

He is a great Lord. He who limits and shows the immeasurable *Brahmam*.

The word *Parama* also means "at a distance". i.e. he is at a distance for those who do not have devotion.

According to *Vishnu Purana*, the supreme being has four forms viz., Male, Twice Born, Time and *Param*. He is in the fourth form *Param*. This name can also be construed as *Paramātma*.

In *Lalitā Sahasranāmam* – 618th name – *Paramā* – One who is the greatest.

In *Gāyatri Sahasranāmam* – 558th name – *Paramā* – One who is the great in all things and in all ways.

In *Śiva Sahasranāmam* – 77th name – *Paramaḥ* – He is very great.

511th name below may also be referred.

119. *Tanuvijñeyāya* – तनुविज्ञेयाय ।

He is the self to be realised by devotion.

120. *Paramātmanisaṃsthitāya* – परमात्मनिसंस्थिताय ।

He is firmly established in the Supreme Atma – i.e. Paramatma.

121. *Prabodhakalanādhārāya* – प्रबोधकलनाधाराय ।

He is the foundation of awakening to wisdom.

122. *Prabhāva Pravarottamāya* – प्रभाव प्रवरोत्तमाय ।

He is the highest of the blessed and powerful.

The above 5 names were taken from the 16th shloka of the *Sahasranāma* Stotram.

123. *Cidambarāya* – चिदम्बराय |

He is the Lord at Cidambaram.

Lord Shiva is the Lord at Cidambaram as Lord Nataraja. Lord Dattatreya is the Lord Shiva and hence, he is also *Cidambarāya*.

If this name is split into *Cid* + *ambara*, it may means he wears consciousness as cloth.

124. *Cidvilāsāya* – चिद्विलासाय |

He is the manifestation of Pure Consciousness.

659th name below may also be referred.

125. *Cidākāśāya* – चिदाकाशाय |

He is the all-pervading Consciousness.

He has the power of removing ignorance and is also termed *chaitanya*. Since he is in the form of knowledge he got this name.

According to the *Svetāsvatara Upanishad* (V–1) – in imperishable and infinite highest universal absolute (*Parabrahmam*), wherein the two, *vidyā* and *avidyā* are hidden, one is imperishable and the other is perishable, he who rules these two is different from either.

Chit, according to the *Yāskar*, who wrote the grammar for the language of *Veda*, means comparison; *Chitiyutmāyām*. The same is written by *Pāŋini* (VIII–2–101) in his grammar book on languages, as; *Chititi Chopamārde Prayujyamāne*. This method is to describe one unknown object by comparing it with a known object. The knowledge of comparison is *Śrī Dattatreya* himself.

In *Lalitā Sahasranāmam* – 416th name – *Cicchaktiḥ* – One who is in the form of energy called *Chit*.

126. *Ciduttamāya* – चिदुत्तमाय |

He is the highest awareness.

127. *Citta Caitanya Cittātmane* – चित्त चैतन्य चित्तात्मने ।

He is the the Embodiment of Consciousness and Pure Intelligence.

He is best worshipped with the offerings of the consciousness – *chaitanya*.

Consciousness is the form of mind. Self–consciousness is the mind form of soul. *Shiva Sūtra* (I–1) says that this is the soul;
Ātma Chaitanyamātma.

Chaitanya (consciousness) means the essence of the form of the potency of knowledge. *Sūta Samhita* says that if one chants the *mantra* called *chaitanya* for 10,000 times, he is removed from all groups of sins.

128. *Devānāṃ Paramāgataye* – देवानां परमागतये ।

He is the final refuge for Devas.

In the 37th name above, it was mentioned that he is the final refuge for all beings. Again, in the 77th name above, it was mentioned that he is the final refuge for all Siddhas. Here it is stressed that he is the final refuge for all Devas.

The above 6 names were taken from the 17th shloka of the *Sahasranāma* Stotram.

129. *Acetyāya* – अचेत्याय ।

He is beyond conception. He can be conceived only through devotion.

130. *Cetanādhārāya* – चेतनाधाराय ।

He is the foundation of awareness for animate things.

131. *Cetanācittavikramāya* – चेतनाचित्तविक्रमाय ।

He is the power of Thoughtless Awareness.

132. *Cittātmane* – चित्तात्मने |

He is the pure intelligent atma.

133. *Cetanārūpāya* – चेतनारूपाय |

He is in the form of consciousness (*chaitanya*).

The *chetana* energy in all the beings is he only. *Chetana* means inner sense. Only because of this, we can recognise the objects shown by eye, ear and mind. Only through the action of this we can recognise the availability of this. Not by any other means.

Kenopanishad (First *Kanḍa*) says;

Srotrasya Srotram Manaso Mano.

Samkshepa Sāreerakam says, the pure *chit shakti* of the supreme Lord is called *chaitanya*;

Chitshaktiḥ Parameshvarasya Vimalā Chaitanya–mevochyate.

In *Lalitā Sahasranāmam* – 417th name – *Cetanārūpā* – She is in the form of consciousness.

134. *Lasatpaṅkajalocanāya* – लसत्पङ्कजलोचनाय |

He has eyes like swaying lotuses.

The above 6 names were taken from the 18th shloka of the *Sahasranāma* Stotram.

135. *Parabrahmaṇe* – परब्रह्मणे |

He is the supreme formless (*niroopa*) consciousness i.e. *Parabrahmam*.

Parabrahmam is beyong cause, effect, eternal, pure, absolute consciousness and free from any attributes. He is in such a form.

859th name below may also be referred.

136. *Parañjyotiye* – परञ्ज्योतिये |

One who is the Supreme transcendent light.

The state without light is darkness. The ignorance is the darkness in the mind. Once the light is on, the darkness goes away. When there is knowledge ignorance is removed. When it is dark neither inside nor outside the world is seen. The outside darkness is removed by Sun, Moon, stars, fire and other light galaxies. In a way, Sound is also light, because we recognise something with the help of sound in darkness also.

The above said Sun, etc., are illuminated only by him. Hence he is called as supreme (*param*).

The *Brhadāraṇya Upanishad* (IV–4–16) says, "That is light of light";

Taddevā Jyotishām Jyotirāya Hopāsadamrutam.

Again, the *Brhadāraṇya Upanishad* (III–9–10) "The supreme light one attains" – *Jyotis* here means the illuminator, for we see the same meaning given in such places, "the illuminator of the mind";

Mano Jyotiḥ

Chāndogya Upanishad (VIII–3–4) – The Sun shines only when he is illuminated by Him; "*Param Jyotirupasampadya*".

Paramjyotis is the eight–syllable *mantra* described in the fifth chapter of the *Dakshiṇāmoorti Samhita*.

In *Lalitā Sahasranāmam* – 806th name – *Parasmaijyotiḥ* – She is in the supreme light.

197th name below may also be referred.

137. *Parandhāmne* – परन्धाम्ने |

One who is in the form of Supreme abode above all.

Here the word *Dhāma* has many a meaning viz., lustre, dwelling place, state (state of mind, etc.). All these meanings fit him.

Let us consider the meaning lustre – It has been mentioned in many names about the lustre of *Śrī Dattatreya* including the above 136th name – *Parañjyotiye*

In *Viṣŋu Sahasranāmam* – 719th name – *Dīptamūrtiḥ* – *Śrī Ādi Śaņkara* in his commentary mentions;

a. He who has the bright form of knowledge.
b. He is self–illuminating, bright and lustrous and hence *Dīptamūrtiḥ*.

The *Śrīmad Bhagavad Geeta* (XV–6) Lord Krihna says, "The Sun never illuminates, nor Moon, nor fire. After reaching it when one does not return, that is my supreme abode".

Śrī Gouḍapādāchārya in his book *Māntookya Kārikai* (I–5) advises, "The man who knows both the object of enjoyment as well as the enjoyer is never stained though he enjoys all the three states (awaken, dream and deep sleep)".

Soota Samhitā (*Yagna Vaibhava Kāṇḍa* – IV–11–32,33) also says, "He who knows the three states, namely waking, dreaming and deep sleeping, he is the Self, that is not the object, the object is super–imposed upon that. I take refuge in the supreme abode which is the evidence of the three abodes, characterized by reality, wisdom, bliss etc., and is the meaning of the word 'I'. *Dhāman*, the states of consciousness, *para*, beyond – he is beyond the states of consciousness.

The *Kaṭopanishad* (III–9) says, "That is the supreme abode of *Viṣŋu*"; *Tadvishnoḥ Paramam Padam*.

138. *Parantapase* – परन्तपसे |

He is the greatest austerity.

He is called as the earliest guru of the Avaduta monastic lineage.

139. *Paraṃsūtrāya* – परंसूत्राय |

He is the supreme bliss.

140. *Paratantrāya* – परतन्त्राय |

He is the highest technique (to attain Moksha).

141. *Pavitrāya* – पवित्राय ।

He is very holy. He is the means of purification.

In *Viṣŋu Sahasranāmam* – 62nd name – *Pavitram* – The holy.

142. *Paramohavate* – परमोहवते ।

He is beyond all the worldly delusions.

By imparting the idea of unity to his devotees he destroys bewilderment.

In *Lalitā Sahasranāmam* – 163rd name – *Mohanāśinī* – She is dispels all delusions/ illusions.

The above 8 names were taken from the 19th shloka of the *Sahasranāma* Stotram.

143. *Kṣetrajñāya* – क्षेत्रज्ञाय ।

He is the knower of the field, the universe.

In Shrimad Bhagavad Gita (13.2), Lord Krishna says, understand Me as the knower of the field.

In *Viṣŋu Sahasranāmam* – 16th name – *Kṣetrajnaḥ* – The knower of the field.

144. *Kṣetragāya* – क्षेत्रगाय ।

He resides in the material plane.

In *Lalitā Sahasranāmam* –

- 341st name – *Kṣetrasvarūpā* – Her body is matter – body of all beings.
- 342nd name – *Kṣetreśī* – She is the ruler of matter.
- 343rd name – *Kṣetra Kṣetragna Pālinī* – She is the protector of matter and the knower of matter.

This name can be read along with names 145, 146 and 148 below.

145. *Kșetrāya* – क्षेत्राय |

He is the fertile ground of spirituality.

146. *Kșetrādhārāya* – क्षेत्राधाराय |

He supports the physical existence of all living beings.

147. *Purāñjyanāya* – पुराञ्ज्यनाय |

He is the governor of the body of all beings.

148. *Kșetraśūnyāya* – क्षेत्रशून्याय |

He has an empty field without any matter.

149. *Lokasākșiņe* – लोकसाक्षिणे |

He is the witness for every action of the entire world.

In *Sūrya Sahasranāmam* – 980th name – *Karmaņām Sākșiņe* – He is the witness for all actions of all.

35th and 52nd names above may also be referred.

150. *Kșetravate* – क्षेत्रवते |

He possess a body with matter.

In reality, as the *parabrahmam*, he is *niroopam* – without any form. But, for his devotees sake, he seemingly has a body (*saroopa brahmam*).

151. *Bahunāyakāya* – बहुनायकाय |

He is the leader of multi-tude.

The above 9 names were taken from the 20th shloka of the *Sahasranāma* Stotram.

152. *Yogīndrāya* – योगीन्द्राय |

He is the master of Yoga. He is the head/ king of Yogis.

Yogis are, normally, obstructed in their progress by Yogic impediments and consequently fall off from their progress or from their position. But he is free from such impediments and hence, he is the Lord of Yogis.

In *Viṣŋu Sahasranāmam* – 850th name – *Yogīśaḥ* – The Lord of Yogis.

663rd name below may also be referred.

153. *Yogapūjyāya* – योगपूज्याय ।

He is worshipped by Yogis.

He can be realised and connected only through Yogas.

154. *Yogyāya* – योग्याय ।

He can be connected only through Yogas and by Yogins.

155. *Ātmavidaṃśucaye* – आत्मविदंशुचये नमः।

He is the Pure Knowledge of the Atma.

156. *Yogamāyādharāya* – योगमायाधराय ।

He possess miraculous powers.

157. *Sthānave* – स्थानवे ।

He is very much eternal, firm, constant and steady.

In *Viṣŋu Sahasranāmam* – 28th name – *Sthāṇuḥ* – 120th name – *Śaśvatasthānuḥ* and 426th name – *Sthāvarasthāṇuḥ* – He is constant firm and motionless.

158. *Acalāya* – अचलाय ।

He is constantly static/ immobile.

In *Sūrya Sahasranāmam* – 793rd name – *Acalāya* – He is static.

958th name below may also be referred.

159. *Kamalāpataye* – कमलापतये |

61st name above may be referred.

The above 8 names were taken from the 21st shloka of the *Sahasranāma* Stotram.

160. *Yogeśāya* – योगेशाय |

152nd name above may be referred.

161. *Yoganimantre* – योगनिमन्त्रे |

He is the origin of yogas.

162. *Yogajñānaprakāśakāya* – योगज्ञानप्रकाशकाय |

He elucidates the direct knowledge of Gods through Yogas.

163. *Yogapālāya* – योगपालाय |

He is the protector of Yogas.

164. *Lokapālāya* – लोकपालाय |

He is the protector of the entire world.

165. *Saṃsāratamonāśanāya* – संसारतमोनाशनाय |

He dispells the darkness of worldly illusion. Unless the darkness called illusion from the mind is removed, the knowledge cannot be obtained.

The above 6 names were taken from the 22nd shloka of the *Sahasranāma* Stotram.

166. *Guhyāya* – गुह्याय |

He is most secretive both in form and meanings.

Guhyā means one who dwells in a cave, i.e. heart.

He is secretive and dwelling in our heart. Hence he can be identified only by inward search.

The word *Guhyā* can be considered to mean *Jeevātma* (soul), *Paramātmā* (supreme) and the union of both. The presiding deity who can bestow these results is called *Guhya*.

Kaṭopanishad (I–2–12) says;

Esha Sarveshu Bhūteshu Kooṭātmā Na Prakāshate.

In *Vişŋu Sahasranāmam* – 542nd name – *Guhyaḥ* and 545th name – *Guptaḥ* – *Śrī Ādi Śaṇkara* in his commentary says, one who can be understood by the secret *Upanishads* or one who dwells in the secret cavity viz., heart. **He** is beyond speech and mind.

In *Lalitā Sahasranāmam* – 624th name – *Guhyā* – She is very secretive.

167. *Guhyatamāya* – गुह्यतमाय ।

He is most secretive, who can be realised only through meditation.

This name can be read in conjunction with the previous name.

168. *Guptaye* – गुप्तये ।

He guards the truth.

Previous two names also can be referred.

169. *Muktāya* – मुक्ताय ।

He is the liberated soul, i.e. Paramatma.

He blesses liberation to his devotees.

The *Brahmānḍa Purāŋa* says, "Those who worship the supreme soul whether regularly or irregularly, are not entangled in *samsāra*. There is no doubt, they are the liberated souls".

In *Lalitā Sahasranāmam* – 736th name – *Muktidā* – She is the giver of salvation.

170. *Yuktāya* – युक्ताय ।

94th name above may be referred.

171. *Sanātanāya* – सनातनाय |

He is the earliest – earlier than Brahma and others.

Since he is the cause of all, he is the ancient.

In *Viṣṇu Sahasranāmam* – 897th name – *Sanātanatamaḥ* – The most ancient.

445th and 457th names below may also be referred.

172. *Gahanāya* – गहनाय |

He is unfathomable and impenetrable.

173. *Gaganākārāya* – गगनाकाराय |

He is as vast as the sky. He is immeasurable.

174. *Gambhīrāya* – गम्भीराय |

He is so gigantic of unfathomable depth.

In every Shiva shrines, at the back, we can see idol of '*Lingotbhava*', whose image is so huge that Lord Brahma and Lord Vishnu went in search of the head and feet in vain, respectively. He is in that form.

This is what was mentioned in the previous name also.

175. *Gaṇanāyakāya* – गणनायकाय |

He is head of all groups of Devas like Kinnara, Ghandarva, etc.

One of the primary meanings of the word *Gaṇa* in Samskrutam is group. In Modern Algebra section of Mathematics also we have something called 'Set', which is a collection of objects. This is called as *Gaṇam*. Hence, *Gaṇanāyakā* is leader or head of that group.

Normally, in practice the word *Gaṇapati* has started to mean by default, Lord *Vinayaka*. Because he is the leader of Deva *Gaṇas* – all the groups of Devas he is called as *Gaṇanāyakā*, here.

The above 10 names were taken from the 23rd shloka of the *Sahasranāma* Stotram.

176. *Govindāya* – गोविन्दाय ।

He is in the form of the protector of the universe *Vişŋu*, who predominantly has *Satva* character, is also *Śrī Dattatreya* only.

Normally, the word *Govindā* will indicate Lord Vishnu more in particular Sri Krishna. Here it indicates Lord Dattatreya. Hence, it is very clear that Lord Dattatreya and Vishnu are one and the same.

Go – speech. *Govinda* – who can be understood by it (speech – chanting Vedas). The supreme being is beyond reach by speech. Since *Govinda* has taken the protection task, once he hears the crying of the soul, he immediately appears before him.

Go – earth. Once the creation of the universe is complete the earth, on account of overweight, became unstable and started to sub–merge in the water. Also when *Hiranyāksha*, the demon, seized the earth *Vişŋu* only took the incarnation as a boar protected it from him. Hence among all the names of *Vişŋu*, the name *Govinda* stresses the task of protection. *Śrī Dattatreya* himself is in the form of *Govinda*.

In *Vişŋu Sahasranāmam* – 197th name and 539th name – *Govindaḥ* – *Śrī Ādi Śaṇkara* in his commentary says;

1. Since he, as a boar takes out the earth that is being destructed, he is *Govinda*.
2. Head of cows.
3. One who enables his devotees to speak.
4. One who can be reached through languages (*Gobhiḥ*)
5. One who understands the souls through the statements of *Vedānta*.

747th name below may also be referred.

177. *Gopataye* – गोपतये ।

He is the lord of cows. He is a shepherd. He is the lord of the earth. He is the lord of senses.

At Gokulam, Lord Krishna was a shepherd and hence he is *Gopati*.

In *Vişŋu Sahasranāmam* – 495th name and 592nd names – *Gopatiḥ* – a shepherd.

178. *Goptre* – गोप्त्रे |

He is the protector of all beings in the universe. He veils his nature with his illusions.

He is the protector of all vidyas.

In *Vişŋu Sahasranāmam* – 496th name and 593rd names – *Goptā* – the protector of the universe.

179. *Gobhāgāya* – गोभागाय |

He is the saviour of cows. As Krishna, he protected the cows and hence this name.

180. *Bhāvasaṃsthitāya* – भावसंस्थिताय |

He has firmly established himself in existence. His existence has been mentioned in many a name in this Stotra.

181. *Gosākşiṇe* – गोसाक्षिणे |

He is the witness of the entire world. He being the witness has been mentioned in many names in this Stotra.

182. *Gotamāraye* – गोतमारये |

He eradicates the enemy of the darkness in devotees.

The ignorance is the darkness with devotees. He lits the light called knowledge and removes the darkness.

183. *Gāndhārāya* – गान्धाराय |

He holds the earth. In the Varaha incarnation he held the Earth in his nose.

In classical music he is in the form of '*Gāndhāram*', the Third Note which awakens the *Sushumnā*.

184. *Gaganākṛtaye* – गगनाकृतये ।

He is all-pervading like the sky. This has been stressed in many other names also.

The above 9 names were taken from the 24th shloka of the *Sahasranāma* Stotram.

185. *Yogayuktāya* – योगयुक्ताय ।

He is well-established in Yoga.

186. *Bhogayuktāya* – भोगयुक्ताय ।

He enjoys wordly enjoyments. This name is in contrast to the previous name.

187. *Śaṅkāmukta Samādhimate* – शङ्कामुक्त समाधिमते ।

He is always in deep meditation and hence, free from any type of anxieties.

188. *Sahajāya* – सहजाय ।

He has a natural disposition.

371st and 873rd names below may also be referred.

189. *Sakaleśanāya* – सकलेशनाय ।

He is the Lord from a noble family.

Unless the family is very noble, the Trimurties will not offer themselves as a child. He was born as a son of Sage Atri and Anusuya. In earlier chapters it has been described how noble they are. Hence, he is from a noble family.

190. *Kārtavīryavarapradāya* – कार्तवीर्यवरप्रदाय ।

He bestowed boons to King Kartavirya(rjuna).

Kartaviryarjuna is thousand handed king and a local monarch. He worshipped Sri Dattatreya with great devotion and was granted boons. He has even become Sri Dattatreya's disciple. That is a different story that he was later killed by Lord Parashurama.

The above 6 names were taken from the 25th shloka of the *Sahasranāma* Stotram.

191. *Sarajase* – सरजसे ।

He is so affectionate with his devotees. He never gets angry with anyone.

192. *Virajase* – विरजसे ।

He is free from any type of passion and ignorance.

He is in the form of Homas as also that of the Viraja River.

The verses of *Mahā Nārāyaṇopanishat* (20th chapter) and *Tattva-Soḍanā* may be connected – *Virajā Vipāpma*..

When such meaning is said, the prefix '*Vi*' has to be taken in the opposite sense – i.e. without the character called *Rajo*.

The word *Rajas* means splendour, water and world. While accepting these meanings the prefix '*Vi*' has to be specifically considered.

The presiding deity in the place called *Virajā* in Utkal state (present Odisha) is called *Virāja*. **She** is in that form.

In *Vişŋu Sahasranāmam* – 396th name – *Viraja* – Pure

In *Lalitā Sahasranāmam* – 779th name – *Virajā* – She is without any stain or sin originated by the *Rajo* character.

In *Gāyatri Sahasranāmam* – 902nd name – *Virajāyai* – She is without any stain or sin originated by the *Rajo* character.

In *Śiva Sahasranāmam* – 956th name – *Virajaḥ* – the pure one.

193. *Puṃse* – पुंसे ।

He is the most courageous.

194. *Pāvanāya* – पावनाय ।

He is the purifier.

The commentary given for the 67th name above may also be referred.

195. *Pāpanāśanāya* – पापनाशनाय ।

He destroys all the sins of his devotees.

By the repetition of his *mantra*, etc., he destroys the sins of devotees.

In *Chāndogya Upanishad* IV–24–3, it is mentioned as; *Yateśikā Tūlamagnou Pradūyataiva Mevāsya Papmanaḥ Pradūyante* – Like the point of a reed in the fire, all the sins are burnt up.

The *Vashisṭa Smruti* says – If a person is always devoted to learning, penance and continually repeating mantras, even if he is always committing sinful actions, he is not afflicted thereby. Sin never touches those who repeat the mantras or offer oblations, or meditate, or make pilgrimages, or who perform *Shirovrata* (the rite of carrying the fire on the head).

The *Padma Purāṇa*, in its *Pushara Kanda* says – The mass of sins though as great as mount Meru is instantly destroyed by worshipping. He, who is devoted, is not stained even by committing heinous crimes, in the manner as the lotus leaf is not affected by water.

The *Vriddhaśātātatapa* says (verse 119) – whatever sins are destroyed by the virtue of observing the vow of fasting for a fortnight, the same is destroyed by the practice of one hundred Pranayamas. Whatever sins are removed by one thousand Pranayamas, are destroyed in a minute by meditation upon Hari.

Valmiki Ramayana says, when Sri Rama is praised, worshipped, meditated upon or even remembered, he destroys all classes of sins.

Brahmāŋḑa Purāŋā says – The sinful actions of those who are devoid of *Varŋa* and *Ashrama* and the wretched also, by mere meditation, become virtuous.

In *Vişŋu Sahasranāmam* – 924th name – *Pāpanāśanaḥ* and 992nd name – *Dushkrutihā* – *Śrī Ādi Śaṇkara* in his commentary says, **He** destroys the bad act of sin or one who does sinful acts. He destroys the sins in bunches, of those people, who sing hymns in praise of him, or worship him or meditate upon him or just remember him.

In *Lalitā Sahasranāmam* – 167th name – *Pāpanāśinī*, 555th name – *Kalikalmaşa Nāśinī*, 743rd name – *Pāpāraŋyadavānalā* and 860th name – *Akānta* – One who destroys the sins of devotees.

In *Lalitā Triśatī* – 31st name – *Enaḥ Kūṭa Vināśinī* and 112th name – *Hatyāti Pāpaśamanī* – *Śrī Ādi Śaṇkara* in his commentary says all the sins including killing of a person, are instantly removed just by thinking about Sri Devi.

196. *Parāvaravinirmuktāya* – परावरविनिर्मुक्ताय ।

He is fully liberated from cause and effect.

76th name above may also be referred.

197. *Parañjyotiye* – परञ्ज्योतिये ।

He is the supreme light.

136th name above may also be referred.

198. *Purātanāya* – पुरातनाय ।

He is the premodel being.

As he transcends time, he is the earliest Atma – earlier to every other being.

In *Vişŋu Sahasranāmam* – 498th name – *Purātanaḥ* – the ancient.

The above 8 names were taken from the 26th shloka of the *Sahasranāma* Stotram.

653rd name below may also be referred.

199. *Nānājyotişe* – नानाज्योतिषे ।

He is endowed with versatile, manifold brilliance.

200. *Anekātmane* – अनेकात्मने ।

He is possessing many forms.

He is formless (*niroopa*) *Brahmam*. On account of illusion, for us he seeming has many forms.

He takes various forms at his own wish, during different incarnations in order to help the world.

In *Vişŋu Sahasranāmam* – 721st name – *Anekamūrtiḥ* – multiple formed.

Thus ends 100 divine names on Lord *Dattātreya* from 101 to 200.

*****

201. *Svayañjyotiṣe* – स्वयञ्ज्योतिषे

He is a self-luminous Lord.

202. *Sadāśivāya* – सदाशिवाय

He is always benevolent, always happy and prosperous.

203. *Divyajyotirmayāya* – दिव्यज्योतिर्मयाय

He shines with a natural divine light.

204. *Satyavijñānabhāskarāya* – सत्यविज्ञानभास्कराय

He is Sun of true wisdom.

The above 6 names were taken from the 27th shloka of the *Sahasranāma* Stotram.

205. *Nityaśuddhāya* – नित्यशुद्धाय

He is eternally pure.

He is beyond any impurity in all the three times (tenses).

Veda says – he does not touch anything, elder to all and always pure; *Asparśaśca Mahān Śuciḥ*

Another verse of *Veda* says – The body is untidy, but the person inside is clean – *Atyanta Malino Deho Dehī Cātyanta Nirmalaḥ*

In *Lalitā Sahasranāmam* – 148th name – *Nityaśuddhā* – she is eternally pure.

435th name below may also be referred.

206. *Parāya* – पराय

He is in the form sound called *Parā*, the transcendent word.

The power of expression depends upon the correspondence of the words and their meanings. Hence, as the unconditioned *Brahmam* also is included in the sound (*Shabdabrahmam*), *Brahmam* indirectly

(*Lakshaņa*) indicates (as the *Vedāntins* say) by the word's existence, etc. The speech is divided into four forms; *Parā*, *Pashyantee*, *Madyamā* and *Vaikharee*.

It is also explained by *Śrīmad Acārya* in his *Prapancha Sāram* (II–43) that sound which first arises in the *Mūlādhāra* is called *Parā*, next the *Paśyanti*; next when it goes as far as the heart and is joined to the understanding Buddhi it is called *Madhyamā*; and the full manifestation is *Vaikharī*. Thus, articulated sound is produced by air.

In *Lalitā Sahasranāmam* – 366th name – *Parā* – she is in the form sound called *Parā*.

207. *Pūrņāya* – पूर्णाय

He is very much complete.

As he possesses all the objects of desire and all energies, he is complete.

He possesses all the knowledge, the Dharma Shastra, etc.

In *Vişņu Sahasranāmam* – 685th name – *Pūrņāḥ* – The full.

208. *Prakāśāya* – प्रकाशाय

He is very bright. He reveals his form to his devotees.

He bestows enlightenment to his devotees.

He gives brightness to the Sun himself. *Sri Dattatreya*, who is in the form of Brahmam, resides within the Sun also.

He shines as the only brilliant ruler of the universe. He shines with all divine qualities.

In *Vişņu Sahasranāmam* – 274th name – *Prakāşanaḥ* – The illuminator.

In *Gāyatri Sahasranāmam* – 561st name – *Prakāśinyai* – She shines like anything.

209. *Prakaţodbhavāya* – प्रकटोद्भवाय

He openly renders his existence.

210. *Pramādavigatāya* – प्रमादविगताय

He is free from infatuation.

211. *Pareśāya* – परेशाय

He is the sovereign supreme.

In *Vişņu Sahasranāmam* – 377th name – *Parameśwaraḥ* – *Sri Adi Shankara* in his commentary says, he is *Parameshwara*, since he has great wealth and supreme ruling power.

In *Lalitā Sahasranāmam* – 396th name – *Parameśvarī* – conveying the same meaning.

393rd and 539th names below may also be referred.

212. *Paravikramāya* – परविक्रमाय

He is possessed of excellent prowess.

The above 8 names were taken from the 28th shloka of the *Sahasranāma* Stotram.

213. *Yogine* – योगिने

He himself is a Yogi.

In the above 2nd name itself it was mentioned that he is a great Yogi. Here again it is being stressed.

The realization of oneness of the individual and the Supreme Atma, by keeping under control the senses of knowledge together with the mind, is called Yoga. Lord Dattatreya is the Yoga because he can be reached by means of it only.

In *Vişņu Sahasranāmam* – 18th name – *Yogaḥ* – He is united with his devotees.

214. *Yogāya* – योगाय

He is an embodiment of Yoga.

666th name below may also be referred.

215. *Yogapāya* – योगपाय

He is an imparter of the practice of Yoga.

In *Viṣṇu Sahasranāmam* – 19th name – *Yogavidāmnetraḥ* – He is the leader of all who know Yoga.

216. *Yogābhyāsaprakāśanāya* – योगाभ्यासप्रकाशनाय

He teaches the discipline of Yoga – a Yoga guru. This name is same as previous name.

Those who enquire into, realise, or acquire Yoga are called the knowers of Yoga. He is their teacher because he takes care of the concerns of the wise ones.

In Shrimad Bhagavat Gita (9.22) Lord Krishna says – to those who are always devout, I secure gain and safety.

The 4 names from 213 can be read together.

217. *Yoktre* – योक्त्रे

He applies effort in all his activities.

218. *Moktre* – मोक्त्रे

He gives liberation to his devotees.

219. *Vidhātre* – विधात्रे

In the form of Brahma, he conceives (*Dhātā*) and supports all.

In *Viṣṇu Sahasranāmam* – 44th name – *Vidhātāḥ* and 484th name – *Vidhātā* – He is the supporter of all.

220. *Trātre* – त्रात्रे

As a guardian, he is the saviour of all from all troubles.

221. *Pātre* – पात्रे

He is the protector of all.

The last 3 names give almost the same meanings.

222. *Nirāyudhāya* – निरायुधाय

He does not possess any weapon.

He is a peace lover and hence do not have any weapon in his hand.

It can be noted that in Kurukshetra battle, Lord Krishna promised that he would drive the chariot of Arjuna, but will not touch any weapon. However still he got the battle won for Pandavas.

The above 10 names were taken from the 29th shloka of the *Sahasranāma* Stotram.

223. *Nityamuktāya* – नित्यमुक्ताय

He is ever-liberated.

Since **His** devotees are bonded to this world and he is in the form of liberation, typically as per the character of *Nityamuktās*.

In *Lalitā Sahasranāmam* – 144th name – *Nityamuktā* – She is ever free from worldly bonds.

224. *Nityayuktāya* – नित्ययुक्ताय

He is ever united with the Supreme Brahmam.

225. *Satyāya* – सत्याय

57th name above and 372nd name below may be referred.

226. *Satyaparākramāya* – सत्यपराक्रमाय

He is courageous for truth.

In *Vişŋu Sahasranāmam* – 213th name – *Satyaparākramaḥ* – he is of real valour.

227. *Sattvaśuddhikarāya* – सत्त्वशुद्धिकराय

He is purified by the truth.

He purifies his devotees with and for the truth.

228. *Sattvāya* – सत्त्वाय

He is the true essence of existence.

229. *Sattvabhṛtāṅgataye* – सत्त्वभृताङ्गतये

He always maintains the sacred fire of truth

The above 7 names were taken from the 30th shloka of the *Sahasranāma* Stotram.

230. *Śrīdharāya* – श्रीधराय

He is endowed with glory. He supports prosperity.

In general, the name *Śrīdhara* will mean Lord Vishnu. But Lord Dattatreya and Lord Vishnu are one and the same and hence this name.

In *Viṣṇu Sahasranāmam* – 610th name – *Śrīdharaḥ* – bearer of *Śrī*. *Śrī* means Goddess Lakshmi. He always has her in his chest and hence this name.

231. *Śrīvapuṣe* – श्रीवपुषे

He has an auspicious, wonderful, admirable and gigantic body.

In *Śiva Sahasranāmam* – 749th name – *Vapuṣaḥ* – He has an auspicious body.

232. *Śrīmate* – श्रीमते

He is a prosperous person. When he has Goddess Lakshmi with him, there cannot be any shortage of prosperity.

233. *Śrīnivāsāya* – श्रीनिवासाय

He is the abode of Śrī – Lakshmi, goddess of wealth.

In general, the name *Śrīnivāsaḥ* will mean Lord Vishnu. But Lord Dattatreya and Lord Vishnu are one and the same and hence this name.

In *Vişŋu Sahasranāmam* – 607th name – *Śrīnivāsaḥ* – abiding always with the wealthy.

234. *Amarārcitāya* – अमरार्चिताय

He is the one who is worshipped by the Devas.

235. *Śrīnidhaye* – श्रीनिधये

The treasure of *Śrī* – the wealth. He protects *Śrī* as a treasure.

In *Vişŋu Sahasranāmam* – 608th name – *Śrīnidhiḥ* – treasure house of all prosperity.

236. *Śrīpataye* – श्रीपतये

The lord of *Śrī* i.e. Goddess Lakshmi.

In general, the name *Śrīpati* will mean Lord Vishnu. But Lord Dattatreya and Lord Vishnu are one and the same and hence this name.

Svetashwata Upanishad (6.8) says – the supreme shakti of Him is declared to be various.

Goddess Lakshmi, having originated during the churning of milky ocean for nectar, has chosen Lord Vishnu as her consort rejecting all the Devas, Asuras and others.

In *Vişŋu Sahasranāmam* – 603rd name – *Śrīpatiḥ* – The lord of *Śrī*, the Parashakti.

237. *Śreşţhāya* – श्रेष्ठाय

He is the eldest, excellent and greatest.

Brahadaranyaka Upanishat (8.1.1) says – The prana is the eldest and the excellent and again Brahma Sutra (2.4.8) says – He is excellent.

This may mean that the chief Prana or Jyeshta, being the universal cause and Shreshta being above all others.

The second of the five-brahma aspect of Lord Shiva is *Vāmadevā*. The corresponding mantra says – he is the *Jyeṣṭha* and *Śreṣṭha*.

In *Viṣṇu Sahasranāmam* – 68th name – *Śreṣṭaḥ* – he is the eldest and excellent.

In *Sūrya Sahasranāmam* – 63rd, 315th and 506th names – *Śreṣṭhāya* – The greatest

575th name below may also be referred.

238. *Śreyaskāya* – श्रेयस्काय

He creates well-being for his devotees. He bestows eternal bliss, being the nature of the supreme.

In *Viṣṇu Sahasranāmam* – 612th name – *Śreyaḥ* – he provides salvation to his devotees.

In *Sūrya Sahasranāmam* – 798th name – *Śreyase* – He bestows welfare and ultimately bliss to his devotees.

239. *Caramāśrayāya* – चरमाश्रयाय

He is the final refuge for all beings.

81st name above may also be referred.

The above 10 names were taken from the 31st shloka of the *Sahasranāma* Stotram.

240. *Tyāgine* – त्यागिने

He is a renouncer. He has renounced everything including his clothes and lived a life of an avadhoota sanyasi.

241. *Tyāgājyasampannāya* – त्यागाज्यसम्पन्नाय

He has achieved the true purpose of renunciation and he set an example for others.

242. *Tyāgātmane* – त्यागात्मने

He is the Pure Atma having forsaken all the worldly affairs.

714th name below may also be referred.

243. *Tyāgavigrahāya* – त्यागविग्रहाय

He has withdrawn from all the worldly affairs and live into isolation.

244. *Tyāgalakṣaṇasiddhātmane* – त्यागलक्षणसिद्धात्मने

He is the realised soul characterised by renunciation.

245. *Tyāgajñāya* – त्यागज्ञाय

He is completely knowledgeable about renunciation.

246. *Tyāgakāraṇāya* – त्यागकारणाय

He is the cause of sacrifice.

The above 7 names from 240th onwards, describes the Lord as the best of sanyasis.

The above 7 names were taken from the 32nd shloka of the *Sahasranāma* Stotram.

247. *Bhogāya* – भोगाय

He enjoys the worldly affairs.

Earlier it was mentioned that he has renounced the worldly affairs. Here it is mentioned that he enjoys the worldly affairs. It is simply an illusion for the devotee's sake.

248. *Bhoktre* – भोक्त्रे

He is the enjoyer of insentient Prakruti or matter. As Virat Purusha he enjoys.

Lord Krishna was the enjoyer of even leaves, etc., offered to him with devotion.

As supreme bliss, he enjoys the task of protection.

Bhogā means bliss. He enjoys it. He is the bliss and the enjoyer as well.

The word *Bhogā* means the body of a snake. He is in the form *Kuṇḍalinī* energy in the human body as a snake.

In *Viṣṇu Sahasranāmam* – 143rd, 500th and 888th names – *Bhoktāḥ* – the enjoyer.

In *Lalitā Sahasranāmam* – 293rd name – *Bhoginī* – She is the enjoyer.

249. *Bhogyāya* – भोग्याय

He is in the form of the things enjoyed.

He is the enjoyer and also, he is the things being enjoyed.

250. *Bhogasādhanakāraṇāya* – भोगसाधनकारणाय

He is the cause of attaining enjoyment.

251. *Bhogine* – भोगिने

He himself is in the form of all the pleasures being enjoyed.

252. *Bhogārthasampannāya* – भोगार्थसम्पन्नाय

He only enables accomplishing the purpose of enjoyment.

The above 6 names were taken from the 33rd shloka of the *Sahasranāma* Stotram.

253. *Bhogajñānaprakāśanāya* – भोगज्ञानप्रकाशनाय

He only elucidates the real knowledge of enjoyment.

Above 7 names starting from 247th, talks about enjoyment. It has to be looked with the perspective that *Vedā* says – *Annam Ca Brahmā Aham Ca Brahmā Bhoktā Ca Brahmā* – the enjoyer, the enjoyment and the enjoyed matter – everything is Brahmam and nothing else.

When we eat our stomach full, the desire for hunger does not exist anymore. Similarly, once the desire is satisfied by enjoyment, we can concentrate on devotion and meditation to realise the Brahmam.

254. *Kevalāya* – केवलाय

He is the absolute, devoid of all attributes (*Nirguna*).

In practice, nowadays, the *kevala* is used to indicate the least or low level. But its actual important meaning is very great, individual and not mingled with any other attribute or righteousness.

He is *Ekā* (single) as he is devoid of any attributes. The only remaining sense of non–duality philosophy is *Kevala*.

Kevalā, a kind of knowledge described in a *Shiva Sūtra* (III–35) – that which is freed from that is the absolute '*Kevalā*'.

There are mainly three objects *dharma* (righteousness), *Artha* (money) and *Moksha* (salvation). The *kāmakala* (i.e. *Im*) enables the worshipper to reach the *turiya* (fourth) state. This is the state of *Kevala* or *Kaivalyam*.

In *Lalitā Sahasranāmam* – 623rd name – *Kevalā* – She is the absolute entity.

255. *Keśavāya* – केशवाय

He is the Lord of Creation with abundant hair

Keśas are the rays which are in the Sun and other stars. As he is the possessor of them, he is called as *Keśavā*.

Whose hairs, *Keśa*, are beautiful – *va*, the termination and is being used in the sense of 'praise'.

Ka means *Brahma*, '*A*' means *Vishnu* and *Īśa* means Rudra. Hence, *Keśavā* denotes the *Trimurtis*. This name is very apt to Lord Dattatreya, because *Trimurtis* were born as Dattatreya.

In Vishnu Purana (5.16.23) Narada says to Krishna – because thou hast slain the impious *Keśin* thou shall be known in the world by the name *Keśavā*.

In Shrimad Bhagavad Gita Lord Krishna says – the rays of mine which illuminate the Sun, etc., are called *Keśas*. The wise Brahmins call me therefore by the name *Keśavā*.

The word *Keśa* means *Shakti* or energy. The energies called Brahma, Vishnu and Rudra are named as *Keśas*. As he rules over them, he is *Keśavā*.

Rig Veda (1.164.44) says – there are three *Keśins*....

In *Harivamśa* Lord Shiva says to Lord Vishnu – *'Ka'* means Brahma and I am *Īśa* or Lord of all embodied being. We (Brahma and myself) sprang your parts of manifestations. Hence, you are *Keśavan*.

In *Viṣṇu Sahasranāmam* – 23rd and 648th names – *Keśavaḥ* – he has a beautiful hair. All the explanations given above applicable here also.

256. *Kṛṣṇāya* – कृष्णाय

He is Dark-skinned Lord who attracts devotees.

Kṛṣṇā means existence, intelligence and bliss.

Vyasa says – The word *Kṛṣ* means existence and *'ṇā'* means bliss. The union of these two is called the eternal Brahmam – *Sadananda Brahmam, Kṛṣṇā*.

Vyasa is called as *Krishnadvaipayana*. *Vishnu Purana* (3.4.5) says – you should know the *Krishnadvaipayana Vyasa* as Lord Narayan himself. Who can be the compiler of Mahabharata other than Lotus eyed Vishnu?

Mahabharata (Shanti Parva 343) says – As my colour is dark blue I am called *Kṛṣṇā*, Oh Arjuna.

In *Viṣṇu Sahasranāmam* – 57th and 550th names – *Kṛṣṇaḥ* – he is in an attractive black colour.

In *Gāyatri Sahasranāmam* – 180th name – *Kṛṣṇāyai* – One who is black in colour.

In *Śiva Sahasranāmam* – 128th name – *Kṛṣṇaḥ* and 453rd name – *Kṛṣṇavarṇaḥ* – He is in the form of Sadananda Brahmam. He is black in colour.

257. *Kaṃvāsase* – कंवाससे

He always resides on the waters. Lord Vishnu is always on the *Ksheera Sagar* – milky ocean. The same is being indicated in this name.

258. *Kamalālayāya* – कमलालयाय

He abides in a temple of Lotus.

Note: The biggest temple tank at Thiruvarur, in Tamil Nadu is called as *Kamalālayam*.

259. *Kamalāsanapūjyāya* – कमलासनपूज्याय

He is always worshipped by the lotus-seated – *Srī Brahma*.

260. *Haraye* – हरये

He is the remover of illusions. He removes all types of sorrows.

He is in the form of Lord Anjaneya.

He is *Sarva Samharda* – he in the form of Lord Rudra, the All-destroyer.

In *Viṣṇu Sahasranāmam* – 650th name – *Hariḥ* – he destroys the disease called samsara with its cause.

In *Śiva Sahasranāmam* – 208th, 375th, 705th and 784th names – *Hariḥ* – He removes the birth-death cycle.

261. *Ajñānakhaṇḍanāya* – अज्ञानखण्डनाय

He is the destroyer of ignorance. Unless the darkness called ignorance is removed the light called knowledge cannot be obtained.

The above 9 names were taken from the 34th shloka of the *Sahasranāma* Stotram.

262. *Mahātmane* – महात्मने

He is the great soul – *Mahātma*.

Ātma is any general soul like us. *Mahātma* is a great soul. Lord Dattatreya is a *Mahātma*.

The word *Ātmā* has several meanings – body, mind, *Brahmam*, nature, firmness and intelligence. All these names apt for him.

In *Lalitā Sahasranāmam* – 617th name – *Atmā* and 618th name – *Paramā* – She is in the form of *Ātman* or *Jeeva* (soul) and also in the form of *Paramātma*.

In *Sūrya Sahasranāmam* – 16th name – *Mahātmane* – He is a great soul.

We used to call Gandhiji as *Mahātma*.

263. *Mahadādaye* – महदादये

He is the bestower of intellect and other faculties to all his devotees.

264. *Maheśottamavanditā* – महेशोत्तमवन्दिता

He is adored by the most excellent Lord Brahma, Vishnu and Shiva.

265. *Manovṛddhivihīnātmane* – मनोवृद्धिविहीनात्मने

His nature is beyond mind and intellect. He can be realised only devotion and dedication.

266. *Mānātmane* – मानात्मने

He is a respected soul – atma.

267. *Mānavādhipāya* – मानवाधिपाय

He is an overseer of human beings. Earlier multiple times we read that he is witness to all activities of all beings. He is an overseer.

The above 6 names were taken from the 35th shloka of the *Sahasranāma* Stotram.

268. *Bhuvaneśāya* – भुवनेशाय

He is the lord of all worlds.

There are seven worlds beneath this earth viz., *Athalam, Vitalam, Sutalam, Talātalam, Mahātalam, Rasātalam* and *Patālam*. There are six worlds above the earth viz., *Bhuvarloka, Suvarloka, Mahālokā, Janolokā, Tapo Lokā* and *Sathya Loka*. These 13 alongwith Earth are the 14 worlds. He steers these 14 worlds as per his wish.

The word *Bhuvanā* has many meanings – earth, heaven, water, etc. He is the head of all these.

In *Lalitā Sahasranāmam* – 294th name – *Bhuvaneśvarī* – She is the sovereign ruler of the universe comprising of fourteen worlds.

In *Gāyatri Sahasranāmam* – 767th name – *Bhuvaneśvarī* – The Shakti due to whom the Universal evolution is made possible and the various Beings are sustained without hassles.

In *Sūrya Sahasranāmam* – 22nd name – *Bhuvaneśvara* – He is the Lord of all the worlds.

269. *Vibhūtaye* – विभूतये

He is so magnificent.

Mundaka Upanishat (1.6) says – He is eternal and multi-form.

He is all pervade – in all the 14 worlds.

In *Viṣṇu Sahasranāmam* – 240th and 880th names – *Vibhuḥ* – he is multi-formed.

270. *Dhṛtaye* – धृतये

He is very steady in all his activities. He is fearless and offers courage to his devotees.

By nature, he is changeless, ever the same, free from birth, etc. By him all the devotees are supported by the gift of his Atma.

In *Viṣṇu Sahasranāmam* – 160th name – *Dṛtātmā* – he is a controlled self.

In *Gāyatri Sahasranāmam* – 485th name – *Dhṛtyai* – She is a courageous lady. She is without fear.

271. *Medhāye* – मेधाये

He is very much Retentive. He is in the form intelligence (*Medhā*). Goddess Saraswati is his tongue.

He is able to grasp several subjects at a time.

Agni Purāṇa says *Medhā* is remembrance.

According to the *Padma Purāṇa*, the deity called *Medhā* is in Kashmir.

In *Viṣṇu Sahasranāmam* – 77th name – *Medhāvīḥ* – he is with powerful memory.

In *Lalitā Sahasranāmam* – 538th name – *Medhā* – She is in the form of special knowledge. We worship *Śrī Devī* through *Medhā Sookta* also.

272. *Smṛtaye* – स्मृतये

He is in the form of *Smrutis*.

Śruti– hearing and *Smruti* – recollection – he is in the form of knowledge obtained through both these.

The *Vedas* and the *Smrutis* of Manu etc., are but his form.

The *Koorma Purāṇa*, says, "*Rig, Yajus, Sāma* and *Atharva* are the inherent form of *Brahmam*, thus is the eternal energy".

The *Vāyu Purāṇa* says, "As he recollects all actions, present, past and future, he is called *Smruti*".

In *Lalitā Sahasranāmam* – 540th name – *Smrutiḥ* – She is in the form of *Smrutis*.

273. *Dayāye* – दयाये

He is the personification of mercy/ compassion.

The famous *Śrī Śrīdara Ayāvāl* has written an epic of poems called *Dayā Shatakam* about compassion. This book has been written metamorphosing the compassion of Lord *Shiva*.

Śrī Parāsara Battar also describes compassion in detail in his book called *Kshamā Śoḍaśī*.

Śrī Vedanta Desikar also in his book called *Dayā Śatakam* (51–14) mentions about the compassion of *Śrī Venkatachalapathi*.

In *Lalitā Sahasranāmam* – 581st name – *Dayāmūrtiḥ* – She is the embodiment of Mercy.

In *Lalitā Triśatī* – 9th name – *Karuŋāmrutasāgarā* and 151st name – *Kārunyavigrahā* – *Śrī Ādi Śaṇkara*'s commentary for these names – the thought of very great people to have mercy on the people in distress is called *Karuŋā* (compassion).

274. *Duḥkhadāvānalāya* – दुःखदावानलाय

He is like a fire that consumes the forest of miseries.

He removes the sorrow, pain caused by wordly affairs.

The *Goutama sutrā* (I–22) says; *Tadatyarta Vomoko Pavarkaḥ* – Salvation is the complete release from that pain.

In *Veda* also – He lives completely free from pain –
"*Dukkhenātyanta Vimuktas Charati*".

In *Lalitā Sahasranāmam* – 191st name – *Duḥkhahantrī* – She is the destroyer of all types of sorrows.

275. *Buddhāya* – बुद्धाय

He is an enlightened soul.

104th name above may be referred.

276. *Prabuddhāya* – प्रबुद्धाय

He is an enlightened and awakened soul.

This name can be read in conjuction with the previous name.

277. *Parameśvarāya* – परमेश्वराय

He is the supreme Lord.

He is the *Ĕshwara*, the *shakti* of the universal absolute.

Usually the word *Parameśvarā* will indicate Lord Shiva. Here it indicates Lord Dattatreya clearly confirming that both are one and the same Lord.

Shrimad Bhagavad Gita (13.17), Sri Krishna says, The supreme Lord remain the same in all beings.

In *Vişṇu Sahasranāmam* – 377th name – *Parameśvaraḥ* – *Śrī Ādi Śaṇkara* in his commentary says that he is *Parameśwaraḥ* since he has great wealth and supreme ruling power.

In *Lalitā Sahasranāmam* – 396th name – *Parameśvarī* – She is the Sovereign Supreme.

In *Sūrya Sahasranāmam* – 982nd name – *Parameśvarāya* – He is the supreme being.

The above 10 names were taken from the 36th shloka of the *Sahasranāma* Stotram.

278. *Kāmaghnāya* – कामघ्नाय

He is the destroyer of lustfulness.

The word *Kāma* will also indicate Cupid (*Manmatan*). In the form of Lord Shiva, he won over Cupid and hence this name.

He destroys other desires and satisfies the desire for salvation.

In *Śiva Sahasranāmam* – 187th name – *Kāmanāśakaḥ* – He killed Cupid.

279. *Krodhaghnāya* – क्रोधघ्नाय

He is the destroyer of anger.

He has no hatred on anyone; he does not get angry also. Only when he does not get angry, he can control the anger of his devotees.

Every human has six internal enemies – lust, anger, stinginess, libidinous, recklessness and amusement. He suppresses the anger of the devotees and destroys the lust in them.

Sage *Āpastambā* explains the cruelty of the anger as, He, who sacrifices, offer obligations, or worships with anger, is deprived of all benefits therefrom like water in a vessel of unbaked clay.

In *Śrīmad Bhagavat Geeta* (II–62/63) and again in III–37 the result of anger is explained. Also in (IX–29) Lord Krishna says;

Na Me Dveshyosti Napriyaḥ

To protect the devotees, Lord destroys the wicked. Still **He** does not get angry with the wicked people.

Anger is a state of mind arising out of the knowledge of an object. He adorns the goad in his hand to control the anger. A weapon will act as intended by the person who takes aim. Here these weapons will act as per the wish of *Śrī Dattatreya*. For worshippers of him, he will make the 'desire' and 'hatred' act according to the wishes of the devotees and ultimately raise them to his level.

In *Vişṇu Sahasranāmam* – 314th name – *Krodhahā* – He destroys anger (in good men). In contrast, again 315th name – *Krodhakṛtkartā* – He creates anger (in wicked men).

In *Lalitā Sahasranāmam* – 9th name – *Krodhā Kārāng Kuśojjvalā* – Her lustre is enhanced by holding the goad symbolising anger.

Again, in *Lalitā Sahasranāmam* – 168th name – *Nişkrodhā* and 169th name – *Krodhaśamanī* – She is without anger and controls the tendency to get angry of her devotees.

280. *Dambhadarpamadāpahāya* – दम्भदर्पमदापहाय

He removes hypocrisy, insolence and pride in his devotees.

281. *Ajñānatimirāraye* – अज्ञानतिमिरारये

He removes the enemy of the darkness called ignorance.

He is so compassionate to his devotes that he removes the darkness called ignorance around the beings and bestows them with well-being. Once the light is lit, the darkness goes away. The light does its duty of encompassing brightness, immediately the darkness escapes. That is, once the knowledge is obtained, the ignorance runs away.

In *Śrīmad Bhagavad Geeta* (X – 11) also Lord Krishna says that out of mere compassion for them, I, dwelling within their selves, destroy the darkness born of ignorance with the luminous lamp of knowledge.

In *Lalitā Sahasranāmam* – 993rd name – *Ajnānadhvānta Dīpikā* – She dispels the darkness of ignorance.

261st name above may also be referred here.

282. *Bhavāraye* – भवारये

He is a foe of the cycle of birth and death.

The word *Bhava* has three meanings – Lord *Mahadeva*, the human life cycle and Cupid. He gives life (*Ānayathee*) to all these three and hence this name.

Since Lord *Paramashiva* creates all the living things his name is *Bhava*. Out of the eight forms of Lord *Paramashiva*, the form of water is called *Bhava*. (*Tayonmruḍa Jeevase – Śrī Rudra* verse). Lord Dattatreya, in the form Lord Shiva also gets that name.

The forest is dense with trees which grow again and again. Similarly this life cycle (*Samsāra* Ocean) also, makes repeated birth again and again on account of cravings on various external objects in this world. The forest will be destroyed only when all the trees are cut. In the same way only if the desires on the worldly matters are destructed the *Samsāra* forest will be shattered. It has to be understood that once we get the knowledge of *Śrī Dattatreya*, the bonding to this world will be cut.

In *Lalitā Sahasranāmam* – 112th name – *Bhavānī* – Lord *Shiva*, the form of water is called *Bhava*. His consort is *Bhavānī*.

Again, in *Lalitā Sahasranāmam* – 114th name – *Bhavāraŋya Kuṭhārikā* – she is like an axe clearing the jungle of trans migratory existence (the ocean of *Samsāra*).

The 22nd*verse* of *Soundaryalaharī*, assuming two usages for the word *Bhavānī* the grace of *Śrī Devī* is explained. The word *Bhavānī* is used as an exclamation and as a predicate.

In *Gāyatri Sahasranāmam* – 733rd and 760th names – *Bhavānī* – same meaning as given for Lalita *Sahasranāma*m 114th name.

In *Sūrya Sahasranāmam* – 1,004th name – *Bhavasāgaratārakāya* – He helps his devotees to cross over the ocean of birth and death cycle and worldly affairs. He ensures liberation to his devotees.

283. *Bhuvaneśvarāya* – भुवनेश्वराय

268th name above may be referred.

The above 6 names were taken from the 37th shloka of the *Sahasranāma* Stotram.

284. *Rūpakṛte* – रूपकृते

He only creates beauty to all beings and to everything in this universe.

285. *Rūpabhṛte* – रूपभृते

He only sustains all the forms.

286. *Rūpiṇe* – रूपिणे

He is the possessor of elegant form.

287. *Rūpātmane* – रूपात्मने

He is the embodied sprit (Atma).

922nd name below may also be referred.

288. *Rūpakāraṇāya* – रूपकारणाय

He only causes the perception of forms.

289. *Rūpajñāya* – रूपज्ञाय

He only knows the senses of the objects.

290. *Rūpasākṣiṇe* – रूपसाक्षिणे

He is the witness of all the forms.

291. *Nāmarūpāya* – नामरूपाय

He has name and fame.

284th name onwards, the above 8 names talk about the forms of Sri Dattatreya. They can be read together. In reality he is *Niroopa* – formless. Only the *Brahmam* is beyond name and form. Hence, he is the *Brahmam* – but, on account of the illusion of his devotees, he seemingly has different forms.

Everything in this world is identified only by name and form. He is without both. He cannot be indicated by name or form.

Everything created in this universe has identification in five forms viz. existence (*Asti*), knowledge (*Pāti*), bliss (affection – *priyam*), name (*nāmam*) and form (*roopam*). The first three indicate the relationship of Chit with this world as a matter. They are called *Chit granti*. The last two, name and form are illusory and they are called A*chit granti*.

The details are;

1. *Asti* – existence – one who exists. The essence of *Brahmam* reflects in the feeling that "I exist" (self). Thus, all actions take place.

2. *Pāti* – knowledge – that could be understood by the knowledge. The chit part of *Brahmam* is 'I'. Only because every object reflects on this, it is understood by the mind.
3. *Priyam* – bliss – affection. Every living being has affection on self just because of the activities of this world. All the activities happen only because of the love on the things where the human being has affection.

   These three are permanent and route for activities.
4. *Nāmam* – name. It is not only the name given to us by others, it is also the feeling that "I am a man", "This is a horse", etc. This is in general applicable to all perceivable matters.
5. *Roopam* – form. Individual person or thing by form. The form is important for all activities.

In *Lalitā Sahasranāmam* – 300th name – *Nāma Rūpa Vivarjitā* – she has neither name nor form.

The above 8 names were taken from the 38th shloka of the *Sahasranāma* Stotram.

292. *Guṇāntakāya* – गुणान्तकाय

He puts an end to the three attributes. He is *Nirguna* – without any attributes. Because he being the universal soul and the Lord of creation, preservation and destruction, by means of Sattva, Rajas and Tamas qualities. As being, in truth, he is devoid of all these attributes.

He is in the form of *Brahmam.* He is earlier to root nature (*moolaprakruti*). Hence, he is also earlier to the three attributes.

The *Sānkhya* doctrine says that though the qualities are specifically three viz. *sattva, rajas* and *tamas*, they have endless modifications.

Guṇa means aggregate (*Vyoohas*). Like nine *nidhies*, these *vyoohas* also are nine in number. Lord *Dattatreya* is of the form of aggregate of these nine qualities. They are; *Kālavyooha* (time), *Kulavyooha* (family race), *Nāmavyooha* (name), *Gnānavyooha* (knowledge), *Chittavyooha* (mind), *Nadavyooha* (*Nātha*), *Binduvyooha* (*Bindu*), *Kalpavyooha* (*Kalpa*) and *Jeevavyooha* (soul). He is of all these forms.

The word *Guṇa* also means rope. The rope called *Vairikā*, which tied the ship during the *pralaya*; He is the deity to whom it was tied. The following story occurs in the *Matsya* and *Kālika Purāṇas* and also in Shrimad Bhagavata, thus; at the time of dissolution all seeds and sages entered the boat at the command of *Manu*, who was directed by the Lord *Viṣhṇu* and the boat was tied to the horn of the fish–incarnation. That rope became firm when the Lord held it. "Make a great rope of hides to be called *Vatrikā*, nine *Yojanas* long and three cubits broad. Lord *Vishnu* who is the protector of the universe, the great *Māyā*, the father of the world, the world itself, will make that rope firm so that it will not give away".

Svetavastara Upanishat (6.15) says – he is pure and devoid of qualities.

In *Viṣṇu Sahasranāmam* – 839th name – *Guṇabhṛt* – He is possessed of all the three attributes. On the contrary – 840th name – *Nirguṇaḥ* – he transcends all the attributes.

In *Lalitā Sahasranāmam* – 604th name – *Guṇanidhiḥ* – she is the treasure house of all the three attributes. On the contrary – 961st name – *Guṇātītā* – She transcends the three qualities.

293. *Aprameyāya* – अप्रमेयाय

He is immeasurable – infante.

Prameya means measurable. This is not possible and hence he is *Aprameya*.

The letter '*A*' indicates *Brahma*, *Viṣhṇu* and all. He is to be known, or measured by them only. *Āpa* = water. *Aprameya* abiding in water. In *Rātri Sūktam* and *Devī Upanishad* also we read as – my origin is in the water of the ocean – *Mama Yonirapsvantaḥ Samudre*.

Since he does not have the qualities like sound, etc., he cannot be practically recognised by organs; not even by inferences, because there are no symbols relating to him; cannot be frozen through comparisons, because there are no comparisons, since he himself is undefined. He cannot be recognised by signification also. If he is not there then what will happen to the auxiliaries/ supporting evidences.

He cannot be recognised by the proof of negation also. He cannot be recognised by form, as witness to a non–form and proof of *sāstras*. There is no surprise for the knowledge understood by proof, then how he is understood by *sāstras* – he is the witness for all the proofs and he is in the form of explanation for all these. There is no room for further proof. Still since it is a great thing, by removing the false matters, which are not of the universal absolute (*tat*), the *Sāstra* becomes the evidence. Thus, since he is in the form of witness, he is *Aprameyaḥ*.

In *Viṣṇu Sahasranāmam* – 46th name – *Aprameyaḥ* – 248th name – *Aprameyātmā* – *Śrī Ādi Śaṇkara* in his commentary mentions he is immeasurable self.

In *Lalitā Sahasranāmam* – 413th name – *Aprameyā* – she is immeasurable.

In *Sūrya Sahasranāmam* – 509th name – *Aprameyāya* and 1,007th name – *Aprameyaparākramāya* – he is immeasurable and his energy and strength are uncountable.

294. *Prameyāya* – प्रमेयाय

He is finite – he seems to be finite as an illusion to his devotees.

This is in contrast to the previous name, which has been described in detail.

295. *Pramāṇāya* – प्रमाणाय

He is provable. As he is the underlying principle of consciousness, he is the authority in all Dharmas and other shastras. He is self-shining lord. He is in the form of wisdom.

Aitreya Upanishat (3.3) says – The wisdom is Brahmam.

The Vishnu Puranam (1.2.6) says – the nature of knowledge is in reality extremely pure. Through illusionary understanding of it, it appears as objects.

In *Viṣṇu Sahasranāmam* – 428th and 959th names – *Pramāṇam* – the proof. He is in the form of wisdom.

In *Śiva Sahasranāmam* – 76th name – *Pramāṇaḥ* – He is the cause of true knowledge.

296. *Praṇavāśrayāya* – प्रणवाश्रयाय

He is the Abode of the *Pranava mantra Oṃ*.

Vedas say – therefore, the worshipper praises him by *'Oṃ'*.

Sanatkumara says – As the Vedas salute Him, he is name Pranava.

In *Viṣṇu Sahasranāmam* – 409th name – *Praṇavaḥ* – He is in the form of *Pranava mantra Oṃ* or *Pranava mantra Oṃ* is his form.

In *Gāyatri Sahasranāmam* – 671st name – *Praṇavāyai* – She is the *Pranava mantra Oṃ*.

Note; General *Pranava mantra* is *'Oṃ'*. *Śākta Pranava mantra* is *'Hrīṃ'*.

297. *Pramāṇarahitāya* – प्रमाणरहिताय

He is devoid of any type limitations or rules.

298. *Acintyāya* – अचिन्त्याय

He is inconceivable – conceivable only through devotion and focused penance.

By any proof, he cannot be thought of in any particular form as separate from this Universe.

Because he is free from connection with the qualities, his nature is unthinkable. He is *Nirguṇā* and hence he cannot be conceived.

In *Viṣṇu Sahasranāmam* – 832nd name – *Acintyaḥ* – He is inconceivable.

In *Lalitā Sahasranāmam* – 554th name – *Acintyarūpā* – she is of unthinkable form or inaccessible to mind.

299. *Cetanāvigatāya* – चेतनाविगताय

He is a sentient Lord.

The *Chetana* energy in all the beings is *Śrī Dattatreya* only. *Chetana* means inner sense. Only because of this, we can recognise the objects shown by eye, ear and mind. Only through the action of this we can recognise the availability of this.

Samkshepa Sāreerakam says, the pure *chit shakti* of the supreme Lord is called *chaitanya*;

Chitshaktiḥ Parameshvarasya Vimalā Chaitanya – Mevochyate.

In the *Taitreeya Upanishad* (II–8–1) – The letter '*SA*' is in the form of *Chit Shakti* only.

In *Lalitā Sahasranāmam* – 417th name – *Chetanārūpā* – she is in the form of consciousness (*chaitanya*).

130th, 131st and 133rd names above may also be referred.

300. *Ajarāya* – अजराय ।

He is ageless and ever young.

The above 9 names were taken from the 39th shloka of the *Sahasranāma* Stotram.

Thus ends 100 divine names on Lord *Dattātreya* from 201 to 300.

*****

301. *Akṣarāya* – अक्षराय

He is imperishable. He is in the form all the alphabet letters.

In Shrimad Bhagavad Gita (15.16), Lord Krishna says – there are two types of persons in this world, the perishable and imperishable. The perishable is made of all creatures and the Brahmam is imperishable.

In *Viṣṇu Sahasranāmam* – 17th name – *Akṣaraḥ* and 481st name – Akṣaram – He is undecaying.

In *Śiva Sahasranāmam* – 410th name – *Akṣaraḥ* – he is indestructible.

302. *Akṣaramuktāya* – अक्षरमुक्ताय

He is eternally liberated. He enables his devotees to get liberated.

He enables his devotees to use the alphabet letters freely.

303. *Vijvarāya* – विज्वराय

He is free from mental afflictions. He removes the distress and anxiety of his devotees.

86th name above may also be referred.

304. *Jvaranāśanāya* – ज्वरनाशनाय

He destroys mental afflictions of his devotees. Jvara does not only mean fever, it means all the distress.

This may also mean that fever is a special type or an important disease – or an indication of some other disease inside the body. Further since there are many types of fevers, it has to be taken as Jara all types of fevers. Chanting of this *Sahasranāma*, is to get rid of the fever(s).

In *Gāyatri Sahasranāmam* – 338th name – *Jvaraghnyai* – and 343rd name – *Jvaradevatāyai* – She is best medicine for any type of fevers – feverish fire. She is the goddess of all fevers.

Some of the types of fevers mentioned in the Puranas are – heat fever, bile fever, vaada fever, sleshma fever, kapha fever, aalapha fever, sannipaada fever, Mahendra fever, krutrima fever, krutyati fever, ekahika fever, dwahika fever, triahika fever, caturthika fever, panchahika fever, paksha fever, maasa fever, shaanmaasa fever, samvatsara fever, sarvaanga fever, etc.

305. *Viśiṣṭāya* – विशिष्टाय

He is the most distinguished/ special Lord.

306. *Vittaśāstriṇe* – वित्तशास्त्रिणे

He is great scholar. He is an expert of all *Sāstras* (scriptures).

In *Lalitā Sahasranāmam* – 845th name – *Śāstrasārā* – she is in the essence of all *Sāstras*.

307. *Dṛṣṭāya* – दृष्टाय

He is perceptible only through ardent devotion and penance.

308. *Dṛṣṭāntavarjitāya* – दृष्टान्तवर्जिताय

He is beyond perceivarance. This name seems to be in a way contracdicting the previous name, but actually not.

He cannot be perceived, since he does not have any attributes that are felt by human senses through objects, qualities, actions, forms and organs. Without any attributes, he can only be seen by the intellect.

In *Lalitā Sahasranāmam* – 650th name – *Druśya Rahitā* – she cannot be seen by normal people with naked eyes.

The above 8 names were taken from the 40th shloka of the *Sahasranāma* Stotram.

309. *Guṇeśāya* – गुणेशाय

He controls the three attributes like Sattva, Rajas and Tamo relating to creation, protection and destruction.

He is the treasure house of all the qualities. In his Saguna form he has all the three qualities and in Nirguna form he without any attributes.

In *Gāyatri Sahasranāmam* –

- 210th name – *Guṇatrayavibhāvitā* – She manifests with all the three gunas
- 218th & 221st names – *Guṇavatī* – She is a personification of good qualities,
- 224th name – *Guṇadāyinī* – she bestows good qualities to her devotees.

316th name below may also be referred.

310. *Guṇakāyāya* – गुणकायाय

His body is composed of all the three moods.

Repeatedly it is being stressed that his *Niroopa* and *Nirguna* – without body or form and without any attributes. But these names talk about him *Saroopa* and *Saguna* – with body or form and with attributes, just for lay men like us.

311. *Guṇātmane* – गुणात्मने

He possess all good qualities.

He bestows good qualities to his devotees. Unless he possess them he cannot bestow to others.

318th name below may also be referred.

312. *Guṇabhāvanāya* – गुणभावनाय

He creates the attributes that are ingredients of Nature.

319th name below may also be referred.

313. *Anantaguṇasampannāya* – अनन्तगुणसम्पन्नाय

He is endowed with infinite virtues.

314. *Guṇagarbhāya* – गुणगर्भाय

He is impregnant with attributes.

315. *Guṇādhipāya* – गुणाधिपाय

He is the overseer of the three qualities, so that they are not misused.

The above 7 names were taken from the 41st shloka of the *Sahasranāma* Stotram.

316. *Guṇeśāya* – गुणेशाय

309th name above may be referred.

317. *Guṇanāthāya* – गुणनाथाय

He is the master of the three, Sattva, Rajas and Tamo moods relating to creation, protection and destruction.

318. *Guṇātmane* – गुणात्मने

311th name above may be referred.

319. *Guṇabhāvanāya* – गुणभावनाय

312th name above may be referred.

320. *Guṇabandhave* – गुणबन्धवे

He is like a kinsman of all the Gunas.

321. *Vivekātmane* – विवेकात्मने

He is a real judge in distinguishing and classifying things according to their real properties.

583rd name below may also be referred.

322. *Guṇayuktāya* – गुणयुक्ताय

He is enjoined only with good qualities.

It is mentioned in Shrimad Bhagavatam (11.9.32) that he learned good qualities from 24 different gurus (teachers), including animals.

323. *Parākramiṇe* – पराक्रमिणे

He possesses enormous power, courage, energy, strength, etc.

The above 15 names, 309 onwards, talk above the characters and attributes of the Lord. They can be read together to get a better understanding.

The above 8 names were taken from the 42nd shloka of the *Sahasranāma* Stotram.

324. *Atarkāya* – अतर्काय

He is beyond any logical reasoning.

Tarkam in Samskrutam is logic. *Atarkam* is illogic or beyond logic.

325. *Ākṛtave* – आकृतवे

He is with a gigantic body.

He is greatly enlightened soul.

326. *Agnaye* – अग्नये

He is in the form of Agni (fire God). He is the dwelling place for *Agni*.

In *Śiva Sahasranāmam* – 432nd name – *Agnijvālaḥ* – He is as bright as the flame of the Agni.

In *Sūrya Sahasranāmam* – 224th name – *Agnaye* – He is in the form of fire god *Agni*.

327. *Kṛtajñāya* – कृतज्ञाय

He is down to earth simple. He is very grateful with those who aided or favoured him.

827th name below may also be referred.

328. *Saphalāśrayāya* – सफलाश्रयाय

He is the abode of compassion.

329. *Yajñāya* – यज्ञाय

He is the Lord of all sacrifices, the one who performs the sacrifices, and the one who is worshipped through sacrifices.

He is in the form of all sacrifices. All Vedic sacrifices are his powers.

Taitrīya Samhita (2-5-5) says – Sacrifice is indeed his form.

Shrimad Bhagwat Gita (9-24) – Bhagawan Krishna says – I am the enjoyer of all the sacrifices and also the lord of them.

In *Viṣṇu Sahasranāmam* – 445th & 971st names – *Yagnaḥ* and 972nd name – *Yajñapatiḥ* – he is the lord or protector of all sacrifices.

In Ramayana, Sri Rama protected the yagnas performed by Vishwamitra and other sages.

In *Sūrya Sahasranāmam* – 109th name – *Yagnaḥ* – and 110th name – *Yajñapataye* – He is the lord of worship or sacrifice or yagna.

330. *Yajñaphaladātre* – यज्ञफलदात्रे

He is the lord who bestows the results of all sacrifices (*yagnas*).

331. *Yajñātmane* – यज्ञात्मने

He is the Lord worshipped through yagnas.

332. *Ījanāya* – ईजनाय

He is the one who has sacrificed everything.

He is an apostate ascetic who sacrificed even his clothes.

333. *Amarottamāya* – अमरोत्तमाय

He is the highest of the Immortal Devas.

The above 10 names were taken from the 43rd shloka of the *Sahasranāma* Stotram.

530th name below may also be referred.

334. *Hiraṇyagarbhāya* – हिरण्यगर्भाय

He is born out of a golden egg.

Usually, Lord Brahma is called as *Hiranyagarbhaḥ*. But here Lord Dattatreya is being called so. This implies that Lord Brahma and Lord Dattatreya are one and the same.

Taitreeya Samhita (4.1.8) says, at the beginning *Hiranyagarbhaḥ* came into existence.

In *Vişṇu Sahasranāmam* – 70th name – *Hiranyagarbhaḥ* – the dweller in the golden egg.

335. *Śrīgarbhāya* – श्रीगर्भाय

As *Śrī* or glory is within him he is *Śrīgarbhā*.

He is pregnant with entire wealth.

In *Vişṇu Sahasranāmam* – 376th name – *Śrīgarbhaḥ* – containing *Śrī* within him.

336. *Svagarbhāya* – स्वगर्भाय

He is self-originated (Svayambhu) and not from the womb of any lady.

Svayambhu means the Supreme Lord as he is independent and not subject to any other.

He is both the person, who is above all others as well as others.

This clearly shows that he alone is the instrumental cause. He is both material and instrumental cause.

Vedanta Sutra (1.4.23) says, he also is the material cause, on account of the promise (instructions) and of the illustrations.

Manu (1.7) says, He manifested himself, because he is foremost of all or self-born.

Katopanishat (4.1) says, the Self existent pierced the openings of the senses.

Isavasya Upanishat (8) says, He is Omnipresent, self-existent.

In *Viṣṇu Sahasranāmam* – 37th name – *Svayambhuḥ* and 986th name – *Svayamjātaḥ* – He is self-born.

337. *Kuṇapeśvarāya* – कुणपेश्वराय

He spears/ controls his body.

He is the lord of his own. Nobody else can be his lord.

338. *Māyogarbhāya* – मायोगर्भाय

He is born out of illusion. He gives rise to illusion

339. *Lokagarbhāya* – लोकगर्भाय

He is of the world, by the world, for the world and shall not perish from the world.

340. *Svayambhuve* – स्वयम्भुवे

336th name above can be referred.

341. *Bhuvanāntakāya* – भुवनान्तकाय

He is the destroyer of the worlds. In the form of Rudra, he does the task of destruction.

The above 8 names were taken from the 44th shloka of the *Sahasranāma* Stotram.

342. *Niṣpāpāya* – निष्पापाय

He is without any sin. Unless he is without any sin, he cannot destroy the sins of his devotees.

By the repetition of his *mantras* (doing japam), etc., he destroys the sins of his devotees.

Any sin or virtue is created only deeds – primarily due to desires on actions. He is without any desires. No actions also for him. Resultantly no sin or virtue also.

In *Śrīmad Bhagavat Geeta* (IV–14) we read as;

Na Mām Karmāni Limpanti Na Me Karmaphale Spruha.

In *Lalitā Sahasranāmam* – 166th name – *Nishpāpā* – She is without any kind of sin. The next 167th name – *Pāpanāśinī* – She destroys the sins of devotees.

343. *Nibiḍāya* – निबिडाय

He is compact and firm.

344. *Nandine* – नन्दिने

He is the supreme Bliss. He rejoices with worship performed by his devotees.

In *Vişṇu Sahasranāmam* – 618th name – *Nandiḥ* – he is the supreme.

345. *Bodhine* – बोधिने

He is the spiritual knowledge.

He causes to know or perceive the Brahmam. He, in the role of a teacher instructs or initiates. He is a friend, a relative and now a *guru* also. He takes all the roles.

In *Gāyatri Sahasranāmam* – 692nd name – *Bodhitā* – she acts as an instructor/ teacher.

346. *Bodhasamāśrayāya* – बोधसमाश्रयाय

He is the Abode of wisdom.

347. *Bodhātmane* – बोधात्मने

He is an awakened/ enlightened soul.

348. *Bodhanātmane* – बोधनात्मने

He is a Natural teacher of enlightenment.

349. *Bhedavaitaṇḍakhaṇḍanāya* – भेदवैतण्डखण्डनाय

He destroys divisions and dualism. This specifies that Lord Dattatreya preaches Advaita philosophy.

The above 8 names were taken from the 45th shloka of the *Sahasranāma* Stotram.

350. *Svabhāvyāya* – स्वभाव्याय

He is self-created. His Swayambhu nature has been insisted earlier also in many names.

351. *Bhāvavimuktāya* – भावविमुक्ताय

He is free from any type of sentiment or emotions. He is emancipated from existence.

Bhāva means the state of existence If the lord is considered as to have the existence status, then it may mean that he is existent. It is only the perseverance. Everything in the world has anyone of the states – existent of non–existent. For instance – rice is existent. After cooking rice is non–existent, but food is existent. Once it is eaten, the food is non–existent and the blood, etc., of the person who consumed the food, is existent. The Lord does not completely have such states. That Supreme Being is eternal.

In *Lalitā Sahasranāmam* – 680th name – *Bhāvā Bhāva Vivarjitā* – she is in the form of existence and non–existence.

352. *Vyaktāya* – व्यक्ताय

He is the manifested/ instantiated individual.

353. *Avyaktasamāśrayāya* – अव्यक्तसमाश्रयाय

He is in an unmanifested form. In the previous name, it was mentioned that he is in a manifested form. Though he has various forms, still he cannot be defined precisely to be in a particular form.

To start with *Vyakta*, the category *Mahat*, is called so because it was first manifested and also from its greatness. Since *Vyakta*, manifested, i.e., egoism the product of the above, *Āvyakta*. Thus, he is in the form of *Mahat* and *Ego*.

The *Linga Purāṇa* says, *Vyakta* is called *sat* (existence), as it is the second modification of the elements; *avyakta* is called *Asat* because it is devoid of that modification.

Vyakta is perishable and *avyakta* is imperishable. He has both the characters. The *Matsya Purāṇa* says;

"Uktam Aksharamavyaktam Vyaktam Ksharam Utāhrutam".

Vyakta is individual and *avyakta* is collective form. This has been mentioned in the *Narasimha Purāṇa* as, the *avyakta* is known as collective and *vyakta*, oh lord of ascetics, is individual;

"Samshtim Viduravyaktam Vyaktam Vyashṭim Munīshvarāḥ" I

According to the *Brahmāṇḍa Purāṇa*, the wise say the twenty-three categories are meant by the word *vyakta* and by the word *avyakta*, the supreme nature.

In *Viṣṇu Sahasranāmam* – 305th name – *Vyaktarūpaḥ* and 722nd name – *Avyaktaḥ* – he is in both manifested and unmanifested forms.

In *Lalitā Sahasranāmam* – 399th name – *Vyaktāvyaktasvarūpiṇī* – she is in a manifest as well as un–manifest state.

89th name above may also be referred.

354. *Nityatṛptāya* – नित्यतृप्ताय

He is eternally contented. He is complete in all respects. He does not need anything. Hence, he is always contented. He is contented with the permanent and eternal form of bliss.

Everything in the world is perishable, excepting himself. Even if those perishable things are offered, he gets satisfied.

In *Śrīmad Bhagavad Geeta* (IX–26) Lord Krishna says; Whoever offers me with devotion, a leaf, a flower, a fruit or water, I accept that, the pious offering of the pure in heart.

In the story of *Kuchela* and *Kaŋŋappa Nāyanar* this has been made very clear.

In *Lalitā Sahasranāmam* – 566th name – *Nityatruptā* and 815th name – *Anityatruptā* – she is eternally contented. She is satisfied even with our perishable offerings. She asks for devotion only and not for costly things.

355. *Nirābhāsāya* – निराभासाय

He is without unreal/fallacious appearances.

481st and 919th names below may also be referred.

356. *Nirvāņāya* – निर्वाणाय

He is in the state of absolute stillness, absolute extinction or annihilation of individual existence or of all desires and passions.

In Tamil language, the word *nirvana* also means without clothes. Since, he was an *Avadhootha* ascetic, it can also be considered in that sense.

In *Vişņu Sahasranāmam* – 577th name – *Nirvāņam* – he is the supreme bliss characterised by the absence of all sorrows.

357. *Śaraņāya* – शरणाय

He is the refuge as he destroys the misery of Misérables.

In *Vişņu Sahasranāmam* – 86th name – *Śaraņam* – he is the refuge.

In *Śiva Sahasranāmam* – 842nd name – *Śaraṇyaḥ* – he well takes care of his devotees.

In *Sūrya Sahasranāmam* – 27th & 316th names – *Śaraṇyāya* – he is the Lord with whom everyone seeks refuge with.

358. *Suhṛde* – सुहृदे

He is very good-hearted. He will not get angry with anyone.

The above 9 names were taken from the 46th shloka of the *Sahasranāma* Stotram.

359. *Guhyeśāya* – गुह्येशाय

He is the master of the secrets. He whose nature and all are concealed on account of illusions. He is to be known only through the secret sciences.

In literal form *Guhya* means secret. But, in tattva sense, he resides in *Guhā*, the ether in the heart. *Guhyā* means one who dwells in a cave, i.e. heart. He is secretive and dwelling in our heart. Hence, he can be identified only by inward search.

The word *Guhyā* can be considered to mean *Jeevātma* (soul), *Paramātmā* (supreme) and the union of both. The presiding deity who can bestow these results is called *Guhya*.

Kaṭopanishad (I–2–12) says;

Eśa Sarveśu Bhūteśu Kūṭātmā Na Prakāśate.

In *Viṣṇu Sahasranāmam* – 383rd name – *Guhaḥ* and – 542nd name – *Guhyaḥ* – he is concealed and mysterious. He can be understood by the secret *Upanishats* or one who dwells in the secret cavity viz., heart. He is beyond speech and mind.

In *Lalitā Sahasranāmam* – 624th name – *Guhyā*, 707th name – *Guhyarūpiṇī* and 720th name – *Guhyakārādhyā* – she is most secretive both in form and meanings.

In *Śiva Sahasranāmam* – 261st & 974th names – *Guhaḥ*, 260th name – *Guhāvāsī* – and 507th name – *Guhyhaḥ* – He is in the form of *Karthikeya*. The one who is hidden.

360. *Guṇagambhīrāya* – गुणगम्भीराय

He is with profound virtues.

361. *Guṇadośanivāraṇāya* – गुणदोशनिवारणाय

He prevents the faults of the three attributes. He investigates the merits and defects of virtues and vices and bestows results accordingly.

362. *Guṇasaṅgavihīnāya* – गुणसङ्गविहीनाय

He is free from involvement of the three moods.

From the above 309th name onwards, 15 names spoke about his qualities. Here again 3 names appreciate his virtues.

363. *Yogārerdarpanāśanāya* – योगारेर्दर्पनाशनाय

He destroys the pride of those without Yoga.

The above 5 names were taken from the 47th shloka of the *Sahasranāma* Stotram.

364. *Ānandāya* – आनन्दाय

He is the bliss, *Paramanandam*.

Brahadaranyaka Upanishat (6.3.32) says – of this happiness, all other beings enjoy only a part.

In *Viṣṇu Sahasranāmam* – 526th name – *Ānandaḥ* – He is the bliss.

365. *Paramānandāya* – परमानन्दाय

He is supreme bliss – in the complete contended form. Hence *Paramānanda*. Nothing greater or bigger than this.

In *Lalitā Sahasranāmam* – 252nd name – *Paramānandā* – she is the Supreme Bliss.

366. *Svānandasukhavardhanāya* – स्वानन्दसुखवर्धनाय

He is promoting happiness by granting the bliss of the Self.

367. *Satyānandāya* – सत्यानन्दाय

He is the real joy of truth.

The word *Sat* means eternal or indestructible. Bliss is pure happiness – form of *Brahmam*. That *Brahmam* is Lord Dattatreya.

The form of *Brahmam* is called as *Satchitānandam* indicated as three *Sat* + *Chit* + *Ānandam*. Among this *Chit* is knowledge.

As per the *Veda* statement – the word *Satyā* indicates *Prāŋan* (breath), *Annam* (food) and *Ādityam* (Sun);

Stiti Prāŋastītyannamayam Ityasāvādityaḥ

In *Lalitā Sahasranāmam* – 646th name – *Satyānandasvarūpiŋī* – she is the Supreme knowledge and bliss.

368. *Cidānandāya* – चिदानन्दाय

He is the Bliss of pure consciousness.

369. *Sarvānandaparāyaṇāya* – सर्वानन्दपरायणाय

He intends to have joy of oneness with everything.

The above 6 names were taken from the 48th shloka of the *Sahasranāma* Stotram.

370. *Sadrūpāya* – सद्रूपाय

He is the embodiment of reality.

371. *Sahajāya* – सहजाय

He is very much natural, without any type of artificial characters.

188th name above and 873rd name below may also be referred.

372. *Satyāya* – सत्याय

He is very much truthful.

57th and 225th names above may also be referred.

373. *Svānandāya* – स्वानन्दाय

He is self-full of joy and always happy.

366th name above may also be referred.

374. *Sumanoharāya* – सुमनोहराय

He is exceedingly charming. He attracts everyone.

571st name below may also be referred.

375. *Sarvāya* – सर्वाय

He is the entirety.

In Mahabharata (Udyoga Parvam 70.12) Vyasa says, as he is the origin and end of all, whether existent or otherwise, and as He at all times, cognizes all, he is called *'Sarva'*.

As he involves all beings at the time of involution of the Universe or causes all beings to involve in himself, he is *'Sarva'*.

In *Vişņu Sahasranāmam* – 25th & 26th names – *Sarvaḥ* – He is the all and he is the destroyer.

49th name above may also be referred.

376. *Sarvāntarāya* – सर्वान्तराय

He pervades in the minds of all beings. He fixes all the organs or provides the orders.

Brahadāraŋya Upanishad (III–7–3) says that this is with you and eternal; *Esha Ta Ātmā Antaryāmyamrtaḥ*.

Mānḍukya Upanishad (6th verse) also conveys the same message; *"Eshontaryāmyesha Yoniḥ Sarvasya"*.

In *Lalitā Sahasranāmam* – 819th name – *Sarvāntaryāminī* – she is omnipresent in the minds of all.

377. *Pūrvātpūrvāntarāya* – पूर्वात्पूर्वान्तराय

He has such a forethought that he anticipates obstacles and take appropriate steps.

The above 8 names were taken from the 49th shloka of the *Sahasranāma* Stotram.

378. *Svamayāya* – स्वमयाय

His nature is the Self.

379. *Svaparāya* – स्वपराय

He is beyond individuality.

380. *Svādaye* – स्वादये

He is the Primordial Self.

381. *Svambrahmaṇe* – स्वम्ब्रह्मणे

He is the Brahmam as the Self of the Universe.

382. *Svatanave* – स्वतनवे

He can be identified with the Self.

383. *Svagāya* – स्वगाय

He resides in the Self.

384. *Svavāsase* – स्ववाससे

He is clothed with the Self. Being an avadhootar, the atmosphere is his dress, i.e., he is naked – clothed with the self.

385. *Svavihīnāya* – स्वविहीनाय

He is without a sense of individuality – he is collective.

386. *Svanidhaye* – स्वनिधये

His treasure is the Self.

387. *Svaparākṣayāya* – स्वपराक्षयाय

He is the Self, the highest refuge.

From 378th onwards, the above 10 names talk about the self of the Lord. They can be read together.

The above 10 names were taken from the 50th shloka of the *Sahasranāma* Stotram.

388. *Anantāya* – अनन्ताय

He is without end in time or space.

He, through his unlimited powers, excel everyone. He being eternal, all-pervading and unlimited by space and time. He is in the form of Ananta, the snake.

Svetavastara Upanishat (6.8) says, the supreme Shakti in him, is declared to be various.

In *Viṣṇu Sahasranāmam* –

307th name – *Anantajit* – He is the conqueror of all
518th name – *Anantātmā* – He is of infinite self.
886th name – *Anantaḥ* – The endless
933rd name – *Anantaśrī* – He is with infinite power.

68th name above may also be referred.

389. *Ādirūpāya* – आदिरूपाय

He is the Primordial Manifestation.

He does the three main tasks of creation, protection and destruction of the entire universe and pervades everything in the form of root cause energy (*shakti*).

In *Lalitā Sahasranāma*m – 615th name – *Ādishakti:* – she is the primordial power.

390. *Sūryamaṇḍalamadhyagāya* – सूर्यमण्डलमध्यगाय

He resides in the midst of Sun's disc.

It is a method of worshipping the Lord meditating upon him in the Sun's disc.

It is said that the golden man seen within the Sun etc., is the supreme Lord *Parameshwarā.* This name indicates that the Lord is in that form; *Ya Esho Antarāditye Hiranmayaḥ Purusho Rudtāte*.

It is also described that *Bhānumaŋḍala* is the *Anāhata cakra* in the human body. Lord Dattatreya lives there in the form of *Kunḍalinī* energy.

In *Lalitā Sahasranāma*m – 275th name – *Bhānumaŋḍalamadhyasthā* – she is in the midst of the solar orbit.

391. *Amoghāya* – अमोघाय

All of his actions are completely effective and fruitful.

He fulfills every desire, when worshipped, praised or remembered and never leaves any of the aspirations unfulfilled. He is always unobstructed.

Chandokya Upanishat (8.1.5) says – truthful is his wish and truth is his resolve.

In *Viṣṇu Sahasranāma*m – 110th name and 154th name – *Amoghaḥ* – worshipping him will be very much fruitful.

392. *Paramāmoghāya* – परमामोघाय

He is extremely infallible.

393. *Pareśāya* – परेशाय

He always completes the past.

211th name above and 539th name below may also be referred.

394. *Parādāya* – परादाय

He grants the supreme state to his devotees.

395. *Kavaye* – कवये

He is a great poet.

In *Sūrya Sahasranāmam* – 402nd name – *Kavaye* – a great poet.

The above 8 names were taken from the 51st shloka of the *Sahasranāma* Stotram.

396. *Viśvacakṣuṣe* – विश्वचक्षुषे

He is the Eyes of the Universe. He perceives everything through his consciousness.

When we visit temples to see the God, it is very important that Lord should see us whether we see the God or not. God seeing the devotees is called "*Netra Deeksha*".

Maha Narayana Upanishat (1) says – He who has eyes on all sides.

In *Viṣṇu Sahasranāmam* – 625th name – *Sarvataścakṣuḥ* – he has eyes everywhere.

397. *Viśvasākṣiṇe* – विश्वसाक्षिणे

He is the witness for the whole universe. He is a witness to everything, as he has eyes in all directions.

35th, 52nd and 149th names above may also be referred.

398. *Viśvabāhave* – विश्वबाहवे

He has arms (shoulders) everywhere, throughout the universe.

399. *Dhaneśvarāya* – धनेश्वराय

He is the Lord of wealth. As Lord Vishnu, he is the consort of Lakshmi, the goddess of wealth. Hence, he is also the lord of wealth.

In *Vişņu Sahasranāmam* – 474th name – *Dhaneśvaraḥ* – he is the Lord of wealth.

526th name below may also be referred.

400. *Dhanañjayāya* – धनञ्जयाय

He is the conqueror of wealth.

Normally, the name *Dhanañjayan* will indicate Arjuna. In Shrimad Bhagavad Gita (10.37), Lord Krishna says – among the sons of Pandu, I am *Dhanañjayan*.

In *Vişņu Sahasranāmam* – 660th name – *Dhananjayaḥ* – he is the conqueror of wealth.

Thus ends 100 divine names on Lord *Dattātreya* from 301 to 400.

*****

401. *Mahātejase* – महातेजसे

He is of great brilliance. He possesses the qualities of velour, etc.

He, by whose light the Sun and other luminaries have become possessed of light, is of great radiance.

In Shrimad Bhagavad Gita (15.12) Lord says – the light which is in the Sun and luminaries is of mine.

In *Viṣṇu Sahasranāmam* – 673rd name – *Mahātejaḥ* – He is of great radiance.

In *Śiva Sahasranāmam* – 118th name – *Tejasaḥ* – He is of great light.

402. *Tejiṣṭhāya* – तेजिष्ठाय

He is the most energetic Lord.

403. *Tejasāya* – तेजसाय

He is the most lustrous Lord.

404. *Sukhine* – सुखिने

He is the happiest and bestows happiness to all.

In *Viṣṇu Sahasranāmam* – 889th name – *Sukhadaḥ* – He is the conferrer of bliss.

The above 9 names were taken from the 52nd shloka of the *Sahasranāma* Stotram.

405. *Jyotiṣe* – ज्योतिषे

He is of brightest light. He that shines of his own.

Maha Narayana Upanishat (13) says Narayana is the supreme Light.

In *Viṣṇu Sahasranāmam* – 877th name – *Jyotiḥ* – He is the light.

406. *Jyotirmayāya* – ज्योतिर्मयाय

He is entirely bright.

In *Śiva Sahasranāmam* – 226th name – *Jyotimayaḥ* – He is full of bright light.

407. *Jetre* – जेत्रे

He is the conqueror.

Nobody else can win over him and hence, he is the conqueror.

He is the conqueror of ignorance (*Avidyā*). He helps his devotees to win over it. He, who is the form of knowledge himself, bestows knowledge and wins over ignorance.

In *Sūrya Sahasranāmam* – 217th name – *Jetre* – He is always triumphant.

In *Gāyatri Sahasranāmam* – 318th name – *Jetrī* – She is always a triumphant.

689th name below may also be referred.

408. *Jyotiṣāṃ Jyotirātmakāya* – ज्योतिषां ज्योतिरात्मकाय

He is the essence of all the astrological bodies. By praying to him, one can come out of any type of Navagraha doshas. No other remedy is needed.

In some versions of *Śiva Sahasranāmam* – 226th name – *Jyotiṣāmayaḥ* – He is the authority in astrology.

409. *Jyotiṣāmapi Jyotiṣe* – ज्योतिषामपि ज्योतिषे

He is the Enlightened Understanding of astrology.

This name can be read in conjunction with the previous name.

410. *Janakāya* – जनकाय

He is the Progenitor. He is the father of all beings.

867th name below may also be referred.

411. *Janamohanāya* – जनमोहनाय

He attracts people with his beauty.

He causes delusion of people.

The above 7 names were taken from the 53rd shloka of the *Sahasranāma* Stotram.

412. *Jitendriyāya* – जितेन्द्रियाय

He has won his organs.

Since he has controlled all his senses, he can be called as an ascetic or Yogi.

Vamana Purana says – Lord promotes righteousness in his devotees, like control of senses, cleanliness, wealth and devotion to God;

Jitendriyatvam Shoucham Cha Māngalyam Bhaktireva Ca I

In *Śiva Sahasranāmam* – 711th name – *Jitendriyaḥ* – He has won his body parts.

In *Sūrya Sahasranāmam* – 9th name – *Jitendriyāya* – He has subjugated his senses.

In *Gāyatri Sahasranāmam* – 324th name – *Jitendriyāyai* – She has her senses sub-judicated.

413. *Jitakrodhāya* – जितक्रोधाय

He has conquered his anger. He enables his devotees also to conquer the anger. He destroys the tendency to get angry of his devotees.

He destroys the foes of Devas, not out of anger, but in order to protect righteousness.

In Shrimad Bhagavad Gita in lot many places, Lord Krishna advises Arjuna, to be a *Jitakrodha* – to control the anger.

In *Viṣṇu Sahasranāmam* – 462nd name – *Jitakrodhā* – He controls his anger.

In *Gāyatri Sahasranāmam* – 325th name – *Jitakrodhāyai* – She has conquered her anger.

414. *Jitātmane* – जितात्मने

He is the Conqueror of the Self.

415. *Jitamānasāya* – जितमानसाय

He is a triumphant over his mind.

Conquering and controlling the mind is very important to become a yogi or sanyasi. He is an expert in this regard.

416. *Jitasaṅgāya* – जितसङ्गाय

He is the Vanquisher of attachments.

A Yogi or sanyasi, should not have any type of attachment on anything. He is very skillful in this regard.

417. *Jitaprāṇāya* – जितप्राणाय

He is the conqueror of the *prāṇas*, the Vital Breaths.

There are five types of pranas; *prāṇan, apānan, vyānan, udānan* and *samānan*. He is the conqueror of all these.

According to the *Taitreeya Upanishat*, the world is *Annamaya, Prāṇamaya,..* He is the conqueror of the same.

418. *Jitasaṃsāra* – जितसंसार

He has overcome the worldly hankerings.

Unless the samsara attachments are overcome, he cannot be sanyasi.

The above 7 names were taken from the 54th shloka of the *Sahasranāma* Stotram.

419. *Nirvāsanāya* – निर्वासनाय

He is free from any type of desires.

As a typical sanyasi, he does not have desire.

420. *Nirālambāya* – निरालम्बाय

He is a Self-supported Lord. Everything in the universe depends on him. He is unsupported, as he supports everything.

In *Lalitā Sahasranāmam* – 877th name – *Nirālambā* – She is self-supported.

In *Sūrya Sahasranāmam* – 976th name – *Nirālambā* – He is self-supported.

421. *Niryogakṣemavarjitāya* – निर्योगक्षेमवर्जिताय

He is free from any attachment to comfort.

416th name above may also be referred.

422. *Nirīhāya* – निरीहाय

He is desireless.

419th name above may also be referred.

423. *Nirahaṅkārāya* – निरहङ्काराय

He is without any type of ego.

Ego is of three kinds; *Vaikharīka*, *Taijasa* and *Bhutādi*, according to *Sattva*, *Rajas* and *Tamo* characters, respectively. He is without any of these.

In *Lalitā Sahasranāmam* – 161st name – *Nirahamkārā* – She is without any type of Egos.

921st name below may also be referred.

424. *Nirāśīnirupādhikāya* – निराशीनिरुपाधिकाय

He is absolutely free from all the types of attachments.

416th and 421st names above can also be referred.

The above 6 names were taken from the 55th shloka of the *Sahasranāma* Stotram.

425. *Nirlābodhyāya* – निर्लाबोध्याय

He is free from any type of greed, because he is exceedingly liberal.

In *Lalitā Sahasranāmam* – 170th name – *Nirlobhā* – She is free from any greed.

426. *Viviktātmane* – विविक्तात्मने

He is a solitary soul i.e. Paramatma.

Though he pervades the Cosmos, yet he is exclusive. He distinguishes himself by his supreme qualities.

The word *Vivikta* indicates the divine places where there is no human being. That is, a holy place, even if people are there around, is called as *Vivikta*. The holy and secluded (both the qualifications) have been mentioned in this name. His blessings are available to those who meditate in those places.

The other meaning can be – He is with those who have the knowledge of soul and non–soul.

In *Vişņu Sahasranāmam* – 263rd name – *Viviktaḥ* – He is solitary.

In *Lalitā Sahasranāmam* – 835th name – *Viviktasthā* – She dwells in secluded places where there is no human being.

115th name above may also be referred.

427. *Viśuddhottama Gauravāya* – विशुद्धोत्तम गौरवाय

He is of the highest purity and venerability.

428. *Vidyārthine* – विद्यार्थिने

He is a learner/ student.

He is called as Adi Guru, the earliest teacher. But still, his thirst for learning does not subsidies. Shrimad Bhagavatam (11.9.32) says that he has learnt from 24 Gurus – both human and animal.

429. *Paramārthine* – परमार्थिने

He is an aspirer of a high or spiritual object or to supreme truth.

430. *Śraddhārthine* – श्रद्धार्थिने

He is always desirous of faith.

431. *Sādhanātmakāya* – साधनात्मकाय

He is the embodied form of accomplishment.

The Vedas say –

"Sarvāṇi Karmāṇi Yadavāptaye Sādhanāni Yasminnithi"

In *Śiva Sahasranāmam* – 988th name – *Sarvasādhanaḥ* – The one who bestows the fruits of all karmas.

80th name above may also be referred.

The above 7 names were taken from the 56th shloka of the *Sahasranāma* Stotram.

432. *Pratyāhāriṇe* – प्रत्याहारिणे

He restrains his senses and enables his devotees also to control their senses.

412th name above may also be referred.

433. *Nirāhāriṇe* – निराहारिणे

He abstains from enjoying the objects of senses. This name is in continuation of the previous name.

434. *Sarvāhāraparāyaṇāya* – सर्वाहारपरायणाय

He is the main aim of all consumption.

435. *Nityaśuddhāya* – नित्यशुद्धाय

He is ever/ eternally pure.

205th name above may also be referred.

436. *Nirākāṅkṣiṇe* – निराकाङ्क्षिणे

He is free from all types of desires.

419th name above may also be referred.

437. *Pārāyaṇaparāyaṇāya* – पारायणपरायणाय

He is the supreme goal.

He is devoted to perusal of the Supreme, from which there is no return.

The above 6 names were taken from the 57th shloka of the *Sahasranāma* Stotram.

438. *Aṇornutarayā* – अणोर्नुतरया

He is subtler than the subtlest, not to be easily recognised, form.

He is in five forms viz., physical, gross, subtle, subtler and subtlest. The sound, etc., are the cause of gross ether and the rest. He is free from physical causes such as sound, etc.

Taitrīya Upanishat (II-20) says – it is subtler than an atom; *Anoranīyān*.

Mundakopanishat (I.1.6) says – he is omnipresent and very subtle – *Sarvagatam Sūkşmam*.

Kaivalyopanishat (16) says – it is subtler than the subtle and eternal; *Sūkşmāt Sūkşmataram Nityam*.

Kaţopanishat (II–20) says – it is subtler than an atom; *Anoranīyān*.

The sacrificial fire done in the fire at *Kunḍalinī*, in the midst of *Mūladhāram*, is subtle. He is in that form.

In *Viṣṇu Sahasranāmam* – 457th name – *Sūkṣmaḥ* – He is very subtle. In *Lalitā Sahasranāmam* – 467th name – *Sūkṣma Rūpiṇī* – She has a very subtle form.

In *Gāyatri Sahasranāmam* – 971st name – *Sūkṣmāyai* – She is so minute in her appearance that one's sensory organs including Mind fail to realise her.

439. *Sūkṣmāya* – सूक्ष्माय

Previous two names can be connected.

928th name below may also be referred.

440. *Sthūlāya* – स्थूलाय

He has a physical and perceptible body/ form.

He pervades the universe and is beyond space and time;
Sthūla Prameya Paryantam Vamantī Viśvamāntaram II

In reality, he is without any form (*nirūpa*). For devotees' sake he seemingly has perceptible physical form.

441. *Sthūlatarāya* – स्थूलतराय

His physical form is extremely solid.

442. *Ekāya* – एकाय

He is the one (Brahmam). He is alone because he is without a backup.

He is devoid of any distinction such as *Sajātīya* – pertaining to the same species, *Vijātīya* – pertaining to different species and *Svāgata* – pertaining to the different parts of the same thing.

Taitrīya Upanishat (I–2–6) says – That supreme being, from which the ether and other things originated, desired to expand very much and grow (as world with name and form). It did penance with this desire and spread the light of knowledge. By doing that penance it created all the things whatever is available now;
Sokāmayata I *Bahusyām Prajāyeyeti* I *SaTapo'tapyata* I

Sa Tapas Taptvā I *Idam Sarvamasrujata* II

Brahma Tanmangalam Viduḥ – *Brahmam* is the only one that is auspicious, says *Viṣŋu Purāŋa*.

Aitreya Upanishad (I–1–1) says – there was only one soul in the beginning. Nothing else was there. It wanted to create the worlds – it created.

Chāndokya Upanishad (6–2–1) says, there is only one and no two; *Ekamevātvtīyam*.

Again, *Chāndogya Upanishad* (VI–2–3) says – It created the light by saying "I will become many and grow in a huge way". According to the saying "I will become many", the Sat in the form of that light created water. There is only one without a second.

In *Viṣṇu Sahasranāmam* – 725th name – *Ekaḥ* – *Śrī Ādi Śaṇkara* in his commentary says, since he is the concluded truth without any kind of differences that are internal or that relates to similar external objects or to dissimilar object, he is *Ekaḥ*.

In *Lalitā Sahasranāmam* – 665th name – *Ekākinī* – She is alone.

451st and 876th names below may also be referred.

443. *Anekarūpāya* – अनेकरूपाय

He has many forms.

He takes many forms at his own wish during his incarnations to protect the living beings.

Mainly, he has four forms viz., *Virāt* (imperishable), *Sūtram* (formulae), *Avyākrutam* (unmanifested) and *Turīyam* (fourth). He has four different colours in each of these forms as white, red, yellow and black.

In reality he, in the form of Supreme Being, is *niroopa* (without any form) *Brahmam*. Ironically, it is mentioned as he has multiple images. Though he is without any form as an actor he takes up different characters and shows different forms.

Veda says *Rudra* has billions of forms. *Śrī Rudram – Asankhyātāḥ Sahasrāni Ye Rudra Atibhūmyām.* He in the form of such a billion forms of *Shiva*.

Many texts like *Varāha Purāŋam, Narasimha Upapurāŋam* and *Tripura Siddhāntam* clearly says that he has many a form.

In *Vişŋu Sahasranāmam* – 721st name – *Anekamūrtiḥ*, 723rd name – *Śatamūrtiḥ* and 765th name – *Chaturmūrtiḥ* – he takes many forms in the self-imposed incarnations to help the human beings and Devas. On account of various alternatives, different forms are created from a single knowledge matter.

In *Lalitā Sahasranāmam* – 824th name – *Bahurūpā* – she has many forms.

In *Sūrya Sahasranāmam* – 551st name – *Anekarūpāya* – He has many forms.

444. *Viśvarūpāya* – विश्वरूपाय

Viśvarūpam is the *Virat* form mentioned in the previous name.

Since he (*Brahmam*) thought "I will take various forms", this world was formed. Hence, he is in the form of this world itself.

The soul is also called as *Pashu*. *Sva* means dog, the lowest kind of form, comparable to that of all beings. Since the soul worships him it is released from *svaroopa*. The *Roopa* becomes *vikatham*, he is called as *Viśvaroopa*.

In the order of creation, i.e. in the formation of all the *tattvas* from nature (*Prakruti*) till universe (*Prithvi*), it has been mentioned that all the subtle *tatvās* one above the other merges with nature. The creation, from the *Brahmam* the first manifestation is darkness (*tamas*), the next is that of intellect called *mahat*, then that of the soul threefold egoism (*ahankārā*), followed by the five subtle elements beginning with sound; among these are the five energies of knowledge and the five energies of action. In these energies the former five individually generate the five senses and collectively the *antahkkaraŋa* (the mind). The latter five generate individually the five organs of action and collectively the *prānās*. The sound and the others – four subtle forces generate the five gross elements. This is an established doctrine. There the *Chaitanya* manifested through the gross, subtle and causal vehicles respectively termed, *Viśva, Taijasā* and *Prāgnā*; these manifested ones (three groups of vehicles) respectively are turned *Vaisvānara, Hiraŋyagarbha* and *Ȅśvara*.

In *Vedanta* the three states are awakened, dream and deep sleep; *Viśva, Taijasā* and *Prāgnā* in those states as forms of soul and creation, protection and destruction as the three tasks; are only accepted. In *Tantra sāstrās* two more states swoon (*Turīyam*) and transcendental (*Turīyātītham*); material pleasure & displeasure (*Tiroḍhāna*) and blessings (*Anugraha*) are two more tasks. Since in the deep sleep state the soul does not completely merge with *Brahmam*, two more states as material pleasure and displeasure and blessings are added. During deep sleep the soul is with the causal body and in the swoon state, the soul takes the subtle body, it mixes completely with *Brahmam* in the transcendental state. Each of these states is being mentioned as names of Lord *Śrī Dattatreya*.

The word *Viśvam* indicates *'Oṃ'*. We all are aware of the *Viśvarūpā* form of Lord Krishna, shown to Arjuna, when he advised Shrimad Bhagavad Gita. Lord Krishna showed *Viśvarūpā* in some other occasions also in Mahabharata.

In *Vişŋu Sahasranāmam* – 717th name – *Viśvamūrtiḥ* – *Śrī Ādi Śaṇkara* in his commentary says – He is this world and its form since everything is himself. First name *Viśvā* can also be compared – this can be interpreted elaborately;

1. Since he is the cause for this world called *Viśvam, Brahmam* is called *Viśvam*.
2. This *Viśvam* is not something different from *Paramapurusha*. Hence *Brahmam* is called as *Viśvam*.
3. Since it pierces in, *Brahmam* is called as *Viśvam*. Being the universal soul, he is in the form of the world.

In *Lalitā Sahasranāmam* – 256th name – *Viśvarūpā* – One who is in the form of the world or *Viśvam*.

445. *Sanātanāya* – सनातनाय

He is the most eternal and oldest. Since, he is earlier than Brahma and others, who are older, he is the oldest.

In *Vişņu Sahasranāmam* – 897th name – *Sanātanatamaḥ* – he is the most ancient.

The above 8 names were taken from the 58th shloka of the *Sahasranāma* Stotram.

171st name above and 457th name below may also be referred.

446. *Naikarūpāya* – नैकरूपाय

He takes many forms.

Brahadaranyaka Upanishat (4.5.19) says, the Lord appears to be manifold by illusion.

The Smruti says, he is the luminaries and all.

In *Vişņu Sahasranāmam* – 271st name – *Naikarūpaḥ* – he has many forms.

200th and 443rd names above may also be referred.

447. *Nirūpātmane* – निरूपात्मने

He is the formless *atman*.

In the previous name, it was mentioned that he takes many a form. But, ironically, in this name it is mentioned that he is formless.

In *Vişņu Sahasranāmam* – 720th name – *Amūrtimān* – **he** is formless because he does not have the bondage and actions (*karmās*).

In *Lalitā Sahasranāmam* – 814th name – *Amūrtā* – she is without any form or shape.

287th name above and 922nd name below may also be referred.

448. *Naikabodhamayāya* – नैकबोधमयाय

He has knowledge of everything in this world.

449. *Naikanāmamayāya* – नैकनाममयाय

He possesses innumerable names.

Since, he is in the form of every being in this world, all the names are his.

450. *Naikavidyāvivardhanāya* – नैकविद्याविवर्धनाय

He promotes several forms of learnings (*Vidyas*).

The above 5 names were taken from the 59th shloka of the *Sahasranāma* Stotram.

451. *Ekāya* – एकाय

442nd name above and 876th name below may be referred.

452. *Ekāntikāya* – एकान्तिकाय

He is the absolute one.

453. *Nānābhāvavivarjitāya* – नानाभावविवर्जिताय

He is free from any type of emotions.

He is a Sanyasi. He should control every type of emotion. He does the same.

454. *Ekākṣarāya* – एकाक्षराय

He is in the form of Pranava mantra *'Oṃ'*.

In *Viṣṇu Sahasranāmam* – 409th and 957th names – *Praṇavaḥ* – he is the monosyllable *'Oṃ'*.

455. *Bījāya* – बीजाय

He is in the form of *Bija* (seed) letter of mantras.

Every mantra is a combination of multiple *Bījāksharas* (seed letters). He is the in the form of all these seed letters.

456. *Pūrṇabimbāya* – पूर्णबिम्बाय

He is the Absolute, complete and Eternal Seed (letter) i.e. the Pranava letter '*Oṃ*'.

The above 6 names were taken from the 60th shloka of the *Sahasranāma* Stotram.

457. *Sanātanāya* – सनातनाय

171st and 445th names above may be referred.

458. *Mantravīryāya* – मन्त्रवीर्याय

He is power of all the Mantras.

Every mantra has lots of powers (*vīryam*) generated by vibrations. He is in the form of all those powers.

459. *Mantrabījāya* – मन्त्रबीजाय

455th name above may be referred.

460. *Śāstravīryāya* – शास्त्रवीर्याय

He is the Power (*vīryam*) generated by all the Scriptures.

461. *Jagatpataye* – जगत्पतये

He is the head of this world.

In *Sūrya Sahasranāmam* – 82nd name – *Jagatpataye* and 787th name – *Jagatāṃ Pataye* – He is the head of this world/ universe.

In *Śiva Sahasranāmam* – 1,008th name – *Jagataḥ* – He is the world.

462. *Nānāvīryadharāya* – नानावीर्यधराय

He possesses multiple powers/ Shaktis (*vīryams*).

463. *Śaktreśāya* – शक्त्रेशाय

He is the master of all powers. He is the master Indra and other Devas.

464. *Pṛthivīpataye* – पृथिवीपतये

He is the Lord of the Earth.

According to the Shrimad Bhagavatam, Sri Krishna is the husband of Goddess Bhumi Devi. Lord Dattatreya, in the form of Sri Krishna, is the husband of Goddess Bhumi Devi.

The above 8 names were taken from the 61st shloka of the *Sahasranāma* Stotram.

465. *Prāṇeśāya* – प्राणेशाय

He is the Controller of the Vital Breaths.

417th name above may also be referred.

466. *Prāṇadāya* – प्राणदाय

He is the giver of *Prāṇan* (life) to all beings.

He destroys (*Da*) the *Asuras*, for the sake Devas (*Suras*).

The *Vişŋu Purana* says, as breath he causes the motion.

Taitreeya Upanishat (2.7) says, who then could live, who could breathe. Because he takes away (*Da* – to kill) the life (*Prana*) in the form of death or he purifies or destroys the Pranas or breaths.

Kenopanishat (1.2) says, He is the life of lives or the principal life.

Taitreeya Āranyakam (2.2.3) says "I am indeed the prana in all".

In *Vişŋu Sahasranāmam* – 65th, 321st, 408th and 956th names – *Prāṇadaḥ* – he is the life giver.

Again, in *Vişŋu Sahasranāmam* – 66th, 320th and 407th names – *Prāṇaḥ* – he is the breath giver. Without him, even the trees become dried.

417th name above may also be referred.

467. *Prāṇāya* – प्राणाय

He is the very life of all.

468. *Prāṇāyāmaparāyaṇāya* – प्राणायामपरायणाय

He is the Ultimate Goal of breath control.

465th name above may also be referred.

469. *Praṇapañcakanirmuktāya* – प्रणपञ्चकनिर्मुक्ताय

He is beyond the five Vital Breaths.

417th name above may also be referred.

470. *Kośapañcakavarjitāya* – कोशपञ्चकवर्जिताय

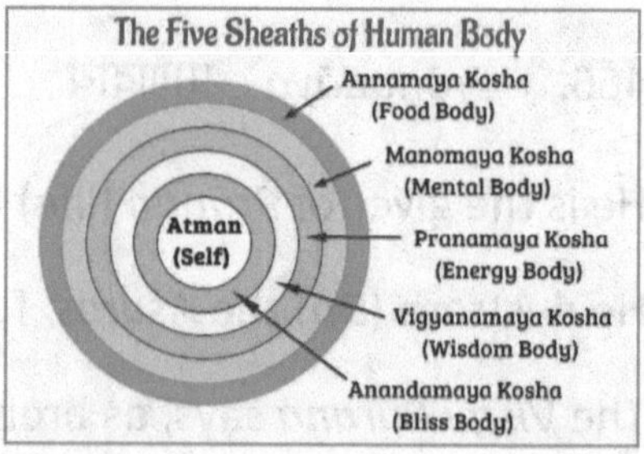

He is above the five sheaths (*Kośas*).

A *Kośa* or sheath is a covering of the Atma or Self according to Vedantic philosophy. The five sheaths or *Pancakośa*, are described in the Taittiriya Upanishat (2.1-5) and they are often visualised as the layers of an onion. The five sheaths, from gross to fine they are;

1. *Annamaya kosha*, 'food' sheath (Anna), the physical body.
2. *Prānamaya kosha*, 'energy' sheath (Prana), the vital principle.
3. *Manomaya kosha* 'mind' sheath (Manas), the mind and the five senses.
4. *Vijñānamaya kosha*, 'discernment' or 'Knowledge' sheath (Vigynana).
5. *Ānandamaya kosha*, 'bliss' sheath (Ananda).

The above 6 names were taken from the 61st shloka of the *Sahasranāma* Stotram.

471. *Niścalāya* – निश्चलाय

He is static and unmoving.

472. *Nişkalāya* – निष्कलाय

He is indivisible – he is partless (organless) unitary whole.

In *Brahma Sūtra* (II–3–43) – *Amsha Athikaran* – It is mentioned as since, some differences are located, the human soul is a part of universal absolute (*param porul* or *Brahmam*).

In *Śrīmad Bhagavat Geeta* (15.7) – *Mamaivamsho Jeevaloke* – the eternal soul in this world is a part of Myself.

Meditating *Brahmam* without any characters is *Nişkalā*.

In *Lalitā Sahasranāmam* – 140th name – *Nişkalā* – She is partless (organless) unitary whole.

473. *Asaṅgāya* – असङ्गाय

He is free from every type of attachments.

416th, 421st and 424th names above may also be referred.

474. *Nişprapañcāya* – निष्प्रपञ्चाय

He is free from mundane existence.

The word *Prapanchā* has three meanings; to unite (*Sanchayaḥ*), to extend (*vistāraḥ*) and to expand (*pratāranaḥ*). Since, he is complete in himself and omnipresent, he is beyond all these three controls of universe.

One thing expanding to many is *Prapanca*. Contraction and expansion are the characters of changing things. The worldly character is not seen in him, who is unchanging.

Or, it can be understood as; he from whom the universe, starting from the Earth, manifested – *Māndukya* Upanishad (7th verse) says;

Prapanchopaśamam Śiva Madhvaitam Chaturtam Manyante.

In *Lalitā Sahasranāmam* – 146th name – *Nişprapajncā* – She is beyond all the controls.

475. *Nirāmayāya* – निरामयाय

He is without any fault or mistake.

He is without any disease. Sickness affects both body and mind. He is without any disease. Since he is the medicine for all the diseases, how can any disease affect him?

In *Lalitā Sahasranāmam* – 876th name – *Nirāmayā* – She is without any disease.

In *Śiva Sahasranāmam* – 984th name – *Nirāmayaḥ* – he is blemishless.

476. *Nirādhārāya* – निराधाराय

He is self-supported. He does not need anyone else to support.

420th name above and 532nd name below may also be referred.

477. *Nirākārāya* – निराकाराय

He has no form at all.

He is the Niroopa Brahmam and hence he has no form.

The various forms of him seen by us are illusions. Reality is he is formless. The sense of this name is; since he is omnipresent there is no form relating to characters.

In *Lalitā Sahasranāmam* – 137th name – *Nirākārā* – She is not limited to and by any form.

478. *Nirvikāryāya* – निर्विकार्याय

He is beyond any modification.

The soul and nature are the two origin–less truths accepted in *Siddanthas*. Out of these the soul is intellect. It is different from body, organs and mind. It lives as witness to the changes in the world and but does not change itself.

Nature is the root for the world. This is origin–less, eternal matter and ever changing. This has the three characters goodness (*sattva*), passion (*rajas*) and ignorance (*tamas*).

The world is created by the unison of the soul and the earth. *Buddhi* (intellect) is the next direct evolute from *Mahat* (intelligence) followed by *ahankara* (ego). This is followed by sense organs, organs for actions, mind, five basic elements and five primary elements. As per the *Sankhya* Philosophy (enumeration or analysis of the Universe) there are 24 principles of creation, starting from nature. The soul is the 25th one.

These philosophies are divided into four parts – that are;

1. Only causes.
2. Only effects.
3. Causes for some and effects for some other.
4. Neither as cause nor as an effect.

Out of these the basic entity (*Moola Prakruti*), also the foremost one, is always a cause. In *Sankhya Tatva Kārikai*, it is very clear that the basic entity is a cause.

Śrī Ādi Śaṇkara, in his commentaries for the *Brahma Sūtra* also mentions about this.

The seven – Intelligence, ego and 5 basic elements are both cause and effects. Five sense organs, 5 organs of action, mind and 5 primary elements are effects. The soul is with neither cause nor effect.

He himself is the universal absolute.

In *Lalitā Sahasranāmam* – 145th name – *Nirvikārā* – She is not subject to any change.

479. *Nirañjanāya* – निरञ्जनाय

He is unstained purity.

Anjana means black collegium used for eyes. Though it is used for beautification, still it is a stain. In this context *Anjana* implies ignorance or illusion. The knowledge disappears due to ignorance (owing to its quality of darkness in mind). It has to be construed that *Śrī Dattatreya* has no relevance to ignorance or illusion.

There are three kinds of ignorant souls (*Pashus*);

(i) The *Vijnanākevala*, he who sees the self in the non–self and has arrogance as the only impurity;

(ii) The *Pralayakevala*, he who has the impurity of *karma*, which is unperceivable and which gives him new births; he also has the impurity mentioned in 'a' above.

(iii) The *sakala*, he who has the impurity of the illusion (*māyā*). He has the idea of duality in all matters. He also has the impurities mentioned in 'b' above.

(iv) He has no impurities of *sakala* and hence *Niranjana*.

(v) One who is – *Ni* (more) – *Ranjanam* (happiness/ delight)

Swetasvatara Upanishad (VI–19) indicates *Brahmam* as;

Niravatyam Niranjanam.

In *Lalitā Sahasranāmam* – 133rd name – *Niranjanā* – She is free from any stain.

The above 9 names were taken from the 62nd shloka of the *Sahasranāma* Stotram.

480. *Nişpratītāya* – निष्प्रतीताय

He is unopposed and unhindered.

481. *Nirābhāsāya* – निराभासाय

He is self-illuminating and make him appear to his devotees.

355th name above and 919th name below may also be referred.

482. *Nirāsaktāya* – निरासक्ताय

He is attached to no-one.

As a typical sanyasi he should not be attached to anyone.

483. *Nirākulāya* – निराकुलाय

He is obvious and unconfused.

484. *Niṣṭhāsarvagatāya* – निष्ठासर्वगताय

He is loyal, steady and all-pervasive.

485. *Nirārambhāya* – निरारम्भाय

He abstains from all works – he does not do any work, but he gets it done from others.

486. *Nirāśrayāya* – निराश्रयाय

He is without help or support.

420th and 476th names above may also be referred.

The above 7 names were taken from the 64th shloka of the *Sahasranāma* Stotram.

487. *Nirantarāya* – निरन्तराय

He is eternal and has no inside or outside

He is without any division (gaps). The word *Antarā* has many a meaning like – gap, extent, end, attire, death and difference. He is in all these forms.

Taitreeya Upanishat (II–7–1) advises – One gets scared if he sees even an iota of difference.

Ya Ethasminnudaramantaram Kurute Thatasya Bhayam Bhavati

In *Lalitā Sahasranāmam* – 151st name – *Nirantarā* – She is eternal.

700th name below may also be referred.

488. *Sattvagoptre* – सत्त्वगोप्त्रे

He is the protector of the truth.

489. *Śāntāya* – शान्ताय

He is the flagship of calm and tranquil.

He has abandoned all the attachments and hence is peaceful.

In *Viṣṇu Sahasranāmam* – 584th name – *Śāntiḥ* – he is peaceful.
In *Gāyatri Sahasranāmam* – 935th name – *Śāntā* – she is very peaceful.

In *Lalitā Sahasranāmam* – 131st name – *Śāntimatī* – 141st name – *Śāntā* – 447th name – *Śānti* and 963rd name – *Śamātmikā* – She is tranquil.

56th name above and 727th name below may also be referred.

490. *Dāntāya* – दान्ताय

He is subdued and restrained.

491. *Mahāmunaye* – महामुनये

5th name above may be referred.

492. *Niḥśabdāya* – निःशब्दाय

He prefers silent without any sound.

493. *Sukṛtāya* – सुकृताय

He performs only virtuous/ meritorious tasks.

934th name below may also be referred.

494. *Svasthāya* – स्वस्थाय

He is an established Self. He is healthy and comfortable.

495. *Satyavādine* – सत्यवादिने

He always tells the truth. He is so adamant in keeping up her words and promises.

He has promised to protect the entire universe and he is stubborn in that.

In *Viṣṇu Sahasranāmam* – 610th name – *Satyasandaḥ* – Since he has the intention to keep up the truth, everything will happen according to his thought.

Chāndogya Upanishat (8–1–5) says – *Satya Sankalpa*.

He is attainable by following the vow to speak and follow the truth.

The truth indicates *Brahmam*. *Vrata* (vow) is, some places, used on edible things. For instance, in *Sruti* statement; "*Payovratam Brāhmanasya*" – the word *vrata* indicates eatables. Hence, like eatables, he has liking on *Brahmam*.

Satyam (truth) also indicates low hanging fruits (which gives faster results). That is, the vows on his give quick results.

In *Lalitā Sahasranāmam* – 693rd name – *Satyasandhā* – 817th name – *Satyavratā* and 818th name – *Satyarūpā* – She is vowed to truth.

496. *Sureśvarāya* – सुरेश्वराय

He is the Lord of all Devas.

The above 10 names were taken from the 65th shloka of the *Sahasranāma* Stotram.

497. *Jñānadāya* – ज्ञानदाय

He is imparter of knowledge.

498. *Jñānavijñānine* – ज्ञानविज्ञानिने

He possesses the wisdom of knowledge.

499. *Jñānātmane* – ज्ञानात्मने

He is the soul of knowledge.

500. *Ānandapūretāya* – आनन्दपूरेताय

He is filled with joy/ bliss.

Thus ends 100 divine names on Lord *Dattātreya* from 401 to 500.

501. *Jñānayajñavidāṃ Dakṣāya* – ज्ञानयज्ञविदां दक्षाय

He is skillful in distributing the knowledge gained from *Yaga* sacrifices.

Knowledge is of two types. First is Attaining the complete form of the Lord, who is not limited by anything. The second is – thinking this un–soul body and universe as soul – this is actually ignorance. He only gives both these.

In *Lalitā Sahasranāmam* – 643rd name – *Jnānadā* – She is the bestower of knowledge.

502. *Jñānāgnaye* – ज्ञानाग्नये

He is the fire of knowledge.

503. *Jvalanāya* – ज्वलनाय

He shines like fire.

504. *Budhāya* – बुधाय

He is so wise and intelligent.

The above 9 names were taken from the 66th shloka of the *Sahasranāma* Stotram.

505. *Dayāvate* – दयावते

He is full of compassion.

The thought of very great people to have mercy on the people in distress is called *Karuṇā* (compassion).

The famous *Śrī Śrīdara Venkatesar* also called as *Ayyāvāl* has written an epic of poems called *Dayā Shatakam* about compassion. This book has been written metamorphosing the compassion of *Shiva* as a personification of compassion.

Śrī Vedanta Desikar also in his book called *Dayā Śatakam* (verse 51–14) mentions about the compassion of *Śrī Venkatachalapathi.*

In *Lalitā Sahasranāmam* – 581st name – *Dayāmūrtiḥ* – She is the personification of mercy/ compassion.

In *Lalitā Triśatī* – 9th name – *Karuṇāmrutasāgarā* and 151st name – *Kārunyavigrahā* – conveys the same meaning.

96th name above may also be referred.

506. *Bhavarogāraye* – भवरोगारये

He is the enemy of the diseases of existence. He is enemy of the birth and death cycle.

Being born again and again is a disease. *Shiva Purāṇa* and *Shrimad Ramayana* say that *Shiva* has the capability of curing it.

In *Shiva Purāṇa*;

Vyādheenām Bheshajam Yadvat Pratipaksha Svabhāvataḥ I
Tadvat Samsārarogānām Pratipakshaḥ Shivādhavaḥ II

In *Śrīmad Rāmāyana*;

Nānyam Pashyāmi Bhaishajyamantrena Vrushdhvajam I

In *Viṣṇu Sahasranāma* – 578th name – *Bheshajam* – The medicine for the disease called *samsara* is he only.

In *Lalitā Sahasranāmam* – 842nd name – *Bhavarogaghnī* – She cures the disease of trans–migratory existence (*samsārā*).

507. *Cikitsā Caramāgalāye* – चिकित्सा चरमा गलाये

He is the best treatment for all malaises.

In *Lalitā Sahasranāmam* – 551st name – *Sarva Vyādhi Praśamanī* – She cures/ alleviates all illness/ diseases.

508. *Candramaṇḍala Madhyasthāya* – चन्द्रमण्डल मध्यस्थाय

He resides in the center of the Moon's disc.

It has been mentioned that the full Moon is present in the *Sahasrāra Kamala* in the head. He is residing in the center of that Moon.

In *Lalitā Sahasranāmam* – 240th name – *Candra Maṇḍala Madhyagā* – She is residing in the center of the Moon's disc.

509. *Candrakoṭisuśīlālaye* – चन्द्रकोटिसुशीलालये

He is very cool like millions of Moons.

The above 5 names were taken from the 67th shloka of the *Sahasranāma* Stotram.

510. *Yantrakṛte* – यन्त्रकृते

He is the activating mechanism of *Kundalini*. We have six chakras in the human body the highest being Sahasrara Chakra in the top of the head. The kundalini energy is woken and risen up from Mooladhara till Sahasrara Chakra. He is the primary mechanism for the rising of Kundalini.

We have *Yantras*, in the form mathematical drawings, which have in themselves, the concerned presiding deities. He is in that form.

In *Lalitā Sahasranāmam* – 206th name – *Sarva Yantrātmikā* – She is in the form of all yantras used in worship.

It is usual to worship Gods through *mantras*, *tantras* and *yantras*. Worshipping through *mantras* is called *Māntrīka* method. Worshipping through *tantras* is called *Tāntrīca* method. Worshipping through *yantras* is called *Vaidhīka* method. Whichever be the method *mantras* are definitely used to worship. But which is predominant is to be considered.

Mantras, the sound form of deities, are integral to *Sādhanas* (worship).

Tantras (Looms or Weavings) refer to numerous and varied scriptures pertaining to any of several esoteric traditions rooted in philosophy of the religion.

Yantras are some mathematical drawings/ patterns used for worship. There are mathematical construction methods explaining the drawing of *yantras*. *Yantras* mean originally the mechanical, mnemonic and musical contraption in the macrocosm. It is a graphic symbol of the contemplative meditation in the tradition, which was intended to be unified with the Gods/ goddesses. *Yantras* area also called as *cakras*. In a human body itself we have seven cakras thought to be an energy point or node in the subtle body viz., *Mūlādhārā, Swādhişţānā, Maņipūrakā, Anāhatā, Viśuddha, Agjnā* and *Sahasrārā*.

Sri Lalita Sahasranama, names 204, 205 and 206, *Sarvamantra Svarūpiŋī, Sarvayantrātmikā* and *Sarva Tantrarūpā*. That is, Sri Lalita herself is in the form of all the mantras, yantras and Tantras.

Usually when consecrating an idol of a deity, it is customary to place the *yantras* of the respective deities beneath the respective idols, duly drawn on copper, five-metals, silver, gold, etc. Properly drawn *yantras* emit micro-vibrations. Those vibrations are not feelable by human beings. However, they have a huge impact on our body, mainly positive impact. It is customary to worship the concerned deity alongwith the respective *chakras/ yantras*.

Yantras are great cosmic conductors of energy, an antenna of Nature, a powerful tool for harmony, prosperity, success, good health, yoga and meditation. *Yantras* are usually made out of copper and consist of a series of geometric patterns. The eyes and mind concentrate at the center of the yantra to achieve higher levels of consciousness.

511. *Paramāya* – परमाय

118th name above may be referred.

512. *Yantriņe* – यन्त्रिणे

He exercises restraint.

He is furnished with harness or trappings.

513. *Yantrārūḍhāparājitāya* – यन्त्रारूढापराजिताय

He has overcome being mounted on the cycle of birth and death.

He enables his devotees to overcome the cycle of birth and death.

514. *Yantravide* – यन्त्रविदे

He knows all the spiritual techniques.

515. *Yantravāsāya* – यन्त्रवासाय

He lives in mathematical diagrams, called yantras or chakras.

516. *Yantrādhārāya* – यन्त्राधाराय

He is the base/ foundation/ source of sacred mechanisms.

517. *Dharādhārāya* – धराधाराय

He is the supporter of the Earth.

464th name above says that he is the Lord of earth and hence he supports the Earth.

The above 8 names were taken from the 68th shloka of the *Sahasranāma* Stotram.

518. *Tattvajñāya* – तत्त्वज्ञाय

He is the knower of the Truth. The connection between the truth and him has been mentioned in many a name in these 1,000 names.

519. *Tattvabhūtātmane* – तत्त्वभूतात्मने

He is the embodiment of truth/ reality.

520. *Mahattattvaprakāśanāya* – महत्तत्त्वप्रकाशनाय

He is the enlightening of the intellectual faculty.

521. *Tattvasaṅkhyānayogajñāya* – तत्त्व सङ्ख्यान योगज्ञाय

He is the knower of the principles of the Sankhya-Yoga philosophy.

522. *Sāṅkhyaśāstrapravartakāya* – साङ्ख्य शास्त्र प्रवर्तकाय

He only propounds the Sankhya philosophy.

The above 5 names were taken from the 69th shloka of the *Sahasranāma* Stotram.

523. *Ananta Vikramāya* – अनन्त विक्रमाय

He possesses infinite valour.

524. *Devāya* – देवाय

He is an immortal being, one of the Devas and head of the Devas.

525. *Mādhavāya* – माधवाय

He is the Sweet-natured Husband of Shri Lakshmi, in the form of Srī Vishnu.

He destroyed the demon Madhu and hence, he is called as *Mādhavan.*

Brahadaranyaka Upanishat (4.5) says, he can be cognised through Madhu Vidya.

Mahabharata, Udyoga Parvam (70.4) says, Oh Bharata! Know Madhava, by silence (Mouna), by meditation (dhyana) and by Yoga.

In *Viṣṇu Sahasranāma* – 72nd and 735th name – *Mādhavāḥ* – born in the family of Madhu.

526. *Dhaneśvarāya* – धनेश्वराय

He is the lord of wealth. Being the consort of Goddess Lakshmi, he is the lord of wealth.

399th name above may also be referred.

527. *Sādhave* – साधवे

He is a virtuous person. He promotes virtuous tasks.

528. *Sādhu Variṣṭhātmane* – साधु वरिष्ठात्मने नमः

He is the most excellent righteous person.

529. *Sāvadhānāya* – सावधानाय

He is the most attentive lord. He gives most attention to his devotees.

530. *Amarottamāya* – अमरोत्तमाय

He is the highest of the Devas.

333rd name above may also be referred.

The above 8 names were taken from the 70th shloka of the *Sahasranāma* Stotram.

531. *Niḥsaṅkalpāya* – निःसङ्कल्पाय

He is free from hankerings. Being a typical sanyasi, he cannot have any desires.

532. *Nirādhārāya* – निराधाराय

476th name above may be referred.

533. *Durdharāya* – दुर्धराय

He is an irresistible lord.

534. *Ātmavide* – आत्मविदे

He only knows the Self.

535. *Pataye* – पतये

He is the protector of all beings. His is an integrated form of all the Tri-murtis. In the form of Lord Vishnu, he protects all.

536. *Ārogyasukhadāya* – आरोग्यसुखदाय नमः

He is the bestower of good health and happiness.

He blesses happiness to the righteous ones and deprives the same to the wicked.

In *Viṣṇu Sahasranāmam* – 459th & 889th names – *Sukhadaḥ* – conferrer of happiness.

In *Lalitā Sahasranāmam* – 502nd name – *Samasta Bhakta Sukhadā* – She bestows happiness to all her devotees.

In *Sūrya Sahasranāmam* – 354th and 357th names – *Sukhadāya* – He is the bestower of pleasures to his devotees.

537. *Pravarāya* – प्रवराय

He is very distinguished.

He is the worthiest of being desired by those who desire worldly pleasures and those who seek salvation.

As mentioned in *Śivānandalahari* (100), when the Devas evaluate those who are worthy of praise, they recognize you as the first.

In *Śiva Sahasranāmam* – 5th name – *Pravaraḥ* – The most excellent.

806th name below may also be referred.

538. *Vāsavāya* – वासवाय

He is in the form of Indra, the king of Devas.

The above 8 names were taken from the 71st shloka of the *Sahasranāma* Stotram.

539. *Pareśāya* – परेशाय

He is the supreme Lord. He is in the form of *Brahmam* called *Parā* (absolute).

Parā – the other person, *Aparā* – dependent on self, i.e., it respectively means an enemy and a friend.

Shrimad Bhagavad Geeta (IX–29) says that the *Brahmam* is of these two types – I have neither foe nor friend;

Na Me Dveshyosti Na Priyaḥ

Parā – superior and *Aparā* – inferior. *Sruti* says, "*Brahmam* is the servant. *Brahmam* is ferry–men; and Brahmam is these gamblers";

Brahmadāsā Brahmadāshā Brahmameme Kitavā Uta.

Parā – he who is far off, *Aparā* he who is near. *Shrimad Bhagavad Geeta* (XIII–15) – "I am far and near".

In general, the *Brahmam* is said to be two types viz., pure form and an adulterated form. *Parāparam* is of third type.

The *Prashno Upanishad* (V–2) says – "This is indeed, Oh *Satyakāma*! *para* and *apara*"; *Etadvai Satyakāma Param Chāparam Cha*. The *Smruti* also says, "Two Brahmams are to be known, one is *Parā* and the other is *Aparā*";

Dve Brahmaŋee Veditavye Param Chāparameva Cha.

Parā – posterior; *Aparā* – anterior. *Shiva* with the unified form of energy is *Parāparam or Parabrahmam*. **He** is in that form.

Parā and *Aparā* are the twofold ether.

The twofold knowledge, as described in the *Muŋḍaka Upanishad* (I–1–4) *Parā Vidyā* and *Aparā Vidya*.

The *Linga Purāŋa* also says, "Two kinds of knowledge should be known, *parā* and *aparā*; the *Vedas* are *Para* and the *Vedāngās* are *Apara*.

Skānda Purāŋa (*Yagna Vaibhava Kānḍa*, 6th chapter) says two types of the *Praŋava* are *Parā* and *Apara*. *Parā* has the qualities of *Sacitānanda* and *Aparā* is pure form, in the form of sound. Since it prays *Parabrahmam*, it is called as *Praŋava* (the word *nava* has such a meaning). Since it is a tool to reach *Parabrahmam*, it is called as *Praŋavam*.

The interpretation of *Vedas* is of two types – the Supreme Being is *Param* and the tool to reach it is called *Aparam*.

In the *Yoga Sāstra* also knowledge is divided into three – *Parā, Aparā* and *Parāpara*. For it is said, "Knowledge is said to be threefold by the division of *para, apara* and *parāpara*. Of these, the first is the supreme knowledge and is the cause of cognizing the Lord, the bondage and the Self. The second, *aparā* knowledge, is simply the cause of cognising the bondage. The *parāparā* knowledge is, just as the change of the sight between a man and cat in the night.

The speech is of two types – *Parā* and *Apara*. *Aparā* includes *Pashyantee, Madyamā* and *Vaikharee*.

Para is the fourth state. *Aparā* is the three states awaken (*Jāgrath*), dream (*Swapna*) and deep sleep (*Sushupti*).

The *homa* (sacrificial fire) is of two types *Parā* and *Apara*. The *Parā* is the state after the destruction of all dualistic interpretations respecting the known, the knower and knowledge. The *Parā homa* is said to be that which being absorbed, does not arise again, in the blaze of the great eternal fire of own Self, which burns forever without fuel. This is done in an imaginative way.

Varāha Purāṇa says when speaking about the *Trimoortis* – The creative energy is said to be *Para* which is the white colour. *Vaishnavee*, which is red and long–eyed is *Apara*. The *Raudri* energy is called *parāpara*.

In *Lalitā Sahasranāmam* – 790th name – *Parāparā* – She is in the form of Brahmam.

211th and 393rd names above may also be referred.

540. *Paramodārāya* – परमोदाराय

He is Supremely generous in bestowing everything to his devotees.

541. *Pratyakcaitanya Durgamāya* – प्रत्यक्चैतन्य दुर्गमाय

He is inaccessible to those turned away from the Supreme Atma. In other words, he is accessible only to those with devotion.

542. *Durādharşāya* – दुराधर्षाय

His presence is hard to attain. As mentioned in the previous name he is attainable only by strong penance.

543. *Durāvāsāya* – दुरावासाय

He is unassailable. But he can be won by a true devotee.

544. *Dūratvaparināśanāya* – दूरत्वपरिनाशनाय

He is the destroyer of distance between him and his true devotee. That is, only his true devotee can easily reach him.

The above 6 names were taken from the 72nd shloka of the *Sahasranāma* Stotram.

545. *Vedavide* – वेदविदे

He is the knower of all Vedas. He spreads the knowledge of Vedas.

In Shrimad Bhagavad Gita (15.15) Lord Krishna says, I am the author of Vedanta and the knower of Vedas.

The Mahabharata says, All the Vedas, all the Vidyas, all the Shastras, all the yagnas and all the offerings are Lord Krishna.

In *Vişŋu Sahasranāmam* – 128th and 131st names – *Vedavit* – He is the knower of all the Vedas.

546. *Vedakṛte* – वेदकृते

He is the creator/ author of all Vedas.

547. *Vedāya* – वेदाय

He is in the form of all Vedas. Vedas are all in his form.

In Shrimad Bhagavad Gita (10.11) Lord Krishna says, out of mere compassion, I, abiding in their self, destroy the darkness of ignorance by the luminous lamp of wisdom called Vedas.

In *Vişŋu Sahasranāmam* – 127th and 131st names – *Vedaḥ* – He is the Vedas.

In *Lalitā Sahasranāmam* – 338th name – *Vedajananī* – She is the mother of all Vedas.

548. *Vedātmane* – वेदात्मने

He is the soul of all the Vedas.

549. *Vimalāśayāya* – विमलाशयाय

He is the abode of purity.

550. *Viviktasevine* – विविक्तसेविने

He is worshipped by variety of devotees.

551. *Saṃsāraśramanāśanāya* – संसारश्रमनाशनाय

He destroys the exertions of mundane existence called Samsara.

The *Brhannāradīya Purāṇa* says, "The Supreme name of *Gangā* is the fire that consumes the forest of sin because Gangā is the remover of the disease of *samsara*".

The stuti called "Mooka Panchashatee" confirms in almost 50+ shlokas that Kamakshi Devi removes bondage called Samsara and bestows moksha to her devotees.

The above 7 names were taken from the 73rd shloka of the *Sahasranāma* Stotram.

552. *Brahmayonaye* – ब्रह्मयोनये

He, in the form of Lord Vishnu, gives birth to Lord Brahma.

553. *Bṛhadyonaye* – बृहद्योनये

He himself has a great origin.

554. *Viśvayonaye* – विश्वयोनये

He only gave origin to the entire universe.

555. *Videhavate* – विदेहवते

He is free from the attachments of the body and enables his devotees also to free from those attachments.

556. *Viśālākṣāya* – विशालाक्षाय

He has broad and powerful eyes.

Normally, goddesses are only called as having broad eyes – *Viśālākṣī*. But here God Dattatreya is mentioned as having broad eyes.

The word *Vishālā* indicates *Badrikāshrama*. Since it is in the Himalayas, it also indicates *Nepala Peeṭa*. *Brahmāṇḍa* and other *Purāŋas* say, that the *Nepala Peeṭa* should be meditated upon as situated in the eyes. The word *Akshee* indicates both the eyes. Hence it can be considered that he has *Vishāla Peeṭa* as his eyes

In *Lalitā Sahasranāmam* – 936th name – *Viśālākṣī* – She has long and large eyes, leading upto the ears.

In *Gāyatri Sahasranāmam* – 918th name – *Viśālākşyaiī* – conveying the same meaning.

557. *Viśvanāthāya* – विश्वनाथाय

He is the Lord of the Universe.

Lord Shiva at Banaras temple, is usually called as *Viśvanāthar*. Here, Lord Dattatreya, in the form of Lord Shiva, is addressed as *Viśvanāthar*.

558. *Hāṭakāṅgadabhūṣaṇāya* – हाटकाङ्गदभूषणाय

He is adorned with golden armlets/ shield.

The above 7 names were taken from the 74th shloka of the *Sahasranāma* Stotram.

559. *Abādhyāya* – अबाध्याय

Noone can oppose him. He is not to be opposed by anyone.

560. *Jagadārādhyāya* – जगदाराध्याय

He is being worshipped by the entire world without any partiality.

561. *Jagadākhilapālanāya* – जगदाखिलपालनाय

He is the protector of the whole world i.e. everything in the world.

562. *Janavate* – जनवते

He is surrounded by people, by his devotees.

563. *Dhanavate* – धनवते

He is the wealthiest. He makes his devotees wealthy.

564. *Dharmiṇe* – धर्मिणे

He is very charitable. He gives away everything to all.

565. *Dharmagāya* – धर्मगाय

He always observes righteousness. He enables his devotees to observe righteousness.

566. *Dharmavardhanāya* – धर्मवर्धनाय

He promotes dharma i.e. virtues.

The above 8 names were taken from the 75th shloka of the *Sahasranāma* Stotram.

567. *Amṛtāya* – अमृताय

He is that Amrutam, drinking which the Devas are immortal.

568. *Śāśvatāya* – शाश्वताय

He is eternal/ permanent.

Narayana Upanishat (13) says, he is ever existing.

He is eternal – impossible to approach, but easy to enjoy.

In *Viṣṇu Sahasranāmam* – 56th name – *Śāśvataḥ*, 120th name – *Śaśvatasthānuḥ* and 627th name – *Śāśvatasthiraḥ* – He is ever-existing. He is eternal, stable and firm.

In *Śiva Sahasranāmam* – 20th name – *Śāśvataḥ* – he is eternal.

569. *Sādhyāya* – साध्याय

He is easily attainable by true devotion.

79th name above may also be referred.

570. *Siddhidāya* – सिद्धिदाय

He grants success and Self-realisation to his devotees.

571. *Sumanoharāya* – सुमनोहराय

He is very charming.

In *Vişṇu Sahasranāmam* – 461st name – *Manoharaḥ* – Being the unlimited bliss, he is charming.

In *Sūrya Sahasranāmam* – 117th name – *Manoharāya* – he is charming.

374th name above may also be referred.

572. *Khalubrahma Khalusthānāya* – खलुब्रह्म खलुस्थानाय

He is both the foundation and the Supreme Spirit.

573. *Munīnāṃ Paramāgataye* – मुनीनां परमागतये

He is the highest goal for refuge of sages.

In the 37th name above, it was mentioned that he is the highest goal for refuge for all living beings. Here it is stressed relating to sages.

The above 7 names were taken from the 76th shloka of the *Sahasranāma* Stotram.

574. *Upadṛṣṭe* – उपदृष्टे

For all those with true devotion he appears very near and whenever needed.

575. *Śreșțhāya* – श्रेष्ठाय

He is the very great lord. He is above all others.

Brahadaranyaka Upanishat (8.1.1.) says – The *Prāŋa* is the eldest and excellent.

The Brahma Sutram (2.4.8.) says – He is the excellent.

237th name above may also be referred.

576. *Śucirbhūtāya* – शुचिर्भूताय

He is the very pure sprit.

He purifies those who worship, meditate on and praise Him.

In *Śiva Sahasranāmam* – 551st and 999th names – *Śuciḥ* – he is very pure and holy.

577. *Anāmayāya* – अनामयाय

He is very hale and healthy.

578. *Vedasiddhāntavedyāya* – वेदसिद्धान्तवेद्याय

He can be known only through the doctrines of the Vedas.

In *Śrīmad Bhagavat Geeta* (XV – 15) Lord *Śrī Krişhŋa* himself says – I am verily that which has to be known by all the *Vedas*;

Vedaiccha Sarvairahameva Vedhyaḥ

In *Lalitā Sahasranāmam* – 335th name – *Vedavedyā* – she can be known through the *Vedas*.

579. *Mānasāhlādavardhanāya* – मानसाह्लादवर्धनाय

He increases the delight of the mind of his devotees.

The above 6 names were taken from the 77th shloka of the *Sahasranāma* Stotram.

580. *Dehādanyāya* – देहादन्याय

He is distinct from the body.

The Vedanta philosophy that the Atma is different from body is being stressed in this name.

In *Śrīmad Bhagavat Geeta* (2.20), Lord *Śrī Krişhŋa* himself says that the soul is neither born, nor does it ever die; nor having once existed, does it ever cease to be. The soul is without birth, eternal, immortal, and ageless. It is not destroyed when the body is destroyed.

581. *Guṇādanyāya* – गुणादन्याय

He is *nirguṇa* – without any of these three attributes viz., Rajo, Tamo and Sattva.

As being in truth, he is devoid of attributes.

Svetashwatara Upanishat (6.15) says – He is pure and devoid of qualities.

In *Vişŋu Sahasranāmam* – 840th name – *Nirguṇaḥ* – he is without any attributes.

582. *Lokādanyāya* – लोकादन्याय

He lives in a different plane, away from these worldly affairs.

583. *Vivekavide* – विवेकविदे

He does not discriminate among His devotees. He treats everyone equally and bestows His grace.

321st name above may also be referred.

584. *Duşṭasvapnaharāya* – दुष्टस्वप्नहराय

He destroys the negative dreams of his devotees, that forebode the forthcoming evils.

In *Vişŋu Sahasranāmam* – 926th name – *Duḥsvapnanāśanaḥ* – he dispels the evil dreams.

In *Śiva Sahasranāmam* – 422nd name – *Susvapnaḥ* – he enables good dreams.

585. *Gurave* – गुरवे

He is the Spiritual Preceptor.

The *mantra sāstras* say – the teacher, the *mantra* and the deity are all one and the same and should not be distinguished.

Aruŋagirināda also sings about Lord Muruga as "*Guruvāi Varuvāi Arulvāi Guhane*". *Lord Dattatreya* himself reaches the devotees in the form of a teacher and gives him invocation of *mantra*.

Gu means darkness of ignorance and *Ru* removes that. Hence the word *Guru* itself means removing of the darkness of ignorance.

The letter *Gu* is an existence (*Sat* letter) and *Ru* is knowledge (of *Brahmam*) and because one is with the knowledge of *Brahmam*, he is called *guru*.

In *Viṣŋu Sahasranāmam* – 209th name – *Guruḥ* and 493rd name – *Devabṛdguruḥ* – **He** is called *Guru* since **he**; (i) invocates/ advises all *Vidyās* or (ii) gave birth to all living beings (as a father). He is the instructor of Indra, who is the king of Devas.

In *Lalitā Sahasranāmam* – 603rd name – *Gurumūrtiḥ*, 713th name – *Gurumaŋḍalarūpiŋī* and 722nd name – *Gurupriyā* – She assumes the form of a teacher. She is in the form of spiritual teachers. She has affection on teachers (*Gurus*).

In *Śiva Sahasranāmam* – 936th name – *Devāsuraguruḥ* – he is the teacher of Devas and Demons as well.

864th name below may also be referred.

586. *Guruvarottamāya* – गुरुवरोत्तमाय

He is the most excellent of teachers.

The above 7 names were taken from the 78th shloka of the *Sahasranāma* Stotram.

587. *Karmiṇe* – कर्मिणे

He is the Performer of religious acts.

He is setting an example for others by demonstrating such acts.

588. *Karmavinirmuktāya* – कर्मविनिर्मुक्ताय

He is fully liberated from the results of actions.

Though he performs religious acts, he does not enjoy the fruits of those acts. He does not at all need those fruits. He performs the acts for his devotee's sake.

589. *Saṃnyāsine* – संन्यासिने

He is an ascetic. That is the reason he does not enjoy the fruits of his religious acts.

590. *Sādhakeśvarāya* – साधकेश्वराय

He is the Lord of aspirants.

591. *Sarvabhāvavihināya* – सर्वभावविहिनाय नमः

He is free of all emotions and sentiments.

As a sanyasi, to set an example for others, he is like that.

592. *Tṛṣṇāsaṅganivāraṇāya* – तृष्णासङ्गनिवारणाय

He wards off all attachments and desires.

This name is in continuation of the previous name to set the qualities of a typical sanyasi.

The above 6 names were taken from the 79th shloka of the *Sahasranāma* Stotram.

593. *Tyāgine* – त्यागिने

He is a renunciant/ Martyr. The qualities of a sanyasi continue.

594. *Tyagavapuṣe* – त्यगवपुषे

He is an embodiment of sacrifice. He has sacrificed everything in this world, including his own cloths.

595. *Tyāgāya* – त्यागाय

This name conveys the same meaning as the previous one.

596. *Tyāgadānavivarjitāya* – त्यागदानविवर्जिताय

He is free from renunciation and charity. He is a renouncer of everything.

597. *Tyāgakāraṇatyāgātmane* – त्यागकारणत्यागात्मने

He is the cause and the essence of relinquishment.

Last 7 names starting from 591, talks about the qualities of a sanyasi especially the sacrificing everything.

598. *Sadgurave* – सद्गुरवे

He is a true master of the world.

585th above and 862nd & 864th names below may be referred.

599. *Sukhadāyakāya* – सुखदायकाय

He is the bestower of happiness to his devotees.

He blesses happiness to the righteous ones and deprives the same to the wicked.

In *Viṣṇu Sahasranāmam* – 459th and 889th names – *Sukhadaḥ* – conferrer of happiness.

In *Lalitā Sahasranāmam* – 502nd name – *Samastabhaktasukhadā* – She bestows happiness to all her devotees.

In *Sūrya Sahasranāmam* – 354th & 357th names – *Sukhadāya* and 769th name – *Sukhapradāya* – He is the bestower of pleasures to his devotees.

The above 7 names were taken from the 80th shloka of the *Sahasranāma* Stotram.

600. *Dakṣāya* – दक्षाय

He is very much adept.

He manifests himself as the Universe. He performs all actions dexterously.

He is in the form of Daksha Prajapati, father of Dakshayani and father-in-law of Lord Shiva.

In *Viṣṇu Sahasranāmam* – 423rd name – *Dakṣaḥ* – he is very clever.

Thus ends 100 divine names on Lord *Dattātreya* from 501 to 600.

*****

601. *Dakṣādi Vandyāya* – दक्षादि वन्द्याय

He is worshipped by Daksha and other *Prajapatis*.

In the previous name, it was mentioned that he is in the form of Daksha Prajapati himself. In this name, it is being mentioned that he is worshipped by Daksha and other *Prajapatis*.

Praja = people. *Pati* = lord. Lord of people or creator of people.

602. *Jñānavādapravatakāya* – ज्ञानवादप्रवतकाय

He propounds the theory of knowledge of justice.

603. *Śabdabrahmamayātmane* – शब्दब्रह्ममयात्मने

He is the embodiment of Shabda Brahmam.

Shatapatha Brahmana III.12.48 defines Shabda-Brahmam or Nada Brahmam as transcendental sound

Shatpatha Brahmana Vi.16.51 defines it as sound vibration or the transcendental sound of the Vedic scriptures

Shabda stands for the word manifested by sound 'verbal' and such a word has innate power to convey a particular sense or meaning.

According to the Nyaya and the Vaisheshika schools, Shabda means verbal testimony. For the Sanskrit grammarians, Yaska, Panini and Katyayana it meant a unit of language or speech or vac.

In the philosophical terms this word appears in the Maitreya Upanishat (VI.22) that speaks of two kinds of Brahmam – Shabda Brahmam (Brahmam with sound) and Ashabda Brahmam (soundless Brahmam).

Bhartruhari speaks about the creative power of Shabda, the manifold universe is a creation of Shabda Brahmam

Brihadaranyaka Upanishat (IV.i.2) says Speech is equated with Brahmam.

The Rig Veda (114.8) states that Brahmam extends as far as Vāc and has hymns in praise of Speech as the Creator and as the final abode of Brahmam. Time is the creative power of Shabda Brahman.

Purva Mimamsa deals with Shabda Brahmam as 'cosmic sound or word', which is endowed with names and forms and is projected in Vedic revelations (the mantras, hymns, prayers etc.). Purva Mimamsa, an esoteric discipline, from the point of view of spiritual growth aims at attaining the heavenly happiness by realising Shabda Brahmam (cosmic sound) by conducting yajnas that help control the senses and the mind; when the mind and the senses are subdued the inner subtle sound is realised as Shabda Brahman.

One has to become well established in Shabda Brahman before realizing Parabrahmam. Vedas are not the product of conventional language but the emanation of reality in form of Shabda (sound, word) which is the sole cause of creation and is eternal.

604. *Śabdabrahmaprakāśavate* – शब्दब्रह्मप्रकाशवते

He elucidates the Divine Knowledge of Shabda Brahmam as explained in the previous name.

The above 5 names were taken from the 81st shloka of the *Sahasranāma* Stotram.

605. *Grasiṣṇave* – ग्रसिष्णवे

He absorbs or swallows everything – during final dissolution/ deluge.

606. *Prabhaviṣṇave* – प्रभविष्णवे

He is endowed with the Grabins've Supreme power. Prabhaviṣṇu refers to the "great lord Viṣṇu".

According to the Śiva purana (2.3.23) – Himavat attempted to dissuade Pārvatī. Accordingly, after Viṣṇu spoke to the Devas and others. Thus, urged by the great lord Viṣṇu i.e., Prabhaviṣṇu, they set out desirous of seeing the Pināka (bow) bearing lord Śiva. At first Viṣṇu and others who were anxious to see the penance of Pārvatī went to her hermitage which was on the way. On seeing the excellent penance of Pārvatī and being enveloped by her refulgence they bowed to her who was engaged in penance and who had brilliant features.

607. *Sahiṣṇave* – सहिष्णवे

He endures/ forbears all the mistakes done by his devotees, of course unconsciously.

In *Viṣṇu Sahasranāmam* – 144th name – *Sahiṣṇuḥ* – he is the subduer of mistakes.

608. *Vigatāntarāya* – विगतान्तराय

He does not distinguish or discriminate among his devotees.

85th name above may also be referred.

609. *Vidvattamāya* – विद्वत्तमाय

He is very much learned.

610. *Mahāvandyāya* – महावन्द्याय

He is highly Adorable.

611. *Viśālottama Vāṅmunaye* – विशालोत्तम वाङ्मुनये

He is such a sage with the most illustrious speech.

The above 6 names were taken from the 82nd shloka of the *Sahasranāma* Stotram.

612. *Brahmavide* – ब्रह्मविदे

He is the knower of Brahmam, the ultimate reality.

In *Viṣṇu Sahasranāmam* – 666th name – *Brahmavit* – he is the knower of Brahmam.

613. *Brahmabhāvāya* – ब्रह्मभावाय

He is absorbed into the supreme soul, i.e. the Brahmam.

614. *Brahmarṣaye* – ब्रह्मऋषये

He knows the Supreme Brahmam directly.

In Ramayana, we know the Sage Vashishta was a *Brahmarṣi* and sage *Vishwamitra* did penance for years together to become *Brahmarṣi* and that too to receive the title of *Brahmarṣi* from the mouth of sage Vasishta.

615. *Brāhmaṇa Priyāya* – ब्राह्मण प्रियाय

He is very fond of Brahmins, who recite the Vedas and seek to know Brahmam.

In *Viṣṇu Sahasranāmam* – 670th name – *Brāhmaṇa Priyaḥ* – he is beloved of Brahmins.

616. *Brahmaṇe* – ब्रह्मणे

He is the Supreme formless (*niroopa*) consciousness, i.e. Brahmam.

617. *Brahma Prakāśātmane* – ब्रह्म प्रकाशात्मने

He is endowed with the light of the Supreme Spirit.

618. *Brahma Vidyā Prakāśanāya* – ब्रह्म विद्या प्रकाशनाय

He shines with the brightness of the Knowledge of the Supreme Atma.

Last 7 names, starting from 612, talk about the Lord Dattareya in different forms of Brahmam.

The above 7 names were taken from the 83rd shloka of the *Sahasranāma* Stotram.

619. *Atri Vaṃśa Prabhūtātmane* – अत्रि वंश प्रभूतात्मने

He is foremost of the lineage of Sage Atri, since he is his son.

620. *Tāpasottam Vanditāya* – तापसोत्तम् वन्दिताय

He is praised as the greatest of ascetics.

621. *Ātmavāsine* – आत्मवासिने

He resides in the soul of everyone.

622. *Vidheyātmane* – विधेयात्मने

He is an established Self.

He is so great and still is submissive to his devotees.

Vaishnavites always call themselves as *Videhan*.

In *Viṣṇu Sahasranāmam* – 621st name – *Avidheyātmā* – he is of unfathomed nature.

In *Sūrya Sahasranāmam* – 464th and 620th names – *Vidheyāya* – he is down to earth subdued.

652nd name below may also be referred.

623. *Atri Vaṃśa Vivardhanāya* – अत्रि वंश विवर्धनाय

He increases the Glory of Sage Atri's dynasty.

619th name above may also be referred.

The above 5 names were taken from the 84th shloka of the *Sahasranāma* Stotram.

624. *Pravartanāya* – प्रवर्तनाय

He always wanders around the world.

As a typical *parivrajaka sanyasi*, he does not stay in a single place for a long time.

625. *Nivṛttātmane* – निवृत्तात्मने

He has renounced the entire world.

626. *Pralayodaka Sannibhāya* – प्रलयोदक सन्निभाय

He only creates consequence of great dissolution.

627. *Nārāyaṇāya* – नारायणाय

He is the only Refuge of Humanity.

Naraḥ = human beings, Atma, the ether and other effects that are produced from it. He, as their cause, pervades them (*Ayana*). Hence, he is *Narayana*.

Narayana Upanishat (13) says, the in and out of this whole Universe, whatever we see or hear, all these are pervaded by Narayana.

The Mahabharata (Udyana Parva 1.1.3) says, the categories (tattvas) are called Nara, as they are sprung from Nara (Atma). He is called Narayana as they are his abode.

Taitreeya Upanishat (3.1) says, whom they approach and enter is Narayana.

Brahma Vaivarta Purana says, as he is the seat of Naras, he is called Narayana.

Manu Smruti (1.10) says, the waters are called Naras, which come of Nara (God). As they are originally his abode, he is called Narayana.

Narasimha Purana says, "*Narayanaya Namaḥ*" this is the real mantra that destroys the deadly poison of Samsara. This I proclaim very loudly with uplifted hands. Let the ascetics with passions curbed and intellects clear listen to me.

Ramanuja loudly preached this mantra (*Om Namo Narayanaya*) to everyone, from the towers of Visnu temple at Tirukkoshtiyoor.

In *Viṣṇu Sahasranāmam* – 245th name – *Nārāyaṇaḥ* – he is the abode of all the *Naras* – human beings.

628. *Mahāgarbhāya* – महागर्भाय

He is pregnant with the entire universe.

629. *Bhārgavapriyakṛttamāya* – भार्गवप्रियकृत्तमाय

He is the highest benefactor of *Parashurama*. *Bhārgava* = *Parashurama* is said to be a disciple of Lord Dattareya.

The Tripura Rahasya is a dialogue between Dattatreya and Parashurama, expounding the teachings of the supreme spiritual truth. According to tradition, this truth was first taught by Shiva to Vishnu.

The above 6 names were taken from the 85th shloka of the *Sahasranāma* Stotram.

630. *Saṅkalpaduḥkhadalanāya* – सङ्कल्पदुःखदलनाय

He has resolved to dispel the sorrows of his devotees.

631. *Saṃsāratamanāśanāya* – संसारतमनाशनाय

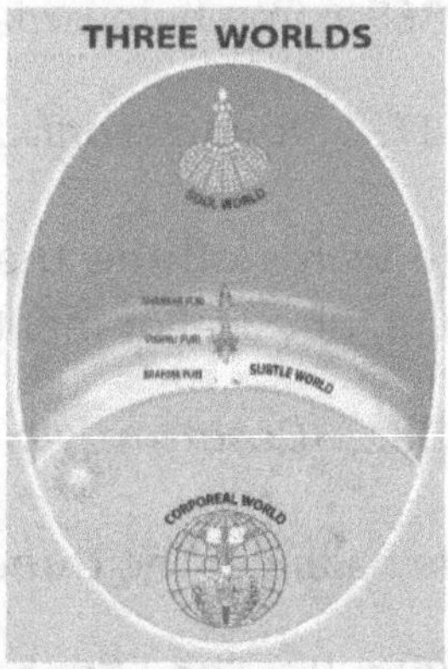

He destroys the darkness of worldly afflictions.

632. *Trivikramāya* – त्रिविक्रमाय

He covered the three worlds in three strides, in the form of Vamana, an incarnation of Shri Vishnu.

Taitreeya Brahmana (2.4.6) says, He stepped (the three worlds) by his three steps of his small feet. He has walked over the three worlds.

The Harivamsa (279.80) says, the sages have named the three worlds as 'Tri' and as you walked them all you are named Tri(vi)krama.

In *Viṣṇu Sahasranāmam* – 530th name – *Trivikramaḥ* – three stepped the three steps were the three worlds.

633. *Tridhākārāya* – त्रिधाकाराय

He is in three forms. We are all aware that Lord Dattatreya in an integrated form of Trimoortis viz., Brahma, Vishnu and Rudra.

634. *Trimūrtaye* – त्रिमूर्तये

As mentioned in the previous name, he and Trimoortis (Brahma, Vishnu and Rudra) are one and the same. He is Trimoorti and Trimoorti is he.

635. *Triguṇātmakāya* – त्रिगुणात्मकाय

He is the essence of the three qualities viz., Sattva, Rajo and Tamo.

The above 6 names were taken from the 86th shloka of the *Sahasranāma* Stotram.

636. *Bhedatrayaharāya* – भेदत्रयहराय

He removes the three distinctions among the Trimurtis and Trigunas as well.

936th name below may also be referred.

637. *Tāpatrayanivārakāya* – तापत्रयनिवारकाय

He wards off the triad of afflictions viz., sufferings stemming from fate, physical or mental disorders.

638. *Doṣatrayavibhedine* – दोषत्रयविभेदिने

He balances the three faults/ calumnies (*Doshas*).

Vāta, *Pitta* and *Kapha* are thee three doshas. For maintaining health and curing disease these three doshas should be stable. When they are vitiated, they cause a disease. The doshas get aggravated by similar properties and they get decreased by opposite properties.

639. *Saṃśayārṇava Khaṇḍanāya* – संशयार्णव खण्डनाय

He annihilates the ocean of doubts.

Doubt – The devil's most lethal weapon. Doubt can be one of the most destructive forces in our spiritual lives, often leading us away from God's promises and plans.

The above 4 names were taken from the 87th shloka of the *Sahasranāma* Stotram.

640. *Asaṃśayāya* – असंशयाय

He is free from doubts.

Unless he is free from doubts, he cannot annihilate the doubts of his devotees, as mentioned in the previous name.

641. *Asaṃmūḍhāya* – असंमूढाय

He has clear thought process without any confusion.

642. *Avādine* – अवादिने

He does not dispute with anyone and is in a peaceful mood and keeps others also in a peaceful mood.

643. *Rājavanditāya* – राजवन्दिताय

He is extolled/ respectfully greeting by Kings.

644. *Rājayogine* – राजयोगिने

He knows the highest deep meditation (*Samadhi*) status of Yogas.

645. *Mahāyogine* – महायोगिने

He is great Yogi.

2nd name above may also be referred

646. *Svabhāvagalitāya* – स्वभावगलिताय

He has relinquished his individual nature itself. Being a sanyasi, he has to do it.

The above 7 names were taken from the 88th shloka of the *Sahasranāma* Stotram.

647. *Puṇyaślokāya* – पुण्यश्लोकाय

His good fame or reputation is well spoken of. His praise confers merit.

648. *Pavitrāṅghraye* – पवित्राङ्घ्रये

His lotus feet are so pure and grants purification to his devotees.

649. *Dhyānayogaparāyaṇāya* – ध्यानयोगपरायणाय

He is devoted to the practice of meditation and absorbed in contemplation.

650. *Dhyānasthāya* – ध्यानस्थाय

He can be realised/ approached through meditation only.

651. *Dhyānagamyāya* – ध्यानगम्याय

He can be attained through meditation only.

Meditation is to keep the mind stuck to one place. When we try to keep Lord's form in mind and focus the thoughts on him, other thoughts would distract the mind. Bringing back again and again this wavering mind back to the thoughts of Lord is called *Dhārana*. Settling this and focusing on him is called meditation. He can be attained only by meditation.

The *Svetāsvatara Upanishad* (1–3) also says the same message as, the sages devoted to meditation, saw the energy of the divine Self– hidden by its own qualities; *Te Dhyānayogānugatā Apashyan Devātmashaktim Svaguṇai Nigoodhām*.

In *Lalitā Sahasranāmam* – 641st name – *Dhyānagamyā* – she can be attained through meditation only.

652. *Vidheyātmane* – विधेयात्मने

622nd name above may be referred here.

653. *Purātanāya* – पुरातनाय

He is the ancient, as he transcends the time.

He was there even before creation of all other beings. He only created all. Hence *Purātana*. It can be compared to the poem in

Tamil – *Thiruvempavai* (9th song) by *Mānickavachagar*;
"Munnai Pazham Porutkum Pazham Porule".

Since he has ancient qualities, he is *Purātana*.

In *Vişņu Sahasranāmam* – 498th name – *Purātanaḥ* – he is the ancient.

In *Lalitā Sahasranāmam* – 802nd name – *Purātanā* – She is the most ancient being. **She** is primordial.

198th name above may also be referred.

The above 7 names were taken from the 89th shloka of the *Sahasranāma* Stotram.

654. *Avijñeyāya* – अविज्ञेयाय

He is incomprehensible to ordinary people. As mentioned earlier, he can be understood only through meditation.

655. *Antarātmane* – अन्तरात्मने

He is the inner soul of every being.

656. *Mukhyabimbasanātanāya* – मुख्यबिम्बसनातनाय

He is the eternal represented form of liberation.

657. *Jīvasañjīvanāya* – जीवसञ्जीवनाय नमः

He gives life to every Soul.

658. *Jīvāya* – जीवाय

He is the soul in every being.

659. *Cidvilāsāya* – चिद्विलासाय

He manifests as the Supreme Consciousness.

124th name above may also be referred.

660. *Cidāśrayāya* – चिदाश्रयाय

He is the abode of Consciousness.

The above 7 names were taken from the 90th shloka of the *Sahasranāma* Stotram.

661. *Mahendrāya* – महेन्द्राय

He is the great ruler.

He is lord of Devas, including Indra, the king of Devas. He is the lord of splendour, strength and prosperity.

In *Viṣṇu Sahasranāmam* – 268th name – *Mahendraḥ* – he is the great Indra.

In *Sūrya Sahasranāmam* – 346th name – *Mahendrāya* – he is a great Indra.

662. *Amaramānyāya* – अमरमान्याय

He is honoured/ worshipped by all the Devas.

663. *Yogīndrāya* – योगीन्द्राय

He is the master/ lord of all the ascetics/ yogis.

152nd name above may also be referred.

664. *Yogavidmayāya* – योगविद्मयाय

He is the most knowledgeable about Yoga. He is expert in Yoga.

665. *Yogadharmāya* – योगधर्माय

He is the right course of Yoga.

666. *Yogāya* – योगाय

He is connected to divine through Yoga.

214th name above may also be referred.

667. *Tattvāya* – तत्त्वाय

He is a true person of principle.

668. *Tattvaviniścayāya* – तत्त्वविनिश्चयाय

He is firmly resolved to the truth.

The above 8 names were taken from the 91st shloka of the *Sahasranāma* Stotram.

669. *Naikabāhave* – नैकबाहवे

He has multiple shoulders (hands).

670. *Anantātmane* – अनन्तात्मने

He is an infinite Self.

671. *Naikanānāparākroṇāya* – नैकनानापराक्रोणाय

He is addressed by innumerable names.

672. *Naikākṣiṇe* – नैकाक्षिणे

He has multiple eyes.

673. *Naikapādāya* – नैकपादाय

He has many a foot.

Puruṣa Sūktam starts with

Oṃ Sahasráśīrṣā Purúṣaḥ | *Sahasrākṣaḥ* *Sahasrápāt* |

The *Virat Purush* – *Parabrahmam* (universal being) has thousand heads, thousand eyes and thousand feet. Thousand signifies innumerable.

In *Viṣṇu Sahasranāmam* – 227th name – *Sahasrapāt* – One who has thousand feet.

In *Śiva Sahasranāmam* – 797th name – *Sahasrapāt* – Conveying the same meaning.

In *Lalitā Sahasranāmam* – 284th name – *Sahasrapāt* – **She** has countless feet.

In *Sūrya Sahasranāmam* – 22nd name – *Sahasrapāde* – he has thousands of feet.

674. *Nāthanāthāya* – नाथनाथाय

He is master of masters.

The above 6 names were taken from the 92nd shloka of the *Sahasranāma* Stotram.

675. *Uttamottamāya* – उत्तमोत्तमाय

He is the Highest of the Highest.

676. *Sahasraśīrṣiṇe* – सहस्रशीर्षिणे

He is with a thousand heads – thousands of heads.

Puruṣa Sūktam starts with

Oṃ Sahasráśīrṣā Purúṣaḥ | Sahasrākṣaḥ Sahasrápāt |

The *Virat Purush* – *Parabrahmam* (universal being) has thousand heads, thousand eyes and thousand feet. Thousand signifies innumerable.

677. *Puruṣāya* – पुरुषाय

He is the Supreme Spirit – *Virat Purush* – *Parabrahmam* (universal being).

678. *Sahasrākṣāya* – सहस्राक्षाय

He has a thousand eyes – thousands of eyes.

Puruṣa Sūktam starts with

Oṃ Sahasráśīrṣā Purúṣaḥ | Sahasrākṣaḥ Sahasrápāt |

The *Virat Purush* – *Parabrahmam* (universal being) has a thousand heads, thousand eyes and thousand feet. Thousand signifies innumerable.

In *Vişņu Sahasranāmam* – 227th name – *Sahasrākşaḥ* – He has a thousand eyes.

In *Sūrya Sahasranāmam* – 123rd name – *Sahasrākşāya* – he has a thousand eyes.

679. *Sahasrapade* – सहस्रपदे

He has thousands of feet.

673rd name above may be referred.

680. *Sahasrarūpadṛśe* – सहस्ररूपदृशे

He is seen in thousands of forms.

In reality he is *Nirupam* (without any form). But for his devotee's sake he takes multiple forms in different incarnations.

The above 6 names were taken from the 93rd shloka of the *Sahasranāma* Stotram.

681. *Sahasrāmaya Udbhavāya* – सहस्रामय उद्भवाय

He originates in the 1,000 petalled lotus.

The Chakra in the top-head of the human body is called Sahasrara chakra – said to be 1,000 petalled lotus. Bringing the Kundalini energy from Mooladharam to the Sahasrara Chakra is the purpose of Kundalini Yoga. Here, Kundalini is drenches in the rain of Amruta. Lord Dattatreya resides in this chakra.

682. *Tripāda Puruşāya* – त्रिपाद पुरुषाय

He is the Supreme manifesting in three stages.

Prakāsha or vyakta (manifest), *Vimarsha* or *avyakta* (unmanifest) and *Sāmarasya* (without any equal or superior) are the three stages of manifestation.

This name can also be construed as; he is in the form of Trivikrama having measured the three worlds with his three feet.

683. *Tripadordhvāya* – त्रिपदोर्ध्वाय

He is above all the three stages mentioned in the previous name – *turiyātītam*.

684. *Tryayambakāya* – त्र्ययम्बकाय

He is endowed with three eyes. He has three eyes represented by the Sun, the Moon and Agni.

Normally, Lord Shiva is called as *Triambaka*, since he has three eyes. His consort Sri Lalita Devi also three eyes. Here Lord Dattatreya is address as *Triambaka*, since he is in the form Lord Shiva.

The *Maha Mrutyunjaya Mantra* (death defeating mantra), is a mantra from Rigveda (7.59.12) addressed to *Triambaka* (three-eyed one). This verse also recurs in Yajurveda.

In *Lalitā Sahasranāmam* – 453rd name – *Trinayanā* and 762nd name – *Triambakā* – She has three eyes.

685. *Mahāvīryāya* – महावीर्याय

He has great prowess/ valour.

686. *Yogavīryaviśāradāya* – योगवीर्यविशारदाय

He is very much proficient in the power of yoga.

The above 6 names were taken from the 94th shloka of the *Sahasranāma* Stotram.

687. *Vijayine* – विजयिने

He is always victorious in all his endeavours.
He is triumphant, in wisdom, dispassion, greatness, etc. No victory anywhere except him.

According to the *Devī Purāṇa*, *Vijayan* is the *Shiva* form in Kashmir, which is one of the sixty–eight sacred places. Since he is in that form, he is called as *Vijaya*.

In *Silpa Sāstra* (sculpture science) a type of building is called *Vijayam*. He is in that form of and hence *Vijaya*.

In *Vişṇu Sahasranāmam* – 147th name – *Vijayaḥ* – He excels in everything.

In *Lalitā Sahasranāmam* – 346th name – *Vijayā* – She is ever with special victories.

In *Śiva Sahasranāmam* – 181st name – *Vijayaḥ* – He is victorious in all.

688. *Vinayine* – विनयिने

He is very modest.

327th and 622nd names above may also be referred.

689. *Jetre* – जेत्रे

He is always the conqueror.

In 687th name above it was mentioned that he is always victorious. The same is being mentioned in different words here in this name.

407th name above may also be referred.

690. *Vītarāgiṇe* – वीतरागिणे

He is free from passions and attachment.

This has been mentioned in many a name in this Stotra, since he is a sanyasi.

691. *Virājitāya* – विराजिताय

He is (self) brightly illuminated.

692. *Rudrāya* – रुद्राय

He is in the form of Rudra, the lord Shiva.

'Rud' = to cry. He causes the beings to cry, when he destroys them. Destruction is the main task of Lord Rudra.

Rudra is supposed to be ferocious form of Lord Shiva. Sri Rudram, hymn from the Yajurveda is dedicated to Rudra and is very important and famous hymn on Lord Shiva. Throughout this hymn Lord Shiva is worshipped and bowed as Rudra.

Rudra is a Rigvedic deity associated with Lord Shiva, the wind or storms, Vayu, medicine and the hunt. One translation of the name is "the roarer". In the Rigveda, Rudra is praised as the "mightiest of the mighty". Rudra means "who eradicates problems from their roots". Depending upon the period, the name Rudra can be interpreted as "the most severe roarer/ howler" or "the most frightening one".

Taittireeya Samhita (4.5), in the first *Anuvaka* of *Namakam*, Rudra is revered as Sadashiva (meaning "mighty Shiva") and Mahadeva. Sadashiva is the Supreme Being, Paramashiva, in the Siddhanta sect of Shaivism.

misery (*Dra*) and its cause (*Ru*).

In *Śiva Sahasranāmam* – 143rd name – *Rudraḥ* – He is Rudra or Lord Shiva.

693. *Raudrāya* – रौद्राय

He is dreadful; hence he is called as Rudra (the previous name).

694. *Mahābhīmāya* – महाभीमाय

He is very much formidable and awesome.

695. *Prājñamukhyāya* – प्राज्ञमुख्याय

He is foremost in wisdom.

696. *Sadāśucaye* – सदाशुचये

He is Ever-*pure*. This has been mentioned in this Stotra in lot many places.

The above 10 names were taken from the 95th shloka of the *Sahasranāma* Stotram.

697. *Antarjyotişe* – अन्तर्ज्योतिषे

He is possessed of inward light.

During meditation inward looking of Gods is very important. In *Lalitā Sahasranāmam* – 870th name – *Antarmukhasamārādhyā* – She is well adored by those who are inward looking.

In *Śrīmad Bhagavad Geeta* (IV chapter) *Śrī Krişhŋa* clearly advises the inward-looking powers.

698. *Anantātmane* – अनन्तात्मने

He is an endless/ infinite Soul.

699. *Pratyagātmane* – प्रत्यगात्मने

He is an internal Self.

700. *Nirantarāya* – निरन्तराय

He is eternal and constant.

487th name above may also be referred.

Thus ends 100 divine names on Lord *Dattātreya* from 601 to 700.

*****

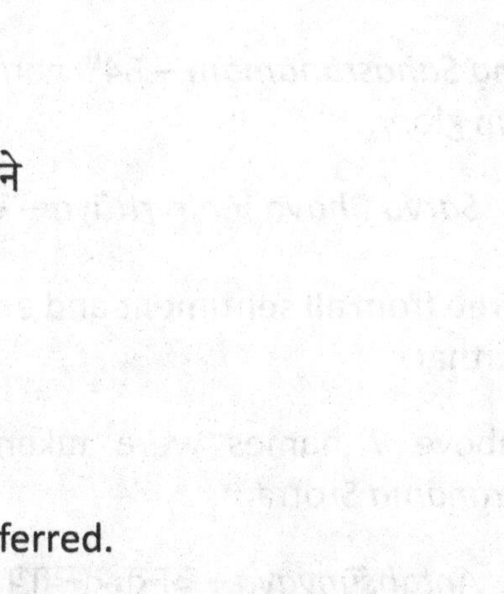

701. *Arūpāya* – अरूपाय

He is formless. Brahmam is *Niroopam* – without any form.

In *Lalitā Sahasranāmam* – 389th name – *Nirūpamā* – she is formless.

In *Gāyatri Sahasranāmam* – 377th name – *Nirūpamāyai* – she is formless.

702. *Ātmarūpāya* – आत्मरूपाय

He has the form of self.

He possesses those souls, who give up the idea that their bodies are Atmans.

Chandokya Upanishat (7.24.1) says, where doth that immensity abide, my Lord! It abideth in its own glory.

In *Viṣṇu Sahasranāmam* – 84th name – *Ātmavān* – He is centered in his own glory.

703. *Sarva Bhāva Vinirvṛttāya* – सर्व भाव विनिर्वृत्ताय

He is free from all sentiment and emotions. He is a sanyasi; he has to be like that.

The above 7 names were taken from the 96th shloka of the *Sahasranāma* Stotram.

704. *Antaḥśūnyāya* – अन्तःशून्याय

He is internally empty in all respects.

705. *Bahiḥśūnyāya* – बहिःशून्याय

He is outwardly empty in all respects.

706. *Śūnyātmane* – शून्यात्मने

His soul is completely empty. In the previous name, it was said that he is internally empty. Here, his soul is explained as empty.

707. *Śūnyabhāvanāya* – शून्यभावनाय

He is devoid of imaginations. We cannot imagine him in any form. He is beyond all these.

708. *Antaḥpūrṇāya* – अन्तःपूर्णाय

He is internally complete in all respects. In the earlier name, it was mentioned that he is internally empty. Here, it is mentioned as he is complete. These are all illusions of devotees.

709. *Bahiḥpūrṇāya* – बहिःपूर्णाय

He is outwardly complete in all respects. In the earlier name, it was mentioned that he is outwardly empty. Here, it is mentioned as he is complete. These are all illusions of devotees.

710. *Pūrṇātmane* – पूर्णात्मने

His Atma is complete in all respects.

711. *Pūrṇabhāvanāya* – पूर्णभावनाय

He is completely absorbed in meditation.

The above 8 names were taken from the 97th shloka of the *Sahasranāma* Stotram.

712. *Antastyāgine* – अन्तस्त्यागिने

He has renounced inwardly everything. Earlier, it was mentioned that he is inwardly empty. Just because he has renounced everything, it was empty.

713. *Bahistyāgine* – बहिस्त्यागिने

He has renounced outwardly everything. Earlier, it was mentioned that he is outwardly empty. Just because he has renounced everything, it was empty.

714. *Tyāgātmane* – त्यागात्मने

He is the embodiment of renunciation. He has renounced everything both inwardly and outwardly.

242nd name above may also be referred.

715. *Sarvayogavate* – सर्वयोगवते

He is endowed – an expert, in/ with all forms of Yoga.

716. *Antaryogine* – अन्तर्योगिने

He is inwardly a Yogi.

717. *Bahiryogine* – बहिर्योगिने

He is outwardly a Yogi.

718. *Sarvayogaparāyaṇāya* – सर्वयोगपरायणाय

He is wholly devoted or destined to Yoga – both inward and outward.

The above 6 names were taken from the 98th shloka of the *Sahasranāma* Stotram.

719. *Antarbhogine* – अन्तर्भोगिने

He is inwardly devoted to enjoyments.

720. *Bahirbhogine* – बहिर्भोगिने

He is outwardly devoted to enjoyments.

721. *Sarvabhigaviduttamāya* – सर्वभिगविदुत्तमाय

He enjoys completely both inward and outward.

722. *Antarniṣṭhāya* – अन्तर्निष्ठाय

He is internally most perfect.

723. *Bahirniṣṭhāya* – बहिर्निष्ठाय

He is outwardly most perfect.

724. *Sarvaniṣṭhāmayāya* – सर्वनिष्ठामयाय

He is an embodiment of all types of devotion.

The above 6 names were taken from the 99th shloka of the *Sahasranāma* Stotram.

725. *Bāhyāntaravimuktāya* – बाह्यान्तरविमुक्ताय

He is liberated from any sense – both inside and outside.

726. *Bāhyāntaravivarjitāya* – बाह्यान्तरविवर्जिताय

He is free or exempted from all emotions and attachments, both external and internal without any exclusion.

727. *Śāntāya* – शान्ताय

He is calm and peaceful.

He, who is freed from every form of avidya, the Brahmam.

In *Viṣṇu Sahasranāmam* – 584th name – *Śāntiḥ* – He is peaceful.

56th and 489th names above may also be referred.

728. *Śuddhāya* – शुद्धाय

He is very pure. This has been mentioned in many a name in this hymn.

729. *Viśuddhāya* – विशुद्धाय

He is completely clean and clear.

Viśuddhi is the chakra in the neck of the human body. He resides there. This is 16 petalled chakra.

In this *chakra*, the soul gets purified by looking at the *Brahmam,* in the form of a swan. Hence this is called as *Vishuddhi Chakra*.

730. *Nirvāṇāya* – निर्वाणाय

He is the final liberation. He bestows liberation to his devotees.

The word *Vāna* or *Bāna* has two meanings – body and bow. Hence, *Nirvāna* means without body. That is the meaning of this name is – He offers bliss indescribable by words to his devotees.

The verses (V–24/25) of *Śrīmad Bhagavat Gita* may be referred; He whose happiness is within, whose delight is within, whose illumination is within only, that Yogi becomes *Brahmam* and gains the beatitude of *Brahmam*.

With sins destroyed, doubts removed, minds disciplined, being delighted in the welfare of all beings, the sages attain the beatitude of *Brahmam*.

In *Vişņu Sahasranāmam* – 577th name – *Nirvāņam* – He is free from all types of sorrows.

In *Lalitā Sahasranāmam* – 390th name – *Nirvāņasukhadāyinī* – She confers the bliss of *Nirvāna*.

731. *Prakŗtice Parāya* – प्रकृतिचे पराय

He is beyond the (Primordial) nature.

The above 7 names were taken from the 100th shloka of the *Sahasranāma* Stotram.

732. *Akālāya* – अकालाय

He is not subject to time (and hence to the death also).

Svetasvatara Upanishad (VI–2) says, omniscient, time of time, possessed of all qualities, all knowing – *Brahmam* is the *Kāla* (death) for *Yama* (God of death) himself;

Gnaḥ Kālakālo Guņī Sarva Vidyāḥ

733. *Kālanemine* – कालनेमिने

He only wields the wheel of time.

He is the destroyer of the demon called *Kālanemi*.

In *Viṣṇu Sahasranāmam* – 642nd name – *Kālaneminihā* – He is destroyer of time.

734. *Kālakālāya* – कालकालाय

He is the destroyer of death.

The word '*Kāla*' means time. But it also means the death or Lord of death (Yama).

This name can mean the Lord Dattatreya killed Yama. Lord Shiva killed Yama to protect Markandeya. Lord Dattatreya only did it in the form of Shiva.

He protects his devotees from the fear of death (untimely).

735. *Janeśvarāya* – जनेश्वराय

He is the Lord of the people. The Lord of beings.

In *Viṣṇu Sahasranāmam* – 341st name – *Janeśvaraḥ* – Lord of people.

736. *Kālātmane* – कालात्मने

He is the soul or the essence of time.

737. *Kālakartre* – कालकर्त्रे

He only creates the time.

Time is calculated based on the revolution and rotation of planets. He only makes the entire universe to revolute and/ or rotate. Hence, he is the creator of the time.

738. *Kālajñāya* – कालज्ञाय

He is the one who knows the death of his devotees in advance.

739. *Kālanāśanāya* – कालनाशनाय

He is the destroyer of (untimely) death of his devotees.

734th name above may also be referred.

740. *Kaivalypadadātre* – कैवल्यपददात्रे

He grants the way to oneness with the Supreme Brahmam.

This state has been described by *Śrī Appayya Deekshitar* in his book called *Ratnatrya Parikshā* as the form of *Brahmam*. He offers that state to his devotees.

There are five kinds of salvation, namely *sālokya, sāroopya, sāmeepya, sāyujya* and *kaivalya*. The *Sālokya* is remaining with the god in the same world. *Sāroopya* is receiving the same form with the god. *Sāyujya* is becoming one with the deity. *Sāmeepya* is remaining near the deity. *Kaivalya*, the state of singleness without attributes. That is the fifth state of consciousness, understanding of self. He bestows all these four *padas* and the *kaivalya* state.

Instead of imagining the form of gods in idols or *yantras*, understanding the form as different from self but still imagining it on the self and by worshipping the same, one can get *Sāroopya*. This is also called as *Sārshtita*. Here the god is imagined with some attributes that are not with oneself, one can get the nearness of the form (*roopa sāmeepyam*) only. *Sāyujya* is worshipping as himself the deity with attributes and he becomes one with the deity. *Sāmeepya* is attained by those celibates who perform the duties as ordained to their states in life.

The *Taitireeya Upanishat* says – those who are peaceful, learned, who live on alms, in the forest performing penance and having faith, without passion, proceed through the Sun to the place of the immortal person, the eternal self. The fourth *pāda* is described in *Muṇḍaka Upanishat* (I–2–II) as to actions and the corresponding results and hence temporary. Hence, they are called *padas* (abode). The fifth one, *Kaivalya*, pertains to the result of knowledge and offers the eternal bliss. Thus says *Taitreeya Sruti*.

The *Yoga Sūtra* (IV–33) says, *Kaivalya* is the establishment in its own nature of the energy of consciousness.

The same message is in brief conveyed in *Shakti Rahasya* as – a mortal who worships by ceremonies, by images, by mind, by identification, by knowing the Self, attains *kaivalya*;

The above 9 names were taken from the 101st shloka of the *Sahasranāma* Stotram.

741. *Kaivalyasukhadāyakāya* – कैवल्यसुखदायकाय

He imparts the happiness of oneness to his devotees.

In *Lalitā Sahasranāmam* – 625th name – *Kaivalyapadadāyinī* – She is the bestower of the solitary abode i.e. non–dual salvation.

742. *Kaivalyālayadharāya* – कैवल्यालयधराय

He possesses the impetus to become one and to enable his devotees also to become one.

It is said that the union of the soul with the Supreme Soul (*Jeevatma* with *Paramatma*) is what becomes one.

743. *Nirbharāya* – निर्भराय

He is with a deep and ardent desire – To bestow his blessings on his devotees. Being an ascetic, he has no other desires.

744. *Harṣavardhanāya* – हर्षवर्धनाय

He increases the joy of his devotees.

The above 4 names were taken from the 102nd shloka of the *Sahasranāma* Stotram.

745. *Hṛdayasthāya* – हृदयस्थाय

He resides in the Heart of the devotees.

Earlier, inward looking was mentioned. The Lord residing in the heart has to be seen inwardly and meditated upon.

The Anahata Chakra in the heart, is a 12-petalled lotus. This is the place of air. He resides there.

In *Lalitā Sahasranāmam* – 303rd name – *Hrudyā* – She lives in the heart of her devotees.

Again, in *Lalitā Sahasranāmam* – 485th name – *Anāhatābja Nilayā* – She abides in the *Anāhata* Lotus. This is in the heart with twelve–petalled lotus.

746. *Hṛṣikeṣāya* – हृषिकेषाय

He is the Lord of the senses, that gives joy.

Hṛṣika = senses. *Īśa* = Lord. He assumes the form of Kshetranjna. Or he who controls the senses, the Supreme Atman.

He, who in the form of Sun and Moon (*Hṛṣi*) delights the world by his (*Keśa*) rays. Mahabharata, Shanti Parvam (343-62 and 53), the Moksha Dharma says, The Sun and the Moon through their rays known as *Keśa* always upholds the Universe as it is by awaking it and causing it to sleep. By such awakening and sleeping the universe is delighted. It is in consequence of these acts Agni and Soma, who upholds the Universe, I am being called as *Hriṣīkeśa*, Oh son of Pandu! Indeed, I am the boon-giver *Iṣāna*, the creator of the Universe.

In *Viṣṇu Sahasranāmam* – 47th name – *Hriṣīkeśaḥ* – He is the lord of senses.

747. *Govindāya* – गोविन्दाय

He is the rescuer of the world.

He resides in waters. In the form of Lord Vishnu, he always resides in the milky ocean, waters.

Mahabharata, Shanti Parvam (343-41), the Moksha Dharma says, I first knew (*Vinda*) and Earth (*Go*), which was carried away and hidden in a cave by Hiranyakshan, a demon. I saved and brought it back. Hence, I am praised by the appellation *'Govinda'*, by all.

The Harivamsha (76.45 and 279.49) says, I am Indra (King) of Devas. I am the Lord of cows. Hence, the world will ever praise as 'Govinda'.

'Go' means speech. Since, he confers the speech, he is called 'Govinda'.

'Vid' = to know. The word *'Go'* has the following 10 meanings;

1. Go = heaven. He transcends from heaven.
2. Arrows. He knows all the Astras (weapons).
3. Cattle. He is the leader of the ignorant ones.
4. Speech. He is to be known by the Vedas.
5. Thunderbolt. He has the Vajra, weapon marks in his feet.
6. Quarters. He is known in all quarters.
7. Eyes. He is the person residing in the eyes.
8. The Sun. He is in the form of Sun.
9. Earth. He recovered the Earth from demon.
10. Waters. He is seated in the waters.

When we go to Tirumala, we can hear people chanting of 'Govinda' loudly.

In *Viṣṇu Sahasranāmam* – 187th name – *Govindaḥ* – He resides in waters.

176th name above may also be referred.

748. *Garbhavarjitāya* – गर्भवर्जिताय

He is not born from any womb. He has no origin.

749. *Sakalāgamapūjyāya* – सकलागमपूज्याय

He is worshipped through all Agama Shastras – all scriptures.

750. *Nigamāya* – निगमाय

He is The Vedas, the scriptures.

751. *Nigamāśrayāya* – निगमाश्रयाय

He is the abode of sacred teachings/ writings.

The above 7 names were taken from the 103rd shloka of the *Sahasranāma* Stotram.

752. *Parāśaktaye* – पराशक्तये

He is the Supreme Power.

Among the elementary substances in the body, skin, blood, flesh, fat and bone were derived from energy (*Shakti*). Marrow, semen, breath and vitality (soul) derived from *Shiva*

Parāshakti can also be interpreted as very great energy. (*Parā – Utkrushṭa* – very great). Just by unison with *Shakti, Shiva attains* enormous greatness. In the first verse of *Soundaryalaharee* (*Shivaḥ Shaktyāyukto*) and other books stress the same principle.

Svetāswara Upanishad (IV–8) says, His supreme *Shakti* is known in different form; "*Parāsya Shaktir Vivdhaiva Shrooyate*".

The *Linga Purāṇa*, says, whatever energy is attributed to any substance is *Śrī Devī* and the ruler of all energised substance is the great *Shiva*. Those substances, which possess energy are the manifestation of *Shiva*. The wise people recognise the energies in substance to be *Śrī Devī*.

The *Shakti* form of the *mantra* called *Para*. Generally, the word *Parāshakti* indicates Goddess Sri Devi. But here it indicates Lord Dattatreya. This means, that there is no different between Sri Devi and Lord Dattatreya.

In *Lalitā Sahasranāmam* – 572nd name – *Parāśaktiḥ* – She is the Supreme energy/ power.

753. *Parākīrtaye* – पराकीर्तये

He is of the highest reputation.

754. *Parāvṛttaye* – परावृत्तये

His conduct is supreme righteousness.

755. *Nidhismṛtaye* – निधिस्मृतये

He is the treasure-house of the scriptures.

756. *Parāvidyā Parākṣāntaye* – पराविद्या पराक्षान्तये

He is the highest knowledge and Supreme forbearance.

757. *Vibhaktaye* – विभक्तये

He is very distinct.

The word *Vibhakti* has several meanings. One meaning is distinct. Another important meaning is, a form of Sama Vedam. He is in that form also.

758. *Yuktasadgataye* – युक्तसद्गतये

He is devoted to the path of truth.

The above 7 names were taken from the 104th shloka of the *Sahasranāma* Stotram.

759. *Svaprakāśāya* – स्वप्रकाशाय

He is self-luminous.

He has luminary powers, which is nothing different from him. With his luster only the other objects get light. There is no object luminating him. He is self–luminous and self splendour.

Brahadāraŋya Upanishat (IV–3–9) says, here this person becomes self–luminous; *Atrāyam Purushaḥ Svayam Jyotiḥ*

Na Tatra Sooryo Bhāti Na Chandra Tārakam
Nemāvidyutobhāntikuto'yamagniḥ Tameva Bhāntamanubhāti
Sarvam Tasya Bhāsā Sarvamidam Vibhāti II

Su – much, *ap* – water, *prakāsha* – manifested. Hence this can also be interpreted as he shines much brighter in water.

In *Lalitā Sahasranāmam* – 414th name – *Svaprakāshā* – She is Sharkesha self–luminous.

760. *Prakāśātmane* – प्रकाशात्मने

He is an enlightened soul.

He reveals brightly his form to his devotees.

As per astronomy, stars are self-illuminating bodies. Sun is a star and hence self-illuminating. He is in that form.

In *Viṣṇu Sahasranāmam* – 274th name – *Prakāṣanaḥ* – He is the illuminator.

In *Śiva Sahasranāmam* – 508th name – *Prakhaśaḥ* – Lord Shiva is illuminating.

In *Gāyatri Sahasranāmam* – 861st name – *Prakāśin* – She shines like anything. *Sri Devi,* who is in the form of Brahmam, resides within the Sun also. *Sri Devi* shines as the only brilliant ruler of the universe. One who shines with all divine qualities.

In *Sūrya Sahasranāmam* – 35th name – *Prakāśakāya* – He shines brightly and make others also to shine. For instance, Moon reflects the light from the Sun and shines.

761. *Parāsaṃvedanātmakāya* – परासंवेदनात्मकाय

He communicates the Supreme Knowledge. He is not only knowledgeable, but also spreads the same to all.

762. *Svasevyāya* – स्वसेव्याय

He is devoted to the Self.

763. *Svavidaṃ Svātmane* – स्वविदं स्वात्मने नमः

He is the essence of Self-knowledge.

764. *Svasaṃvedyāya* – स्वसंवेद्याय

He is the Self that is to be known by all.

765. *Anaghāya* – अनघाय

He is sinless.

The name of the consort of Lord Dattatreya is *Anaghā*. There is a story that the Lady form of Lord Dattatreya himself is *Anaghā*.

Chandokya Upanishat (8.1.5) says, He is free from sin.

In *Viṣŋu Sahasranāmam* – 146th and 831st names – *Anaghaḥ* – He is sinless and painless.

861st name below may also be referred.

766. *Kṣamiṇe* – क्षमिणे

He forbears the mistakes, unknowingly committed by his devotees.

The quality of compassion is to forgive the sins and protect. He is to the core in this regard.

He is the highest in all these – the elevation of mind, regard, the expression indicating the forgiveness of sin, proof, or measurement.

He is our father and we are his children. He does not mind the mistakes done by children, forgives them and still bless us.

In Valmiki Ramayana (1.1.18), when Narada explains the qualities of Sri Rama to Valmiki says, Sri Rama is equal to the Earth in patience.

In *Viṣŋu Sahasranāmam* – 442nd name – *Kṣamaḥ* – He has lots of patience and forgives the mistakes committed by his devotees.

In *Gāyatri Sahasranāmam* – 1,000th name – *Kṣamāyai* – Devi Gayatri is the embodiment of Forgiveness and Tolerance.

The above 8 names were taken from the 105th shloka of the *Sahasranāma* Stotram.

767. *Svānusandhāna Śīlātmane* – स्वानुसन्धान शीलात्मने

He always investigates/ enquiring into his own Atma/ nature.

768. *Svānusandhāna Gocarāya* – स्वानुसन्धान गोचराय

He always enquires into his own perceptions to make it update and current.

769. *Svānusandhāna Śūnyātmane* – स्वानुसन्धान शून्यात्मने

His mind is free from any type of thinking – devoid of personal systems.

770. *Svanusandhānāśrayāya* – स्वनुसन्धानाश्रयाय

His mind is always intent on Self-investigation or self-introspection.

The above 4 names were taken from the 106th shloka of the *Sahasranāma* Stotram.

771. *Svabodhadarpaṇāya* – स्वबोधदर्पणाय

He is the mirror of Self-knowledge.

Last 5 names explain how he self-introspects his own Atma. This is basically a guide for us and nothing for him.

772. *Abhaṅgāya* – अभङ्गाय

He is without any type of separation/ division.

773. *Kandarpa Kula Nāśanāya* – कन्दर्प कुल नाशनाय

He destroys the multitude of lusts and desires of his devotees. Only by destroying the desires one can attain salvation.

774. *Brahmacāriṇe* – ब्रह्मचारिणे

He is the celibate on the path to God.

Brahmacharya is the concept that literally means "conduct consistent with Brahmam" or "on the path of Brahmam". Brahmacharya, a discipline of controlling the senses, is seen as a way to liberation. Though sexual restraint is a part of brahmacharya, brahmacharya encompasses all striving toward a passionless state.

In one context, brahmacharya is the first of four ashramas of a human life. The brahmacharya (bachelor student) stage of life – from childhood – was focused on education and included the practice of celibacy. In this context, it connotes chastity during the student stage of life for the purposes of learning from a guru (teacher) and during later stages of life for the purposes of attaining spiritual liberation or moksha.

In the Hinduism, Jain and Buddhist monastic traditions, brahmacharya implies, among other things, the mandatory renunciation of sex and marriage. It is considered necessary.

- Earlier in one name, it was mentioned that Angha is his consort. That means, he is married and here he is called as Brahmacari.
- Lord Krishna, though married to Satya Bama, Rukmini, Radha and many more Gopika Devis, he is called as "Anadhi Brahmacari" or "Nitya Brahmacari".
- Lord Ganesha is celebrated as a Brahmacari. But it is said that he has two consorts Siddhi and Buddhi.
- Lord Hanuman is worshipped as a Brahmacari. But there is a story that he has a son by name *'Makaradwajan'*.

Is all the above being contradictions? Definitely not. Stories that Gods, have consorts or sons are all for the sake of devotees. In reality they are Niroopa-Nirguna Brahmam. We need to understand and realise this truth.

Brahma also means Vedas. He moves in Vedas or meditates upon the Brahmam.

In *Śiva Sahasranāmam* – 362nd name – *Brahmacārīḥ* – He is in meditation upon Brahmam – (Brahma Nishta)

775. *Brahmavetre* – ब्रह्मवेत्रे

He is the witness of the Supreme Reality. Nobody else has realised the same.

776. *Brāhmaṇāya* – ब्राह्मणाय

He is the knower of the Brahmam.

Brāhmaṇas is a branch of Vedas. He is in that form.

In *Vişŋu Sahasranāmam* – 667th name – *Brāhmaṇaḥ* – He instructs Vedas to the whole world through *Brāhmaṇas.*

In *Śiva Sahasranāmam* – 858th name – *Brāhmaṇaḥ* – He teaches Vedas to the world in the form of *Brahmin.*

777. *Brahmavittamāya* – ब्रह्मवित्तमाय

He is the best among the knowers of Brahmam.

The above 7 names were taken from the 107th shloka of the *Sahasranāma* Stotram.

778. *Tattvabodhāya* – तत्त्वबोधाय

He only has the knowledge of Reality.

779. *Sudhāvarşāya* – सुधावर्षाय

He only enables the shower of the divine nectar.

Earlier in the 681st name, it was mentioned that at the top of the head, in the Sahasrara Chakra, the Kundalini energy gets wet in the rain of divine nectar. He only enables that the shower of the divine nectar.

780. *Pavanāya* – पवनाय

He is the purifier.

In lot many places in this *Sahasranāmam*, it has been mentioned that he is very pure. Here it is mentioned that he purifies others.

In every karma at the start, to clean the areas, the things used, self and others, etc., Punyahavacanam will be performed. The mantra used for the same is called as "*Pavamana Sooktam*"

781. *Pāpapāvakāya* – पापपावकाय

He purifies the sins of his devotees.

By the repetition of his *mantra*, etc., he destroys the sins of his devotees.

Chāndogya Upanishat (IV–24–3), it is mentioned as – Like the point of a reed in the fire, all the sins are burnt up.

In the *Vashisţa Smruti*; If a person is always devoted to learning, penance and continually repeating mantras, even if he is always committing sinful actions, he is not afflicted thereby. Sin never touches those who repeat the mantras or offer oblations, or meditate, or make pilgrimages, or who perform sirovrata (the rite of carrying the fire on the head).

The *Padma Purāņa*, in its *Pushara Kanda* it is said that – The mass of sins though as great as mount Meru is instantly destroyed by worshipping. He, who is devoted, is not stained even by committing heinous crimes, in the manner as the lotus leaf is not affected by water.

In *Brahmāņḍa Purāņā*, it is said that, The sinful actions of those who are devoid of *Varņa* and *Ashrama* and the wretched also, by mere meditation, become virtuous.

In *Vişņu Sahasranāmam* – 992nd name – *Pāpanāśanaḥ* – he destroys the sins in bunches, of those people, who sing hymns in praise of him, or worship him or meditate upon him or just remember him.

Again, in *Vişņu Sahasranāmaa* – 924th name – *Dushkrutihā* – He destroys the bad act of sin or one who does sinful acts.

In *Lalitā Sahasranāmam* – 167th name – *Pāpanāśinī* – She destroys the sins her devotees.

In *Lalitā Triśatī* – 31st name – *Enaḥ Kooţa Vināshinī* and 112th name – *Hatyāti Pāpashamanī* – she destroys all the sins, including the sin of murder, of her devotees.

782. *Brahmasūtra Vidheyātmane* – ब्रह्मसूत्र विधेयात्मने

He is submissive to the tenets of Vedanta (Brahma Sutra) Religion

783. *Brahmasūtrārthanirņayāya* – ब्रह्मसूत्रार्थनिर्णयाय

He is determined to achieve the Goal of the Brahma Sutram, i.e. realising the Brahmam.

The above 6 names were taken from the 108th shloka of the *Sahasranāma* Stotram.

784. *Atyantikāya* – अत्यन्तिकाय

He is extremely close to his devotees.

785. *Mahākalpāya* – महाकल्पाय

He is the cause of the great destruction (*Pralayam*) and the subsequent creation.

786. *Saṅkalpāvarta Nāśanāya* – सङ्कल्पावर्त नाशनाय

He destroys the whirling of bad thoughts of his devotees.

787. *Ādhivyādhiharāya* – आधिव्याधिहराय

He removes the mental and physical afflictions of his devotees.

There are five types of afflictions explained in detail in the *Yoga Sūtra*, (III.3–9);

(1) Nescience, ignorance or *Avidyā* – the absence of discrimination between the self and the non–self.
(2) Egoism or *Asmitā* – thinking that the body, mind and organs as 'I', on account of ignorance and thinking that I am in that form (for instance eyes) – assumption of that body, etc., which are non–self as self.
(3) Strong desire for worldly things or *rāgā* due to *Asmitā* – having interest on the things, which are perceived by the organs and self–involvement in it. Desire is the craving for flowers, scents, etc., which are the means of bodily enjoyment.
(4) Anger, hatred or *Dwesham* on account of *rāgā*; when the interest is affected or if one does not get the things of interest, it results in anger and consequent hatred. Even if the interested things are got, but not the expected results, frustration is created. This is *dwesham* (created on account of *rāgā*).

(5) Ardent attachment is not renouncing a thing even though one knows it is not beneficial. The *dwesha* discussed above is temporary; however the affect in the mind on account of it is a long standing one. Even if the person knows that this is not good or not a suggested one, he cannot leave it. This is *Abhinivesam*.

His devotees are freed from all these afflictions.

788. *Saṃśayārṇava Śoṣakāya* – संशयार्णव शोषकाय

He dries up the ocean of doubts.

Muṇḍaka Upanishad (II–2–8) says, all doubts are removed;
Bhidyate Hrudayagranthiḥ Chdyante Sarva Samshayā

The above 5 names were taken from the 109th shloka of the *Sahasranāma* Stotram.

789. *Tattvātmajñānasandeśāya* – तत्त्वात्मज्ञानसन्देशाय

He announces/ explains the knowledge of the truth about the Self.

790. *Mahānubhāvabhāvitāya* – महानुभावभाविताय

He is established in the great experience of the self realisation.

791. *Ātmānubhavasampannāya* – आत्मानुभवसम्पन्नाय

He is enriched with the experience of the Self.

792. *Svānubhavasukhāśrayāya* – स्वानुभवसुखाश्रयाय

He is the abode of the happiness of experiencing the Self.

The above 4 names were taken from the 110th shloka of the *Sahasranāma* Stotram.

793. *Acintyāya* – अचिन्त्याय

He is beyond mental conception.

By any proof, being the witness of the knower, etc., he cannot be thought of in any particular form as separate from this expanded universe.

Because he is free from connection with the qualities, his nature is unthinkable.

In *Viṣṇu Sahasranāmam* – 832nd name – *Acintyaḥ* – he is inconceivable.

In *Lalitā Sahasranāmam* – 554th name – *Acintyarūpā* – she is of unthinkable form or inaccessible to mind.

In *Śiva Sahasranāmam* – 950th and 997th names – *Acintyaḥ* – he cannot be conceived by any means.

794. *Bṛhadbhānave* – बृहद्भानवे

He shines brightly.

In many a place the *Veda* says, one who knows this (*Brahmam*), his face shines; *Brahmavidiva Te Soumya Mukhamābhāti.*

Chāndogya Upanishat (IV–14–2) – Oh dear child, your face shines like that of a sage – *Shobhatesya Mukhamya Evam Veda*.

53rd name above may also be referred.

795. *Pramadotkarṣanāśanāya* – प्रमदोत्कर्षनाशनाय

He destroys intoxication and self-boastfulness of his devotees.

796. *Aniketa Praśāntātmane* – अनिकेत प्रशान्तात्मने

He is the Serene Soul without a residence.

797. *Śūnyavāsāya* – शून्यवासाय

He resides in the state of emptiness.

He is the subtle ether in the empty cave called heart. There is a subtle hidden cave in the heart of every soul. He dwells there in the form of ether.

798. *Jagadvapuṣe* – जगद्वपुषे

He possesses the Universe itself, as the body.
The above 6 names were taken from the 111th shloka of the *Sahasranāma* Stotram.

799. *Cidgataye* – चिद्गतये

He alone, is the abode of Consciousness.

800. *Cinmayāya* – चिन्मयाय

He is consisting only of pure consciousness.

The *Brahmam,* which is without origin and eternal, shines in two ways viz., with and without qualities. This is called as *chit* (pure consciousness).

The pure consciousness in form of bliss, which is eternal, does not even have an iota of ignorance, does not have anything else as equal or greater, is the Brahmam.

Thus ends 100 divine names on Lord *Dattātreya* from 701 to 800.

*****

801. *Cakriṇe* – चक्रिणे

He holds the *cakra* (Disc).

In the form of Lord Vishnu, he holds the *Sudarshana* Cakra in his hand.

He holds in his hand the cakra, which represents the principle of mind, for the purpose of protecting the whole world.

The *Vişŋu* Purana (1.22.71) says – Vishnu holds in his hand the cakra, which represents the mind, which is unsteady and which is swifter than the wind.

He, whose order, sets the wheel of samsara, in motion.

Caknotīti Cakra – he has enormous powers.

In *Vişŋu Sahasranāmam* – 908th and 995th names – *Cakrī* – holding the disc.

In *Śiva Sahasranāmam* – 414th name – *Cakraḥ* – The one who has enormous powers.

972nd name below may also be referred.

802. *Māyācakrapravartakāya* – मायाचक्रप्रवर्तकाय

He only sets the wheel of illusion in motion.

803. *Sarvavarṇavidārambhiṇe* – सर्ववर्णविदारम्भिणे

He only knows the injunctions of every caste – *varnashrama*.

804. *Sarvārambhaparāyaṇāya* – सर्वारम्भपरायणाय

He is beyond all efforts. He does not need any effort.

We need lots of efforts to realise him.

The above 6 names were taken from the 112th shloka of the *Sahasranāma* Stotram.

805. *Purāṇāya* – पुराणाय

He is the most ancient. As he transcends time, he is the ancient.

16th, 380th, 389th and 653rd names above may also be referred.

806. *Pravarāya* – प्रवराय

He is the most Eminent Lord.

537th name above may also be referred.

807. *Dātre* – दात्रे

He gives liberally to his devotees.

In the form of Brahma, he conceives all.

In *Vişṇu Sahasranāmam* – 44th name – *Dātā* – In the form of Ananta snake (Adishesha) he supports this world.

In *Sūrya Sahasranāmam* – 50th and 673rd names – *Dātre* – He holds a sort of sickle or crooked knife.

808. *Sunarāya* – सुनराय

He is a very good human being.

For the devotee's sake, he is mentioned as a human (*Nara*) in this name.

In Badrikashrama, *Nara* and *Narayana*, two incarnations of Lord Vishnu are doing penance.

Arjuna and Lord Krishna are said to be *Nara* and *Narayana*.

The Virat Purush, who runs the universe –

Nayati Prābhayati Brahmāŋdamiti Naro Virāt.

Sage Vyasa says, the eternal Paramatman is called as Nara, as he leads everything.

He who does not like anything – The non-attached person –

Na Rāti Ādatte Iti Naraḥ

In *Vişņu* Sahasranāmam – 246th name – *Naraḥ* – Jeevas are part of him and hence he is a Naran.

In *Śiva Sahasranāmam* – 716th and 871st names – *Naraḥ* – The one who runs everything.

809. *Kanakāṅgadine* – कनकाङ्गदिने

He wears golden bracelets.

810. *Anasūyātmajāya* – अनसूयात्मजाय

He is the son of *Anasūyā*, wife of sage Atri.

811. *Dattāya* – दत्ताय

He gives away everything to his devotees.

812. *Sarvajñāya* – सर्वज्ञाय

He is omniscient.

He knows everything. He is the witness of all happenings.

Svetasvatara Upanishat (VI.2), says – Omniscient, time of time, possessed of all qualities, all knowing – *Brahmam* is the *Kāla* (death) for *Yama* (God of death) himself –

"*Gnaḥ Kālakālo Guņī Sarva Vidyāḥ*".

Muŋḍako Upanishat (I–1–9) says – one who perceives all and knows all – "*Yaḥ Sarvagnaḥ Sarva Vid*"

Brahadaranyaka Upanishat (6-5-7) says "All this is the self....".

In *Vişņu Sahasranāmam* – 453rd name – *Sarvajñaḥ* – All knowing. He recognises all his manifestations.

In *Sūrya Sahasranāmam* – 272nd and 624th names – *Sarvajñāya* – He is omniscient.

In *Lalitā Sahasranāmam* – 196th name – *Sarvajñā* – She is omniscient.

813. *Sarvakāmadāya* – सर्वकामदाय

He grants all the desired of his devotees.

Brahma Sūtra (3.2.38) says, from him (i.e. the Lord, there comes) the fruit (of works); for (that only) is possible.

In *Viṣṇu Sahasranāmam* – 851st name – *Sarvakāmadaḥ* – The bestower of all wishes.

In *Śiva Sahasranāmam* – 298th name – *Sarvakāmadaḥ* – He fulfills all the desires of his devotees.

The above 9 names were taken from the 113th shloka of the *Sahasranāma* Stotram.

814. *Kāmajite* – कामजिते

He is the conqueror of lust.

He is a sannyasi. Therefore, he has to conquer his lust.

Having conquered lust, he helps his devotees to conquer their lust.

815. *Kāmapālāya* – कामपालाय

He protects his devotees from desires.

Instead of fulfilling the desires of His devotees, he avoids his devotees to desire.

816. *Kāmine* – कामिने

He loves his devotees. Devotees love him like anything.

He has an attractive form.

817. *Kāmapradāgamāya* – कामप्रदागमाय

He fulfills all the desires of his devotees according to *Āgama* principles.

In *Lalitā Sahasranāmam* – 63rd name – *Kāmadāyinī* – She fulfills all the desires of Her devotees.

818. *Kāmavate* – कामवते

He appears wantonly. He appears at his will, only when he wants.

819. *Kāmapoṣāya* – कामपोषाय

He nurtures his devotees with love.

820. *Sarvakāmanivartakāya* – सर्वकामनिवर्तकाय

He removes all the desires of his devotees.

Fulfilling of desires is different from removing the desires. If a desire is fulfilled, one other desire will evoke. When the desire is removed, then his mind focusses/ concentrates on the God and lead to liberation.

939th name below may also be referred.

The above 7 names were taken from the 114th shloka of the *Sahasranāma* Stotram.

821. *Sarvakāmaphalotpattaye* – सर्वकामफलोत्पत्तये

He gives rise to the fruits of all desires of his devotees.

In *Viṣṇu Sahasranāmam* – 652nd – *Kāmapālaḥ* and – 653rd names – *Kāmī* – He fulfills the desires of those that seek happiness.

In *Lalitā Sahasranāmam* – 989th name – *Vānchitārthapradiyinī* – She fulfills all the desires of her devotees.

In *Lalitā Triśatī* – 43rd name – *Īpsithārthapradiyinī* – conveys the same message.

822. *Sarvakāmaphalapradāya* – सर्वकामफलप्रदाय

He satisfies all the wishes of his devotees.

In *Viṣṇu Sahasranāmam* – 851st name – *Sarvakāmadaḥ* – the bestower of all wishes.

823. *Sarvakāmaphalaiḥ Pūjyāya* – सर्वकामफलैः पूज्याय

He is worshipped for all (beautiful) fruits.

Different Gods/ Goddess are worshipped for some specific desires/ fruits – for instance, goddess Saraswati for education, goddess Lakshmi for wealth, etc. But single Lord Datattatreya is worshipped for all types of desires.

824. *Sarvakāmaphalāśrayāya* – सर्वकामफलाश्रयाय

He is the refuge for the fruits of all desires.

The above 4 names were taken from the 115th shloka of the *Sahasranāma* Stotram.

825. *Viśvakarmaṇe* – विश्वकर्मणे

Viśvakarma is the architect for Devas. He is in that form.

He is called *Viśvakarma* being possessed of wonderful powers of creation. From his resembling *Tvashta*, the celestial architect.

In *Viṣṇu Sahasranāmam* – 50th name – *Viśvakarmāḥ* – his act is the Universe.

826. *Kṛtātmane* – कृतात्मने

He is self-disciplined.

827. *Kṛtajñāya* – कृतज्ञाय

He knows only good behaviour.

He is the Atma of the entire universe.

Krita = the created universe and *Jna* = the knower. i.e. *Atman.*

In *Viṣṇu Sahasranāmam* – 532nd name – *Kṛtagnaḥ* – he is the universe and the soul.

327th name above may also be referred.

828. *Sarvasākşikāya* – सर्वसाक्षिकाय

He is the witness of all activities of the entire universe.

He sees the entire world. **He** sees the entire world as his own form.

In *Lalitā Sahasranāmam* – 384th name – *Viśvasākşiņī* – She is the witness for everything.

In *Sūrya Sahasranāmam* – 442nd name – *Sarvasākşine*, 861st name – *Lokasākșiņe* and 980th name – *Karmaņāṃ Sākșiņe* – he is the witness for everything happening in this world.

35th, 52nd, 149th and 397th names above may also be referred.

829. *Sarvārambhaparityāgine* – सर्वारम्भपरित्यागिने

He renounces the fruits of actions.

He only does the actions and does not expect any fruits.

Shrimad Bhagavad Gita (2.47) also says;

1. Do your duty, but do not concern yourself with the results.
2. The fruits of your actions are not for your enjoyment.
3. Even while working, give up the pride of doership.
4. Do not be attached to inaction.

830. *Jaḍonmattapiśācavate* – जडोन्मत्तपिशाचवते

He is seemingly, idiotic, mad and demonic. Noone should be judged just by the look.

The above 6 names were taken from the 116th shloka of the *Sahasranāma* Stotram.

831. *Bhikşave* – भिक्षवे

He is a mendicant.

6th name above may also be referred.

832. *Bhikşākarāya* – भिक्षाकराय

Being a typical sanyasi, he begging his food and eat.

Bhikṣā = begging. *Kara* = hands. He has to obtain the meals in his hands only and not in any vessel.

Usually, bhiksha is the meal served to a *sadhu* sanyasi or monk when that person visits a devout Hindu household. Bhiksha signifies a Hindu tradition of asking for alms with the purpose of self-effacement or ego-conquering.

Bhiksha is incorporated into religious rituals as well, a prominent one being the bhikshacaranam, which includes begging for alms. In such a ritual, after thread ceremony must beg for alms, stating, "*Bhavati Bhiksham Dehi*".

There are lot many rules and procedures prescribed for a sanyasi[3] to obtain Bhiksha and eat.

833. *Bhīkṣṇāhāriṇe* – भीक्ष्णाहारिणे

He is eating only the food offered to him by others. A sanyasi should not cook.

It is the duty of the Grahastas (married family people) to offer food to Brahmacaris and Sanyasis. The description in the previous name may also be referred.

834. *Nirāśramaṇe* – निराश्रमणे

He is without any of the *Ashramas* – beyond all the stages of life.

Brahmacari, Grahasta, Vanaprasta and Sanyasi are the four ashramas (stages) prescribed. He is beyond all these four called – turiateetam.

835. *Akulāya* – अकुलाय

He is without any clan/ race.

Kulā = clan. *Akulā* = without any clan. He does not follow any clan.

---

[3] The author of this book has written a separate book "Ascetism – an Analysis", wherein this has been detailed at length.

Kula means the birth place, parents, family tree, etc. Since he is beyond birth, he has no *kula* and hence *Akula*.

*Akul*ā also means the *Sahasrāra* Lotus at the top of the *Sushumna Nāḍi*. He resides there.

In *Lalitā Sahasranāmam* – 96th name – *Akulā* – *Kula* also means parents, family etc. and *Śrī Devī* is beyond all these.

836. *Anukūlāya* – अनुकूलाय

He is conveniently/ comfortably well disposed.

He moves friendly with all and does everything favourable for them.

In Mahabharata, he, in the form of Krishna, was friendly to Pandavas, especially to Arjuna and did everything favourable to them.

Because of his being the Self of all and as none does anything unfavourable to him.

In *Viṣṇu Sahasranāmam* – 342nd name – *Anukūlaḥ* – he is friendly with all.

837. *Vikalāya* – विकलाय

He is without separate parts – i.e. he is in *Niroopa* – formless.

838. *Akalāya* – अकलाय

He is in an undivided form. Since he has no form, he cannot be divided.

The above 8 names were taken from the 117th shloka of the *Sahasranāma* Stotram.

839. *Jaṭilāya* – जटिलाय

He is with matted hair. Since, he is an *Avadhoota Sanyasi*, he cannot shave his head or body. Hence, his hair is matted.

He mixed with his devotees. There is no difference between *Atman* and himself - Both are one and the same. This is real *Advaitam* –

merging of *jeevatma* and *paramatma*.

In *Gāyatri Sahasranāmam* – 317th name – *Jaṭilāyai* – she mixes with her devotees as a friend.

840. *Vanacāriṇe* – वनचारिणे

He wanders in the forests/ jungles.

841. *Daṇḍine* – दण्डिने

He holds a Danda (staff-stick) of an ascetic.

Lot many sanyasis hold a Danda in their hands. But some, customarily do not hold. Those holding it are called *Dandee* sanyasi.

Lord Dattatreya also would have been given a Danda, while assuming the Sannyasa. But, while become an avadhoota sanyasi, he would have sacrificed the Danda also.

842. *Muṇḍine* – मुण्डिने

His head is clean-shaven.

While assuming the Sannyasa, his head would have been tonsured (clean shaven). But, after becoming an avadhoota sanyasi, no such shaving is permitted.

843. *Gandhine* – गन्धिने

He has a very little of everything.

He does not hold anything more than required.

844. *Dehadharmavihīnātmane* – देहधर्मविहीनात्मने

He is devoid of the obligations of having a body.

He does not care about his body. For instance, Ramana Maharishi had a tumor in his back. Doctors had to do an operation to remove it. Ramana Maharishi asked the doctors to perform the operation without any anesthesia. He did not care about his body.

845. *Ekākine* – एकाकिने

He is only-one no two – typical Advaita philosophy.

He is alone because he is without a backup. The *Brahmam* without any quality (*Nirguna*) is called *Ekā*.

Chāndokya Upaniihat (6-2-1) says – Only one, no two – *Ekamevātvteeyam*.

In *Devi Upanishat* also we read as;
Ekaiva Sarvatra Vartate, Tasmāduchyate Ekā I

The *Brahma Sūtra* says – *Ekam Brahma, dvitīya naste neḥ na naste kincan* – There is only one God, not the second; not at all, not at all, not an iota.

In *Viṣṇu Sahasranāmam* – 726th name – *Ekaḥ* – since he is the concluded truth without any kind of differences that are internal or that relates to similar external objects or to dissimilar object, he is *Ekaḥ*.

In *Lalitā Sahasranāmam* – 665th name – *Ekākinī* – She is only one.

In *Gāyatri Sahasranāmam* – 104th name – *Ekāyai* – She is only one – no-two.

846. *Saṅgavarjitāya* – सङ्गवर्जिताय

He is without any companions.

The above 8 names were taken from the 118th shloka of the *Sahasranāma* Stotram.

847. *Āśramiṇe* – आश्रमिणे

He has completed all the four stages of life and beyond all these.

In *Viṣṇu Sahasranāmam* – 852nd name – *Āśramaḥ* – he is like a resting place for all those who wander in the forests.

848. *Anāśramārambhāya* – अनाश्रमारम्भाय नमः

He is beyond the duties of each stage (*ashrama*) of life.

683rd name above may also be referred.

849. *Anācāriṇe* – अनाचारिणे

He is not performing customary observances/ duties.

Ācāram = duties prescribed. *Anācāram* = not following the duties. He is a sanyasi – renounced everything in this world. There is no prescriptions or restrictions for an avadhoota sanyasi. Hence, he has no customary observances prescribed,

850. *Karmavarjitāya* – कर्मवर्जिताय

He has been released from the fruits of past actions.

It has been mentioned in this Stotra, in lot many places, that he is not been affected by fruits of any action. It is being stressed here.

851. *Asandehine* – असन्देहिने

He is beyond any doubts. There is no ambiguity or uncertainty about him.

852. *Sandehine* – सन्देहिने

There is some uncertainty about him.

He is not clearly visible and he cannot be realised by all. The devotees have to struggle hard to realise him.

This name is in contradiction to the previous name.

853. *Nakiñcanāya* – नकिञ्चनाय

He possessing nothing.

Everything in this world is his. But he does not own anything. He is a sanyasi and he should not own anything.

The above 7 names were taken from the 119th shloka of the *Sahasranāma* Stotram.

854. *Nṛdehine* – नृदेहिने

He does not have body.

He is *Niroopa Brahmam*. Hence, he has no form (body).

855. *Dehaśūnyāya* – देहशून्याय

He has no body. The message of the previous name is being stressed here.

856. *Nābhāvine* – नाभाविने

He is not bound by any destiny.

857. *Bhāvanirgatāya* – भावनिर्गताय

He is free from any sentiment.

351st, 591st and 703rd names above may also be referred.

858. *Nābrahmaṇe* – नाब्रह्मणे

He is not ignorant of the formless Supreme. In other words, he is very much knowledgeable about the Supreme Brahmam.

859. *Parabrahmaṇe* – परब्रह्मणे

He himself is the Supreme Brahmam.

135th name above may also be referred.

860. *Svayameva Nirākulāya* – स्वयमेव निराकुलाय

He is without any confusion about the Self.

The above 7 names were taken from the 120th shloka of the *Sahasranāma* Stotram.

861. *Anaghāya* – अनघाय

765th name above may be referred.

862. *Agurave* – अगुरवे

He had no guru. He was the guru of all.

In the Shrimad Bhagavatam (11.9.32), it is said that he had 24 gurus – that is, he learned many good things from every insect, animal and even a prostitute. He does not have a master.

585th & 598th names above and 864th name below may also be referred.

863. *Nāthanāthottamāya* – नाथनाथोत्तमाय

He is the highest preceptor of all other Gurus.

864. *Gurave* – गुरवे

585th, 598th and 864th names above may be referred.

865. *Dvibhujāya* – द्विभुजाय

He is two armed, similar to other human beings.

In 669th name above, it was mentioned that he has multiple shoulders (arms). But here it is mentioned that he has 2 shoulders. All these are illusions of the devotees.

866. *Prākṛtāya* – प्राकृताय

He is natural and primordial. He is the nature and he is this universe

He only dissolves this universe and recreates it.

In *Sūrya Sahasranāmam* – 426th name – *Prakṛtisthitāya* and 502nd name – *Prakṛtaye* – He is always in the original and natural state. He is the nature. He is this world.

In *Śiva Sahasranāmam* – 828th name – *Vikṛtaḥ* – conveying the same meaning.

867. *Janakāya* – जनकाय

He is the father of this world. He only created this world.

In Ramayana, Sita's father is Janakar.

410th name above may also be referred.

868. *Pitāmahāya* – पितामहाय

He is the paternal grand-father of this world. In the previous name he was referred as father. Here, he is indicated as grand-father.

Usually, Lord Brahma is addressed as *Pitāmahar*. He is in that form.

In Mahabharata, Bheeshma is addressed as *Pitāmahar* by all.

In *Viṣṇu Sahasranāmam* – 970th name – *Prapitāmahaḥ* – he is great grand-father. He is father of Brahma. Brahma is grand-father of all. Hence, he is great grand-father.

The above 8 names were taken from the 121st shloka of the *Sahasranāma* Stotram.

869. *Anātmane* – अनात्मने

He has no sense of Individual Self/ Atman.

870. *Nacanānātmane* – नचनानात्मने

He is of many different personalities.

For his devotee's sake, he takes various incarnations and hence seen as different personalities.

871. *Nītaye* – नीतये

He behaves with propriety and hence, has carried away the minds of his devotees.

In *Śiva Sahasranāmam* – 415th name – *Nītiḥ* and 416th name – *Anītiḥ* – One who is a king of justice. One who is not treated by others.

872. *Nītimatāṃ Varāya* – नीतिमतां वराय

He is the most excellent in moral behaviour. He is a king of justice.

The embodiment of justice who punishes those who deserve punishment – *Dandyeshu Danda Pranayanathi*.

873. *Sahajāya* – सहजाय

He is in his own natural and original way.

188th and 371st names above may also be referred.

874. *Sadṛśāya* – सदृशाय

He is worthy of his behaviour.

875. *Siddhāya* – सिद्धाय

He is a realised soul. He is a Siddhar.

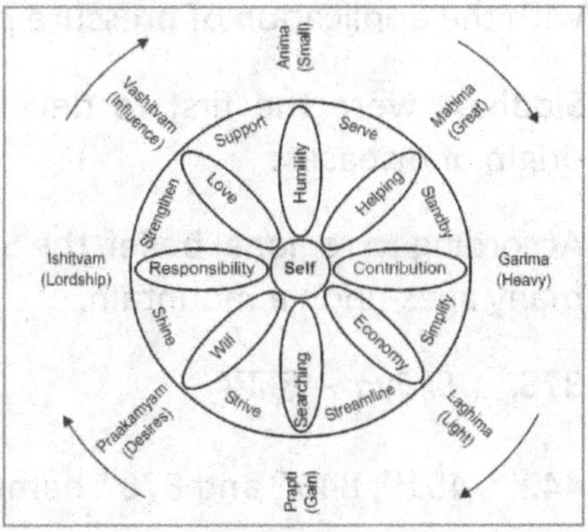

A Siddhar is a perfected individual who has attained spiritual powers called *Siddhis*. There are 8 great Siddhis. They are;

1. Anima – Anima siddhi gives the individual the ability to shrink down one's body.
2. Mahima – Mahima grants the user the ability to attain gigantic forms.
3. Garima – Garima siddhi lets user to alter the weight of their body.
4. Laghima – Laghima siddhi is opposite to Garima, allows its user to decrease the body weight.
5. Prapti – Prapti is very different from previous siddhis. Prapti siddhi gives one ability to instantly get the things they desire.
6. Prakamya – Prakamya siddhi provides wide range of abilities to its user. It allows its user to increase their life length dramatically, teleportation, ability to live underwater.
7. Isitva – The individual obtaining this siddhi gets the ability to influence the nature as per ones will.
8. Vasitva – Vasitva the last of ashta siddhi allows the user to control other people's minds.

In Valmiki Ramayana, we read about Anjaneya Swami manifesting all these eight siddhis.

Historically, Siddhars were knowledgeable in science, technology, astronomy, literature, fine arts, music, drama, and dance and provided solutions to common people's illnesses and advice for their future.

Siddhars are also believed to be the founders of *Varma Jalai* - a martial art for self-defense and medical treatment at the same time with the application of pressure points.

Siddhars were the first to develop pulse-reading to diagnose the origin of diseases.

According to regional belief, the Siddhars are said to have resided for many ages upon a mountain.

876. *Ekāya* – एकाय

442nd, 451st, 845th and 876th names above may also be referred.

877. *Cinmātrāya* – चिन्मात्राय

He is the pure intelligence.

Chit – knowledge. He is in the form of knowledge itself. That is, pure knowledge without the distinction of the knower, the known and the intellect.

In *Lalitā Sahasranāmam* – 251st name – *Cinmayī* – She is in the form of *chit* (pure consciousness itself).

800th name above may also be referred.

The above 9 names were taken from the 122nd shloka of the *Sahasranāma* Stotram.

878. *Nakartre* – नकर्त्रे

He is non-doer. This name has to be read in conjunction with the next name.

879. *Kartre* – कर्त्रे

He is the doer of all karmas. This name may seem contradictory to the previous name.

He is the instrumental cause and also independent.

In *Vişņu Sahasranāmam* – 380th name – *Kartā* – he is the doer.

In *Śiva Sahasranāmam* – 292nd name – *Kartā* – he is the creator and preserver of all things.

880. *Bhoktre* – भोक्त्रे

He is the enjoyer. The enjoyments of his devotees are very great.

In reality he does not enjoy any of the fruits of all karmas. But, for devotees' sake he seems to be enjoying.

In *Vişņu Sahasranāmam* – 433rd name – *Mahābhogaḥ* – he is the great bliss.

881. *Bhogavivarjitāya* – भोगविवर्जिताय

He has completely abandoned indulgences.

882. *Turīyāya* – तुरीयाय

He is in the fourth state of pure spirit.

The bliss obtained in the fourth state makes the enjoyer feels that this is the true state and other three are not. The soul which has reached this state still has the other states, based on the worldly trends. But still he would not be affected by those.

The state mentioned in *Vedas* is called *Tureeya*;
Śiva Matvaitam Caturttam Manyante.

It is mentioned in *Soundaryalaharee* as, the *Sadāshiva* form is above *Brahma, Vişņu* and *Rudra* – the fourth form *Mahāmāyā* is above the three forms *Saraswathee, Lakshmi* and *Parvathi.*

In *Lalitā Sahasranāmam* – 262nd name – *Turyā* – She is the soul in the fourth state (state of ecstasy).

883. *Turīyātītāya* – तुरीयातीताय

He is beyond the fourth stage called *Turīyātītam*.

This *Turīyātītam* stage has been discussed in many a place in this Stotra.

884. *Svacchāya* – स्वच्छाय

He is pure and transparent.

885. *Sarvamayāya* – सर्वमयाय

He has the universal form.

He is in the form of all things. This universe has within it, thirty–six *tattv*as – the universal absolute and the incarnations.

In *Lalitā Sahasranāmam* – 203rd name – *Sarvamayī* – she is omnipresent and omnipotent.

The above 8 names were taken from the 123rd shloka of the *Sahasranāma* Stotram.

886. *Sarvādhişțhānarūpaya* – सर्वाधिष्ठानरूपय

His form is the basis for everything.

887. *Sarvadhyeyavivarjitāya* – सर्वध्येयविवर्जिताय

He is beyond all things that can be conceptualised – He cannot be conceptualised.

888. *Sarvalokanivāsātmane* – सर्वलोकनिवासात्मने

His soul is residing in all the worlds. The soul of all beings is his.

889. *Sakalottamavanditāya* – सकलोत्तमवन्दिताय

He is worshipped as the highest manifestation.

He is worshipped by every soul of the world.

The above 4 names were taken from the 124th shloka of the *Sahasranāma* Stotram.

890. *Dehabhṛte* – देहभृते

He possesses a body (for the sake of his devotees). In reality he is Niroopa Brahmam.

In *Śiva Sahasranāmam* – 296th name – *Dehaḥ* – he is the body of every soul.

891. *Dehakṛte* – देहकृते

He only creates the body of every being.

892. *Dehātmane* – देहात्मने

He is the soul in every body.

893. *Dehabhāvanāya* – देहभावनाय

He is the enlightener of the body.

894. *Dehine* – देहिने

He is embodied.

895. *Dehavibhaktāya* – देहविभक्ताय

He is detached from his body. As mentioned in multiple places, he is without form (*niroopa*). But for devotees' sake, he seemingly has a body.

896. *Dehabhāvaprakāśanāya* – देहभावप्रकाशनाय

He is the enlightening bodily consciousness.

The irony here is that the last 7 names describe the body of a person who has no body at all.

The above 7 names were taken from the 125th shloka of the *Sahasranāma* Stotram.

897. *Layasthāya* – लयस्थाय

He is absorbed in deep concentration.

898. *Layavide* – लयविदे

He only knows the state of dissolving/ merging with the Supreme.

899. *Layabhāvāya* – लयभावाय

He only creates the state of dissolution.

Laya, a peculiar state of mind, greater than ten meditations. The state of mind focusing on seeing, hearing and thinking and do not understand anything else. When we listen to good music, we forget ourselves and do not even know what is happening near us. In the same way the mind absorbs with the Supreme Being. This happens infrequently and also in a temporary way. For a very few people it is of permanent nature also. He only enables that experience.

Bifurcating the songs and dances according to time of drums is also called as *Laya*. He is in that form. The sage called *Bharata*, treated song and dance as separate arts and a tool for the salvation. The trinity (three geniuses) of classical music also used to sing as a tool for salvation.

In *Lalitā Sahasranāmam* – 739th name – *Layakarī* – she causes absorption.

900. *Bodhavate* – बोधवते

He possesses great wisdom.

121st, 346th, 348th and 771st names above may also be referred.

Thus ends 100 divine names on Lord *Dattātreya* from 801 to 900.

*****

901. *Layātītāya* – लयातीताय

He has gone beyond dissolution. He only survives during *pralaya*.

Mahākalpa is the great dissolution (*Pralayā*) of this universe. Destruction means – the entire universe sub–merged with Lord himself. This is the fourth task of the Lord called *Tirodana*. He is the only witness right before creation till complete destruction.

In *Lalitā Sahasranāmam* – 232nd name – *Maheśvara Mahākalpa Mahā Tānḍava Sākşiŋī* – she is the witness to the great awesome destructive cosmic dance of Lord *Maheshvarā* at the end of creative cycle.

902. *Layasyāntāya* – लयस्यान्ताय

He only creates the end of time and death.

903. *Layabhāvanivāraṇāya* – लयभावनिवारणाय

He prevents the sense of dying.

From 897th name 6 names (excepting 900) talk about Layam – merging with Brahmam.

The above 7 names were taken from the 126th shloka of the *Sahasranāma* Stotram.

904. *Vimukhāya* – विमुखाय

He is mouthless/ faceless. He is everywhere and hence, faceless.

In *Śrīmad Bhagavat Geeta* (XIII–13) it is mentioned as; *Sarvatokshishiromukham* – Everywhere eyes, heads and mouths.

In *Purusha Sooktam* also it is mentioned as;

Sahasra Şīrśāḥ Puruşaḥ Sahasrākşaḥ Sahasrapād

In *Lalitā Sahasranāmam* – 532nd name – *Sarvatomukhī* – she has faces in all round directions.

In *Śiva Sahasranāmam* – 249th name – *Amukhaḥ* – since, he is everywhere, he is faceless.

905. *Pramukhāya* – प्रमुखाय

He is the foremost among the lords.

112th name above may also be referred.

906. *Pratyaṅmukhavadācāriṇe* – प्रत्यङ्मुखवदाचारिणे

He has the nature of speaking face to face.

907. *Viśvabhuje* – विश्वभुजे

He enjoys the Universe.

908. *Viśvaghṛṣe* – विश्वघृषे

He grinds the Universe.

909. *Viśvāya* – विश्वाय

He is the universe or he is the cause of this universe.

He is the *Brahmam*, *Oṃkāram*, the world, or the creator of it or the indweller or involver of all in him.

In *Vişŋu Sahasranāmam* – the very first name – *Viśwam* – he is the universe.

In *Lalitā Sahasranāmam* – 256th name – *Viśvarūpā* – she is in the form of universe.

In *Śiva Sahasranāmam* – 40th and 92nd names – *Viśvarūpā* – he is in the form of universe.

910. *Viśvakṣemakarāya* – विश्वक्षेमकराय

He confers happiness to the whole world.

He protects, what has been acquired by his devotees. He destroys the evils of his devotees.

In *Vişŋu Sahasranāmam* – 599th name – *Kşemakṛt* – he is the doer of good to his devotees.

The above 7 names were taken from the 127th shloka of the *Sahasranāma* Stotram.

911. *Avikşiptāya* – अविक्षिप्ताय

He is without any type of confusion or anger.

912. *Apramādine* – अप्रमादिने

He has great wisdom.

He is the underlying principles of consciousness – proof or evidence.

In *Vişŋu Sahasranāmam* – 428th and 959th names – *Pramāṇam* – he is the authority of all dharmas.

295th name above may also be referred.

913. *Parārdhaye* – परार्धये

He is possessed with Supreme Intelligence.

877th name above may also be referred.

914. *Paramārthadṛśe* – परमार्थदृशे

He is the knower of Supreme Reality.

70th and 92nd names above may also be referred.

915. *Svānubhavavihīnāya* – स्वानुभवविहीनाय

He is free from self-derived perceptions.

916. *Svānubhavaprakāśanāya* – स्वानुभवप्रकाशनाय

He publicises the experience of Self. That is, he teaches self-experience to his disciples.

The above 6 names were taken from the 128th shloka of the *Sahasranāma* Stotram.

917. *Nirindriyāya* – निरिन्द्रियाय

He is beyond the senses.

Earlier it was mentioned that he has no body – he is beyond the organs. Here it is indicated as he is beyond his senses.

918. *Nirbuddhaye* – निर्बुद्धये

He is beyond intellect. His intellect cannot be conceived by anyone.

919. *Nirābhāsāya* – निराभासाय

He is beyond appearance. He is, in a way, invisible.

355th and 481st names above may also be referred.

920. *Nirākṛtāya* – निराकृताय

He is beyond any action. He does all the actions, but he is beyond those actions neither the fruits of the action as well.

930th name below may also be referred here.

921. *Nirahaṅkārāya* – निरहङ्काराय

He is without any type of ego. He does not have the concept of individuality.

Ego is of three kinds; *Vaikhareeka*, *Taijasa* and *Bhutādi*, according to *sattva*, *rajas* and *tamas* characters, respectively. He does not any of these.

In *Lalitā Sahasranāmam* – 161st name – *Nirahaṅkārā* – she is without any ego.

423rd name above may also be referred.

922. *Rūpātmane* – रूपात्मने

His form is the *Atma* itself. He is *Niroopa* (formless) *Paramatma*.

287th name above may also be referred.

923. *Nirvapuṣe* – निर्वपुषे

He has no body.

His body has been described in lot many names in this Stotra. Also, in many a place it has been mentioned he has no organ neither a body.

It is being reiterated here, that he is *niroopa* (formless) *brahmam*.

924. *Sakalāśrayāya* – सकलाश्रयाय

He is the refuge for everyone.

In *Vişŋu Sahasranāmam* – 614th name – *Lokatrayāśrayaḥ* – he is the refuge for the three worlds.

In *Śiva Sahasranāmam* – 825th name – *Sarvāśrayakramaḥ* – he is the refuge for all.

The above 8 names were taken from the 129th shloka of the *Sahasranāma* Stotram.

925. *Śokaduḥkhaharāya* – शोकदुःखहराय

He is the dispeller of sorrow and pain.

274th and 630th names above can also be referred here.

926. *Bhogamokṣaphalapradāya* – भोगमोक्षफलप्रदाय

He gives the fruits of enjoyment of liberation.

Lots of benefits/ fruits are mentioned in the *phalashruti* part of every *Stotra, mantra* and all. He bestows all those benefits for all who chant them with focused mind and devotion.

In *Gāyatri Sahasranāmam* – 674th name – *Phaladā* – she bequeaths the results of the mantras and all.

927. *Suprasannāya* – सुप्रसन्नाय

He is a very gracious minded God. He is ever merciful.

His *Antaḥkaraŋa* (inner mind) is untainted by qualities of Rajas and Tamas. He is ever-merciful, on account of his having no desire to be satisfied.

In *Vişŋu Sahasranāmam* – 237th name – *Prasannatmāḥ* – he is of delightful nature.

In *Sūrya Sahasranāmam* – 407th name – *Prasannātmane* – she bequeaths

928. *Sūkşmāya* – सूक्ष्माय

He is very subtle. His form is so subtle.

The ether and all are material causes. Since there is no material cause like sound, etc., he is subtle.

Muŋḍakopanishad (I–1–6) says; "*Sarvagatam Sūkşmam*".

Kaivalyopanishad (16) says – it is subtler than the subtle and eternal; *Sookshmāt Sookshmataram Nityam*.

Kaţopanishad (II–20) says – it is subtler than an atom, the subtlest; *Anoranīyān*.

The sacrificial fire done in the fire at *Kunḍalinī*, in the midst of *Mooladhāram*, is subtle. It is called *Rahoyāgam*.

In *Vişŋu Sahasranāmam* – 457th name – *Sūkşmaḥ* – he is very subtle.

In *Śiva Sahasranāmam* – 895th name – *Sūkşmātmaḥ* and 966th name – *Sūkşmaḥ* – He is a very subtle soul (*Atma*).

In *Lalitā Sahasranāmam* – 467th name – *Sūkşma Rūpiŋī* – She has a very subtle, not to be easily recognised, form.

In *Sūrya Sahasranāmam* – 663rd name – *Sūkşmadhiye* – He is subtly intelligent.

In *Gāyatri Sahasranāmam* – 971st name – *Sūkṣmāyai* – She is very subtle.

439th name above may also be referred.

929. *Śabdabrahmārthasaṃgṛhāya* – शब्दब्रह्मार्थसंगृहाय

He fulfills the purpose of life of his devotees, revealed in the Vedas.

Tantra Sāstras (with a little modification) explain the creation of *Shabda Brahmam* as follows;

The supreme being can be imagined in two ways viz., with attributes and without. The *Sat Chit Ānanda Shakti* (energy) originated from qualified supreme being. From energy the *nādam* (sound) originated, from sound the *mahā Bindu*. This *mahābindu* split into three viz., *Bindu, Nādam* (sound – different from the above said *nādam*) and *Beejam* (seed). *Bindu* is *Shiva*. *Beeja* is *Shakti*. Their union is *Nādam*. The same is cryptically mentioned as various three–folds like; These triplets are considered as three vertices of a triangle.

- *Prakāsham, Vimarsham and Mishram*
- *Rakta caraŋam, Śukla caraŋam and Miśra caraŋam*
- *Moon*, Fire (*Agni*) and Sun
- *Ichā, Gnāna* and *Kriyā*
- *Brahma, Viṣhŋu* and *Rudra*

The above 5 names were taken from the 130th shloka of the *Sahasranāma* Stotram.

930. *Āgamāpāya Śūnyāya* – आगमापाय शून्य

He has no interest in transitory things.

931. *Sthānadāya* – स्थानदाय

He assigns various roles to different Lords and maintains the whole universe.

For instance, Brahma is assigned the creation task, Vishnu is assigned the protection task, Rudran is assigned the destruction task and so on.

932. *Satāṅgataye* – सताङ्गतये

He maintains the sacred fire of truth.

933. *Ākṛtāya* – आकृताय

He is beyond actions.

920th name above may also be referred here.

934. *Sukṛtāya* – सुकृताय

He does only righteous deeds.

493rd name above may also be referred.

935. *Kṛtakarmavinirvṛtāya* – कृतकर्मविनिर्वृताय

He has finished with actions and work. He has no further action or works to do.

The above 6 names were taken from the 131st shloka of the *Sahasranāma* Stotram.

936. *Bhedatrayaharāya* – भेदत्रयहराय

He removes the three distinctions. He enables his devotees to realise that there is no distinction between body, mind and senses.

636th name above may also be referred.

937. *Dehatrayavinirgatāya* – देहत्रयविनिर्गताय

He has gone beyond the three bodies.

The body being is composed of three – emanating from Brahmam by *avidya* (ignorance or nescience). They are often equated with the five koshas (sheaths), which cover the *atman*.

- *Kāraṇa Śarīra* – causal body
- *Sūkṣma Śarīra* – subtle body
- *Sthūla Śarīra* – gross body

938. *Sarvakāmapradāya* – सर्वकामप्रदाय

He is the bestower of all the desired objects of his devotees.

813th and 822nd names above may also be referred.

939. *Sarvakāmanivartakāya* – कामनिवर्तकाय

He removes all the desires of his devotees.

820th name above may also be referred.

The above 4 names were taken from the 132nd shloka of the *Sahasranāma* Stotram.

940. *Siddheśvarāya* – सिद्धेश्वराय

He is the Lord of realised souls.

941. *Ajarāya* – अजराय

He is beyond old age – never become old.

He is exempt from the states of life – childhood, boyhood, youth etc.; because he is eternal.

In *Lalitā Sahasranāmam* – 470th name – *Vayosvasthā Vivarjitā* – She is devoid of old age and other changes.

942. *Pañcabāṇadarpahutāśanāya* – पञ्चबाणदर्पहुताशनाय

He has the sacrificial fire for the pride of the five-arrowed God of Love – Cupid (Manmadan).

Cupid has a sugarcane bow and an arrow made of five flowers viz., Lotus, Red Lotus, Red Lily, Red Jasmine and Mango flower.

943. *Caturākṣarabījātmane* – चतुराक्षरबीजात्मने

He is the essence of the four-syllabled Seed Mantra.

Oṃ Drām Hrīm Krom – is the powerful four lettered *Beeja* (seed) mantra of Lord Dattatreya. This has to be got initiated through an appropriate guru.

944. *Svabhuve* – स्वभुवे

He is self-born. The *Brahmam* has no origin.

336th and 748th names above may also be referred here.

945. *Citkīrti Bhūṣaṇāya* – चित्कीर्ति भूषणाय

He shines wearing the jewel of the glory of consciousness

The above 6 names were taken from the 133rd shloka of the *Sahasranāma* Stotram.

946. *Agādhabuddhaye* – अगाधबुद्धये

He possesses unfathomable Intellect.

947. *Akṣubdhāya* – अक्षुब्धाय

He is unperturbed.

948. *Candrasūryāgnilocanāya* – चन्द्रसूर्याग्निलोचनाय

His three eyes are the Moon, the Sun and Agni (Fire god).

Lord Shiva is also called as *Triambaka* – three eyed.

In *Lalitā Sahasranāmam* – 453rd name – *Trinayanā* and 762nd name – *Triambikā* – She is endowed with three eyes. Bhaskararaya comments that the Moon, Sun and the fire god are the three eyes of *Śrī Devī*.

949. *Yamadaṃṣṭrāya* – यमदंष्ट्राय

He is the jaws of death.

950. *Atisaṃhartre* – अतिसंहर्त्रे

He is the extreme destroyer – during final deluge he destroys everything and recreates.

951. *Paramānanda Sāgarāya* – परमानन्द सागराय

He is the Ocean of Beatitude or bliss. He is the complete contended form. Hence *Paramānanda*. Nothing greater or bigger than this.

In *Lalitā Sahasranāmam* – 252nd name – *Paramānandā* – and 879th name – *Sudhāsrutiḥ* – She is the Supreme Bliss. She is like a stream of nectar or flow of bliss.

The above 6 names were taken from the 134th shloka of the *Sahasranāma* Stotram.

952. *Līlā Viśvambharāya* – लीला विश्वम्भराय

He sustains the unfolding drama of the world.

In *Lalitā Sahasranāmam* – the very name Lalita is Playful (*Līlā*) – Lalanāt *Lalita* – She is in the form of *Leela*. She is predominantly pleasure oriented.

953. *Bhānave* – भानवे

He shines like the Sun.

It is also described that *Bhānumaṇḍala* is the *Anāhata chakra* in the chest. He is in the form of *Kunḍalinee* there.

In *Viṣṇu* sahasranamam – 284th name – *Bhānuḥ* – He shines.

In *Sūrya Sahasranāmam* – 254th name – *Bhānumate* – His splendid rays are so beautifully luminous.

954. *Bhairavāya* – भैरवाय

He is a formidable lord. Since *Bhairavā* does the three functions, he is in terrific form.

In *Gāyatri Sahasranāmam* – 741st name – *Bhairavāyai* – She is the consort of *Bhairava*.

In *Lalitā Sahasranāmam* – 276th name – *Bhairavī* – The consort of *Bhairava*.

955. *Bhīmalocanāya* – भीमलोचनाय

He has dreadful eyes.

He takes terrible forms to annihilate the demons.

In *Vişņu Sahasranāmam* – 948th and 949th names – *Bhīma* and *Bhīma Parākrama* – he is dreadful.

In *Śiva Sahasranāmam* – 4th name – *Bhīma* – conveying the same meaning.

In *Gāyatri Sahasranāmam* – 734th name – *Bhīşņavatī* – She is in a dreadful form.

956. *Brahmacarmāmbarāya* – ब्रह्मचर्माम्बराय

He wears the garb of an ascetic. And since, he is an *avadootha* ascetic, he is without any clothes.

957. *Kālāya* – कालाय

He is the destructive power of time and death.

Lord *Parameshwara*, when he swallowed the venom, it stayed in his neck and hence his throat is coloured in black. Hence, he is called *Nīlakaŋţar* or *Kālakaŋţar*.

Vāyu purāŋa says, "In the presence of a multitude of *Devas*, *Pishāchas*, serpents and demons, the virulent poison became transfixed in the throat; hence I am called *Kālakaŋţar*".

Kāla – a soft low sound, *kanta* – throat, i.e. a soft low sound proceeds from her throat.

In *Lalitā Sahasranāmam* – 464th name – *Kāla Kaŋţhī* – The consort of *Kāla Kanḍar*.

958. *Acalāya* – अचलाय

He is steady and constant without moving. He is static as he has no deuteriation in his nature, power, wisdom or any other attributes.

In *Viṣŋu Sahasranāmam* – 745th name – *Acalaḥ* – He is static.

158th name above may also be referred.

959. *Calanāntakāya* – चलनान्तकाय

He is the destroyer of restlessness (always keep on moving). This confirms the previous name. He avoids continuous moving and hence, *Acalaḥ*.

The above 8 names were taken from the 135th shloka of the *Sahasranāma* Stotram.

960. *Ādidevāya* – आदिदेवाय

He is primordial divine lord.

15th name above may also be referred.

961. *Jagadyonaye* – जगद्योनये

He is the origin of the world. From him only the whole world originated.

962. *Vāsavāri Vimardanāya* – वासवारि विमर्दनाय

He destroys the foes of Indra (Devas). He takes various incarnations to kill different demons.

963. *Vikarmakarmakarmajñāya* – विकर्मकर्मकर्मज्ञाय

He discriminates between unlawful action, good action and inaction and bestows results accordingly.

964. *Ananya Gamakāya* – अनन्य गमकाय

He gives understanding that there is no 'other' – no two – *Advaita*.

965. *Agamāya* – अगमाय

He is Unapproachable. He is Agama Shastra personified.

The above 6 names were taken from the 136th shloka of the *Sahasranāma* Stotram.

966. *Abaddhakarmaśūnyāya* – अबद्धकर्मशून्याय

He is free from nonsensical actions.

967. *Kāmarāga Kulakṣayāya* – कामराग कुलक्षयाय

He destroys the mass of desires and passions.

968. *Yogāndhakāramathanāya* – योगान्धकारमथनाय

He dispels the darkness of attachments.

Usually, the ignorance is called as darkness. But here it is mentioned that the attachment is due to ignorance. He clears this darkness.

The creation, from the *Brahmam* the first manifestation is darkness (*tamas*).

The *Íshāvāsya* Upanishat (9th verse) says, they who worship ignorance enter blind darkness;

Andham Tamaḥ Pravishanti Y'vidyā Mupāsate.

In *Lalitā Sahasranāmam* – 361st name – *Tamopahā* – She is the remover of darkness.

969. *Padmajanmādivanditāya* – पद्मजन्मादिवन्दिताय

He is worshipped by Lord Brahmā and others.

The above 4 names were taken from the 137th shloka of the *Sahasranāma* Stotram.

970. *Bhaktakāmāya* – भक्तकामाय

He is very much beloved by his devotees. He loves his devotees.

971. *Agrajāya* – अग्रजाय

He is the first-born. Then he only created the entire universe.

Taitireeya Upanishat (III–10–6) says – I am the first born of truth or I am the first born out of truth; *Ahamasmi Prathama Jā Rutasya*.

He is the first movement of consciousness towards creation, as *Iccha Shakti*, also known as *Avyakta*.

In *Lalitā Sahasranāmam* – 975th name – *Pūrvajā* – She is the first born.

972. *Cakriṇe* – चक्रिणे

The Ruler of the Chakras.

In a human body itself we have seven cakras thought to be an energy point or node in the subtle body viz., *Mūlādhārā, Swādhişţānā, Maṇipūraka, Anāhatā, Viśuddha, Agjnā* and *Sahasrārā*. He resides in all these chakras.

In the 510th name above the chakras, also called as *yantras*, were discussed at length.

801st name above may also be referred.

973. *Bhāvanirbhāvakāya* – भावनिर्भावकाय

He only is responsible for existence and non-existence of the entire universe.

974. *Bhedāṅkāya* – भेदाङ्काय

He ends duality and division and stabilises Advaita philosophy.

975. *Mahate* – महते

He is very great.

He is the biggest – i.e. bigger than very big. *Mahā Nārāyaŋa Upanishat* (I–1) says; *Mahato Mahīyān*.

The meaning of this name according to *Yāskar's Nirukta* is – one that is to be worshipped; *Mahanīyo Bhavati*.

In *Lalitā Sahasranāmam* – 774th name – *Mahatī* – She is very big/ great.

976. *Agragāya* – अग्रगाय

He is eldest and foremost.

Since he is the root cause for the entire universe, he has to be treated as first.

He is enjoyed supremely by his devotees.

Taitreeya Samhita (4.1.8) says, first Hiranyagarbha only came into existence.

In *Vişņu Sahasranāmam* – 891st name – *Agrājaḥ* – he is the first born.

In *Lalitā Sahasranāmam* – 553rd name – *Agragaņyā* – She is to be reckoned as first.

977. *Niguhāya* – निगुहाय

He is the hidden principle.

Guha means cave or secret. He dwells in the subtle hidden cave in the heart of every soul.

The word *Guhyā* can be considered to mean *Jeevātma* (soul), *Paramātmā* (supreme) and the union of both. The presiding deity who can bestow these results is called *Guhya.*

In *Vişņu Sahasranāmam* – 542nd name – *Guhyaḥ* – one who can be understood by the secret *Upanishads* or one who dwells in the secret cavity viz., heart.

In *Lalitā Sahasranāmam* – 624th name – *Guhyā* – She is most secretive both in form and meanings.

978. *Gocarāntakāya* – गोचरान्तकाय

He is the destroyer of sensual objects.

The above 9 names were taken from the 138th shloka of the *Sahasranāma* Stotram.

979. *Kālāgniśamanāya* – कालाग्निशमनाय

He allays the destructive fire of time.

The *Kālāgni* Rudra Upanishat, is one of the minor Upanishats, attached to the Krishna Yajurveda. It is one of 14 Shaiva Upanishads. It is a discourse by Kalagni Rudra (Shiva) to sage Sanatkumara on the Tripundra, the three horizontal lines of sacred ash on the forehead.

980. *Śaṅkha Cakra Padma Gadā Dharāya* – शङ्ख चक्र पद्म गदा धराय

He holds conch, chakram (discus), lotus and maze in his four hands.

Usually, Lord Vishnu is depicted to have all these four in his four hands. Here Lord Dattatreya in the form Lord Vishnu, holds all these.

981. *Dīptāya* – दीप्ताय

He gives light to the entire world like a great deepam.

The *Taijasa* form, assumed by him at his own will is radiant.

In *Viṣṇu Sahasranāmam* – 719th name – *Dīptamūrtiḥ* – he possesses the brightness of a thousand Suns.

In *Sūrya Sahasranāmam* – 261st name – *Dīptadīdhitaye* and 440th name – *Dīpāya* – he shines like a very big huge lamp.

982. *Dīnapataye* – दीनपतये

He is the protector of poor.

In *Śiva Sahasranāmam* – 73rd name – *Dīnasādhakaḥ* – he helps the poor by satisfying their needs.

983. *Śāstre* – शास्त्रे

He is great scholar.

984. *Svacchandāya* – स्वच्छन्दाय

He is self-willed. Noone needs to or can command him.

985. *Muktidāyakāya* – मुक्तिदायकाय

He is the bestower of liberation.

In *Lalitā Sahasranāmam* – 201st name – *Sadgati Pradā* – She leads along the path of liberation.

The above 7 names were taken from the 139th shloka of the *Sahasranāma* Stotram.

986. *Vyomadharmāmbarāya* – व्योमधर्माम्बराय

He is clothed in the sky and in righteousness.

Being an avadhoota sanyasi, he does not wear any cloths and hence, sky clothed.

987. *Bhettre* – भेत्त्रे

He is the destroyer.

He destroys;

- the enemies of his devotees.
- the sins of his devotees
- the time and death
- the entire universe during dissolution for further creation.

988. *Bhasmadhāriṇe* – भस्मधारिणे

He wears sacred ash (*vibhooti*).

In *Śiva Sahasranāmam* – 537th name – *Bhasmāśayaḥ* – He who rests on the ashes called *Vibhooti*.

989. *Dharādharāya* – धराधराय

He is the upholder of the Earth.

In the form of Lord Vishnu, in the *Varāha* incarnation he lifted the Earth in his horns.

As Adiseshan snake, he supports the Earth.

In *Vişŋu Sahasranāmam* – 756th name – *Dharādharaḥ* – he is the supporter of Earth.

990. *Dharmaguptāya* – धर्मगुप्ताय

He is the protector of virtues/ righteousness.

Righteousness can be defined as the mode of life laid down in each country, according to the respective time, by the tradition of the wise and not contrary to the *Vedas*.

The *Mahā Nārāyaŋa Upanishat* (XXII–1) says – Everything is established in *dharma* or by whom *dharma* is supported, i.e., *dharma* becomes the support of all things by him;

Dharme Sarvam Pratishtitam.

The *Samvarta Smruti* also says, in each country that rule of conduct, which is handed over by tradition and is not contrary to the *Vedas* is distinguished as righteousness.

He makes the righteousness to be the support for everything.

In *Vişŋu Sahasranāmam* – 404th name – *Dharma Viduttamaḥ* – He is the best of the knowers of Dharma.

In *Lalitā Sahasranāmam* – 884th name – *Dharmādhārā* – She is the supporter of *Dharma* (righteousness).

991. *Anvayātmane* – अन्वयात्मने

He is the essence of non-difference.

In Vedanta philosophy this plays a vital role in explaining the indicatory mark in respect of the unity of the individual self with the Infinite or Brahmam.

Difference and non-difference explore the nuanced relationship between mutually exclusive states, emphasizing that while they may coexist in reality, asserting one inherently negates the other, revealing the complexity of perception and understanding.

992. *Vyatirekārtha Nirṇayāya* – व्यतिरेकार्थनिर्णयाय

He comes to conclusions by means of differences.

Deduction and inference are both methods of reasoning that involve drawing conclusions based on available information. However, deduction typically involves drawing specific conclusions from general principles or premises, while inference involves drawing more general conclusions based on specific evidence or observations. Deduction is often seen as a more formal and structured process, while inference is more flexible and open to interpretation. Both deduction and inference are important tools in logic and critical thinking, helping us to make sense of the world around us and draw logical conclusions from the information available to us.

The above 7 names were taken from the 140th shloka of the *Sahasranāma* Stotram.

993. *Ekoneka Guṇabhāsā Bhāsa Nirbhāsavarjitāya* –
एकोनेक गुणभासा भास निर्भासवर्जिताय

He is the one free of the many intentions, false appearances *a*nd mental impressions of the three moods.

The three moods are indicative, imperative and subjective. He is free from all these.

994. *Bhāvābhāva Svabhāvātmane* – भावाभाव स्वभावात्मने

He enables the devotees to realise that the Soul as existence, non-existence and the innate characters.

995. *Bhāvābhāva Vibhāvavide* – भावाभाव विभावविदे

He is the knower of feelings, non-feeling and the causes of emotions of all.

996. *Yogīhṛdayaviśrāmāya* – योगीहृदयविश्रामाय

He is the tranquility in the hearts of sages/ Yogis.

The above 4 names were taken from the 141st shloka of the *Sahasranāma* Stotram.

997. *Anantavidyāvivardhanāya* – अनन्तविद्याविवर्धनाय

He promotes/ propagates the knowledge of the Eternal

998. *Vighnāntakāya* – विघ्नान्तकाय

He destroys the obstacles of his devotees in their holy path.

He has the ability of removing all the obstacles in the *Upasana* of his devotees.

It is a practice to worship *Ganapati* in all activities at the beginning to get rid of all obstrucles. He is in the form of *Ganapati*, who destroys all the obstacles.

In *Lalitā Sahasranāmam* – 451st name – *Vighnanāshinī* – She removes all obstacles.

999. *Trikālajñāya* – त्रिकालज्ञाय

He only knows the past, present and future.

Because his greatness consists in his having an absolute existence unassociated with any idea of time.

The *Vayu Purana* says – As he recollects all actions, past, present and future, he is called *Smruti*.

In *Viṣṇu Sahasranāmam* – 4th name – *Bhūta Bhavya Bhavat Prabhuḥ* and 290th name – *Bhūta Bhavya Bhavannātha* – He is the lord of past, present and future.

In *Gāyatri Sahasranāmam* – 433rd name – *Trikālajñānadāyinyai* – She bestows the knowledge of all the three periods – past, present and future.

In *Śiva Sahasranāmam* – 265th name – *Trikāladṛtaḥ* – He wears/ lives in all the three times.

1000. *Tattvātmajñānasāgarāya* – तत्त्वात्मज्ञानसागराय

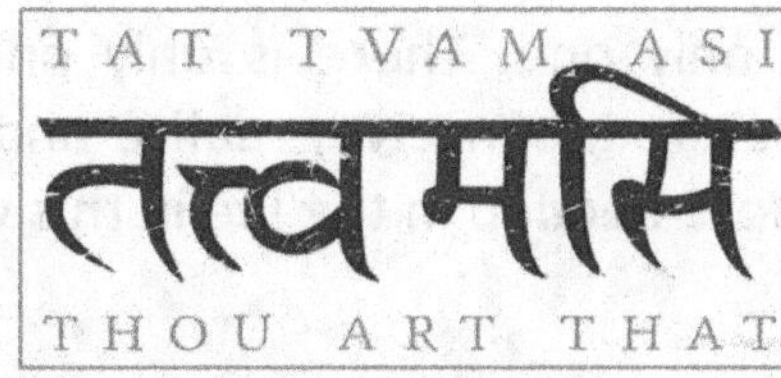

He is the ocean of knowledge of the oneness of the Soul with the Supreme Spirit.

The great sentence (*mahā vākya*) *'Tatvamasi'* from *Sāma Veda, Chandogya Upanishat* (6.8.7), is a typical Advaita philosophy in a single phrase, translated as "I am that" or "Thou Art That".

These 1,000 names are ended with an apt name connecting the Lord Dattatreya and Advaita philosophy.

The above 4 names were taken from the 142nd shloka of the *Sahasranāma* Stotram.

Thus ends 100 divine names on Lord *Dattātreya* from 901 to 1,000.

Iti Śrīmad Dattātreya Sahasranāmāvalī Sampūrṇam ||

इति श्रीमद् दत्तात्रेय सहस्रनामावली सम्पूर्णम् ॥

The above 1,000 names were taken from 142 verses of *Sahasranāma* Stotram available in Brahmanda Puranam as a dialogue between Sanatkumara and Brahmarishi.

An analysis of these 1,000 names reveals the below. There are;

- 41 names appearing 2 times and
- 7 names appearing 3 times

From the comparisons and explanations given above, it is obvious that most of the names are same or conveying the same message with that *Lalitā, Gāyatri, Viṣṇu* and *Śiva Sahasranāmams, Lalitā, Rudra Trishatis* and other Vedic statements. This clearly evidences that all the Gods are one and the same and that is *Niroopa/ Nirguna Brahmam* – without any form or without any attributes. On account of our ignorance, we create various forms of Gods/ Goddesses and try to distinguish/ differentiate among them. Once we get matured, we will realise the single Brahmam, who is without any form neither any qualities.

This has been stressed in multiple names in this Stotra as *'Ekam'*, that is only one. There is only one God or Brahmam. Let us all get matured, conceive, realise and understand this reality and get all those needed in the life in this world and in the upper world.

*****

Śrī Dattatreya Sahasranāma Stotram

Stotram

Nikhilāgamatattvajña Brahmajñānaparāyaṇa |
Vadāsmākaṃ Muktyupāyaṃ Sūta Sarvopakārakam || 1

Sarvadeveṣu Ko Devaḥ Sadyo Mokṣaprado Bhavet |
Ko Manurvā Bhavettasya Sadyaḥ Prītikaro Dhruvam || 2

Sūta Uvāca –

Nigamāgamatattvajño Hyavadhūtaścidambaraḥ |
Bhaktavātsalyapravaṇo Datta Eva Hi Kevalaḥ || 3

Sadā Prasannavadano Bhaktacintaikatatparaḥ |
Tasya Nāmānyanantāni Vartante'thāpyadaḥ Param || 4

Dattasya Nāmasāhasraṃ Tasya Prītivivardhanam |
Yastvidaṃ Paṭhate Nityaṃ Dattātreyaikamānasaḥ || 5

Mucyate Sarvapāpebhyaḥ Sa Sasdyo Nātra Saṃśayaḥ |
Ante Taddhāma Saṃyāti Punarāvṛttidurlabham || 6

Nyāsam

Asya Śrīmad Dattātreya Sahasranāma Stotra Mantrasya
Avadhūta Ṛṣiḥ | Anuṣṭupchandaḥ | Digambaro Devatā |
Oṃ Bījam | Hrīṃ Śaktiḥ | Krauṃ Kīlakam |
Śrī Dattātreya Prītyarthe Jape Viniyogaḥ ||

Dhyānam

Digambaraṃ Bhasmavilepitāṅgaṃ Bodhātmakaṃ Muktikaraṃ Prasannam |
Nirmānasaṃ Śyāmatanuṃ Bhaje'haṃ Dattātreyaṃ Brahma Samādhiyuktam ||

Sahasra Nāma Stotram |

Dattātreyo Mahoyogī Yogeśaścāmaraprabhum |
Munirdigambaro Bālo Māyāmukto Madāpahaḥ || 1

Avadhūto Mahānāthaḥ Śaṅkaro'maravallabhaḥ |
Mahādevaścādidevaḥ Purāṇaprabhurīśvaraḥ || 2

Sattvakṛtsattvabhṛdbhāvaḥ Sattvātmā Sattvasāgaraḥ |
Sattvavitsattvasākṣī Ca Sattvasādhyo'marādhipaḥ || 3

Bhūtakṛdbhūtabhṛccaiva Bhūtātmā Bhūtasambhavaḥ |
Bhūtabhāvo Bhavo Bhūtavittathā Bhūtakāraṇaḥ || 4

Bhūtasākṣī Prabhūtiśca Bhūtānāṃ Paramā Gatiḥ |
Bhūtasaṅgavihīnātmā Bhūtātmā Bhūtaśaṅkaraḥ || 5

Bhūtanātho Mahānāthaścādinātho Maheśvaraḥ |
Sarvabhūtanivāsātmā Bhūtasantāpanāśanaḥ || 6

Sarvātmā Sarvabhṛtsarvaḥ Sarvajñaḥ Sarvanirṇayaḥ |
Sarvasākṣī Bṛhadbhānuḥ Sarvavitsarvamaṅgalaḥ || 7
Śāntaḥ Satyaḥ Samaḥ Pūrṇo Hyekākī Kamalāpatiḥ |
Rāmo Rāmapriyaścaiva Virāmo Rāmakāraṇam || 8

Śuddhātmā Pāvano'nantaḥ Pratītaḥ Paramārthabhṛt |
Haṃsasākṣī Vibhuścaiva Prabhuḥ Pralaya Ityapi || 9

Siddhātmā Paramātmā Ca Siddhānāṃ Paramā Gatiḥ |
Siddhisiddhastathā Sādhyaḥ Sādhano Hyuttamastathā || 10

Sulakṣaṇaḥ Sumedhāvī Vidyāvānvigatāntaraḥ |
Vijvaraśca Mahābāhurbahulānandavardhanaḥ || 11

Avyaktapuruṣaḥ Prājñaḥ Parajñaḥ Paramārthadṛk |
Parāparavinirmukto Yuktastattvaprakāśavān || 12

Dayāvānbhagavānbhāvī Bhāvātmā Bhāvakāraṇaḥ |
Bhavasantāpanāśaśca Puṣpavānpaṇḍito Budhaḥ || 13

Pratyakṣavasturviśvātmā Pratyagbrahma Sanātanaḥ |
Pramāṇavigataścaiva Pratyāhāraniyojakaḥ || 14

Praṇavaḥ Praṇavātītaḥ Pramukhaḥ Pralayātmakaḥ |
Mṛtyuñjayo Viviktātmā Śaṅkarātmā Paro Vapuḥ || 15

Paramastaṇuvijñeyaḥ Paramātmani Saṃsthitaḥ |
Prabodhakalanādhāraḥ Prabhāvapravarottamaḥ || 16

Cidambaraścidvilāsaścidākāśaściduttamaḥ |
Cittacaitanyacittātmā Devānāṃ Paramā Gatiḥ || 17

Acetyaścetanādhāraścetanācittavikramaḥ |
Cittātmā Cetanārūpo Lasatpaṅkajalocanaḥ || 18

Parabrahma Paraṃ Jyotiḥ Paraṃ Dhāma Parantapaḥ |
Paraṃ Sūtraṃ Paraṃ Tantraṃ Pavitraṃ Paramohavān || 19

Kṣetrajñaḥ Kṣetragaḥ Kṣetraḥ Kṣetrādhāraḥ Purañjanaḥ |
Kṣetraśūnyo Lokasākṣī Kṣetravānbahunāyakaḥ || 20

Yogendo Yogapūjyaśca Yoga Ātmavidāṃ Śuciḥ |
Yogamāyādharaḥ Sthāṇuracalaḥ Kamalāpatiḥ || 21

Yogeśo Yoganirmātā Yogajñānaprakāśanaḥ |
Yogapālo Lokapālaḥ Saṃsāratamanāśanaḥ || 22

Guhyo Guhyatamo Gupto Mukto Yuktaḥ Sanātanaḥ |
Gahano Gaganākāro Gambhīro Gaṇanāyakaḥ || 23

Govindo Gopatirgoptā Gobhāgo Bhāvasaṃsthitaḥ |
Gosākṣī Gotamāriśca Gāndhāro Gaganākṛtiḥ || 24

Yogayukto Bhogayuktaḥ Śaṅkāmuktasamādhimān |
Sahajaḥ Sakaleśānaḥ Kārtavīryavarapradaḥ || 25

Sarajā Virajāḥ Puṃso Pāvanaḥ Pāpanāśanaḥ | Pumān
Parāvaravinirmuktaḥ Parañjyotiḥ Purātanaḥ || 26

Nānājyotiranekātmā Svayañjyotiḥ Sadāśivaḥ |
Divyajyotirmayaścaiva Satyavijñānabhāskaraḥ || 27

Nityaśuddhaḥ Paraḥ Pūrṇaḥ Prakāśaḥ Prakaṭodbhavaḥ |
Pramādavigataścaiva Pareśaḥ Paravikramaḥ || 28

Yogī Yogo Yogapaśca Yogābhyāsaprakāśanaḥ |

Yoktā Moktā Vidhātā Ca Trātā Pātā Nirāyudhyaḥ || 29

Nityamukto Nityayuktaḥ Satyaḥ Satyaparākramaḥ |
Sattvaśuddhikaraḥ Sattvastathā Sattvambhṛtāṃ Gatiḥ || 30

Śrīdharaḥ Śrīvapuḥ Śrīmān Śrīnivāso'marārcitaḥ |
Śrīnidhiḥ Śrīpatiḥ Śreṣṭhaḥ Śreyaskaścaramāśrayaḥ || 31

Tyāgī Tyāgārthasampannastyāgātmā Tyāgavigrahaḥ |
Tyāgalakṣaṇasiddhātmā Tyāgajñastyāgakāraṇaḥ || 32

Bhogo Bhoktā Tathā Bhogyo Bhogasādhanakāraṇaḥ |
Bhogī Bhogārthasampanno Bhogajñānaprakāśanaḥ || 33

Kevalaḥ Keśavaḥ Kṛṣṇaḥ Kaṃvāsāḥ Kamalālayaḥ |
Kamalāsanapūjyaśca Harirajñānakhaṇḍanaḥ || 34

Mahātmā Mahadādiśca Maheśottamavanditaḥ |
Manobuddhivihīnātmā Mānātmā Mānavādhipaḥ || 35

Bhuvaneśo Vibhūtiśca Dhṛtirmedhā Smṛtirdayā |
Duḥkhadāvānalo Buddhaḥ Prabuddhaḥ Parameśvaraḥ || 36

Kāmahā Krodhahā Caiva Dambhadarpamadāpahaḥ |
Ajñānapatimirāriśca Bhavārirbhuvaneśvaraḥ || 37

Rūpakudrūpabhṛdrūpī Rūpātmā Rūpakāraṇaḥ |
Rūpajño Rūpasākṣī Ca Nāmarūpo Guṇāntakaḥ || 38

Aprameyaḥ Prameyaśca Pramāṇaṃ Praṇavāśrayaḥ |
Pramāṇarahito'cintyaścetanāvigato'jaraḥ || 39

Akṣaro'kṣaramuktaśca Vijvaro Jvaranāśanaḥ |
Viśiṣṭo Vittaśāstrī Ca Dṛṣṭo Dṛṣṭāntavarjitaḥ || 40

Guṇeśo Guṇakāyaśca Guṇātmā Gaṇabhāvanaḥ |
Anantaguṇasampanno Guṇagarbho Guṇādhipaḥ || 41

Gaṇeśo Guṇanāthaśca Guṇātmā Gaṇabhāvanaḥ |
Gaṇabandhurvivekātmā Guṇayuktaḥ Parākramī || 42

Atarkyaḥ Kraturagniśca Kṛtajñaḥ Saphalāśrayaḥ |
Yajñaśca Yajñaphaldo Yajña Ijyo'marottamaḥ || 43

Hiraṇyagarbhaḥ Śrīgarbhaḥ Khagarbhaḥ Kuṇapeśvaraḥ |
Māyāgarbho Lokagarbhaḥ Svayambhūrbhuvanāntakaḥ || 44

Niṣpāpo Nibiḍo Nandī Bodhī Bodhasamāśrayaḥ |
Bodhātmā Bodhanātmā Ca Bhedavaitaṇḍakhaṇḍanaḥ || 45

Svābhāvyo Bhāvanirmukto Vyakto'vyaktasamāśrayaḥ |
Nityatṛpto Nirābhāso Nirvāṇaḥ Śaraṇaḥ Suhṛt || 46

Guhyeśo Guṇagambhīro Guṇadoṣanivāraṇaḥ |
Guṇasaṅgavihīnaśca Yogārerdarpanāśanaḥ || 47

Ānandaḥ Paramānandaḥ Svānandasukhavardhanaḥ |
Satyānandaścidānandaḥ Sarvānandaparāyaṇaḥ || 48

Sadrūpaḥ Sahajaḥ Satyaḥ Svānandaḥ Sumanoharaḥ |
Sarvaḥ Sarvāntaraścaiva Pūrvātpūrvatarastathā || 49

Khamayaḥ Khaparaḥ Khādiḥ Khambrahma Khatanuḥ Khagaḥ |
Khavāsāḥ Khavihīnaśca Khanidhiḥ Khaparāśrayaḥ || 50

Anantaścādirūpaśca Sūryamaṇḍalamadhyagaḥ |
Amoghaḥ Paramāmoghaḥ Parokṣaḥ Varadaḥ Kaviḥ || 51

Viśvacakṣurviśvasākṣī Viśvabāhurdhaneśvaraḥ |
Dhanañjayo Mahātejāstejiṣṭhastaijasaḥ Sukhī || 52

Jyotirjyotirmayo Jetā Jyotiṣāṃ Jyotirātmakaḥ |
Jyotiṣāmapi Jyotiśca Janako Janamohanaḥ || 53

Jitendriyo Jitakrodho Jitātmā Jitamānasaḥ |
Jitasaṅgo Jitaprāṇo Jitasaṃsāravāsanaḥ || 54

Nirvāsano Nirālambo Niryogakṣemavarjitaḥ |
Nirīho Nirahaṅkāro Nirāśīrnirupādhikaḥ || 55

Nityabodho Viviktātmā Viśuddhottamagauravaḥ |
Vidyārthī Paramārthī Ca Śraddhārthī Sādhanātmakaḥ || 56

Pratyāhārī Nirāhārī Sarvāhāraparāyaṇaḥ |
Nityaśuddho Nirākāṅkṣī Pārāyaṇaparāyaṇaḥ || 57

Aṇoraṇutaraḥ Sūkṣmaḥ Sthūlaḥ Sthūlatarastathā |
Ekastathā'nekarūpo Viśvarūpaḥ Sanātanaḥ || 58

Naikarūpo Virūpātmā Naikabodhamayo'pi Ca |
Naikanāmamayaścaiva Naikavidyāvivardhanaḥ || 59

Ekaścaikāntikaścaiva Nānābhāvavivarjitaḥ |
Ekākṣarastathā Bījaḥ Pūrṇabimbaḥ Sanātanaḥ || 60

Mantravīryo Mantrabījaḥ Śāstravīryo Jagatpatiḥ |
Nānāvīryadharaścaiva Śakreśaḥ Pṛthivīpatiḥ || 61

Prāṇeśaḥ Prāṇadaḥ Prāṇaḥ Prāṇāyāmaparāyaṇaḥ |
Prāṇapañcakanirmuktaḥ Kośapañcakavarjitaḥ || 62

Niścalo Niṣkalo'saṅgo Niṣprapañco Nirāmayaḥ |
Nirādhāro Nirākāro Nirvikāro Nirañjanaḥ || 63

Niṣpratīto Nirābhāso Nirāsakto Nirākulaḥ |
Niṣṭhāsarvagataścaiva Nirārambho Nirāśrayaḥ || 64

Nirantaraḥ Sattvagoptā Śānto Dānto Mahāmuniḥ |
Niḥśabdaḥ Sukṛtaḥ Svasthaḥ Satyavādī Sureśvaraḥ || 65

Jñānado Jñānavijñānī Jñānātmā''nandapūritaḥ |
Jñānayajñavidāṃ Dakṣo Jñānāgnirjvalano Budhaḥ || 66

Dayāvānbhavarogāriścikitsācaramāgatiḥ |
Candramaṇḍalamadhyasthaścandrakoṭisuśītalaḥ || 67

Yantakṛtparamo Yantrī Yantrārūḍhaparājitaḥ |
Yantravidyantravāsaśca Yantrādhāro Dharādharaḥ || 68

Tattvajñastattvabhūtātmā Mahattattvaprakāśanaḥ |
Tattvasaṅkhyānayogajñaḥ Sāṅkhyaśāstrapravartakaḥ || 69

Anantavikramo Devo Mādhavaśca Dhaneśvaraḥ |
Sādhuḥ Sādhuvariṣṭhātmā Sāvadhāno'marottamaḥ || 70
Niḥsaṅkalpo Nirādhāro Durdharo Hyātmavitpatiḥ |
Ārogyasukhadaścaiva Pravaro Vāsavastathā || 71

Pareśaḥ Paramodāraḥ Pratyakcaitanyadurgamaḥ |
Durādharṣo Durāvāso Dūratvaparināśanaḥ || 72

Vedavidvedakṛdvedo Vedātmā Vimalāśayaḥ |
Viviktasevī Ca Saṃsāraśramanāśanastathā || 73

Brahmayonirbṛhadyonirviśvayonirvidehavān |
Viśālākṣo Viśvanātho Hāṭakāṅgadabhūṣaṇaḥ || 74

Abādhyo Jagadārādhyo Jagadārjavapālanaḥ |
Janavāndhanavāndharmī Dharmago Dharmavardhanaḥ || 75

Amṛtaḥ Śāśvataḥ Sādyaḥ Siddhidaḥ Sumanoharaḥ |
Khalubrahmakhalusthāno Munīnāṃ Paramā Gatiḥ || 76

Upadraṣṭā Tathā Śreṣṭhaḥ Śucirbhūto Hyanāmayaḥ |
Vedasiddhāntavedyaśca Mānasāhlādavardhanaḥ || 77

Dehadanyo Guṇādanyo Lokādanyo Vivekavit |
Duṣṭasvapnaharaścaiva Gururguruvarottamaḥ || 78

Karmī Karmavinirmuktaḥ Saṃnyāsī Sādhakeśvaraḥ |
Sarvabhāvavihīnaśca Tṛṣṇāsaṅganivārakaḥ || 79

Tyāgī Tyāgavapustyāgastyāgadānavivarjitaḥ |
Tyāgakāraṇatyāgātmā Sadguruḥ Sukhadāyakaḥ || 80

Dakṣo Dakṣādivandyaśca Jñānavādapravartakaḥ |
Śabdabrahmamayātmā Ca Śabdabrahmaprakāśavān || 81

Grasiṣṇuḥ Prabhaviṣṇuśca Sahiṣṇurvigatāntaraḥ |
Vidvattamo Mahāvandyo Viśālottamavāṅmuniḥ || 82
Brahmavidbrahmabhāvaśca Brahmarṣirbāhmaṇapriyaḥ |
Brahma Brahmaprakāśātmā Brahmavidyāprakāśanaḥ || 83

Atrivaṃśaprabhūtātmā Tāpasottamavanditaḥ |
Ātmavāsī Vidheyātmā Hyatrivaṃśavivardhanaḥ || 84

Pravartano Nivṛttātmā Pralayodakasannibhaḥ |
Nārāyaṇo Mahāgarbho Bhārgavapriyakṛttamaḥ || 85

Saṅkalpaduḥkhadalanaḥ Saṃsāratamanāśanaḥ |
Trivikramastridhākārastrimūrtistriguṇātmakaḥ || 86

Bhedatrayaharaścaiva Tāpatrayanivārakaḥ |
Doṣatrayavibhedī Ca Saṃśayārṇavakhaṇḍanaḥ || 87

Asaṃśayastvasammūḍho Hyavādī Rājananditaḥ |
Rājayogī Mahāyogī Svabhāvagalitastathā || 88

Puṇyaślokaḥ Pavitrāṅghrirdhyānayogaparāyaṇaḥ |
Dhyānastho Dhyānagamyaśca Vidheyātmā Purātanaḥ || 89

Avijñeyo Hyantarātmā Mukhyabimbasanātanaḥ |
Jīvasañjīvano Jīvaścidvilāsaścidāśrayaḥ || 80

Mahendro'maramānyaśca Yogendro Yogavittamaḥ |
Yogadharmastathā Yogastattvastattvaviniścayaḥ || 81

Naikabāhuranantātmā Naikanāmaparākramaḥ |
Naikākṣī Naikapādaśca Nāthanāthottamottamaḥ || 82

Sahasraśīrṣā Puruṣaḥ Sahasrākṣaḥ Sahasrapāt |
Sahasrarūpadṛkcaiva Sahasrāramayoddhavaḥ || 83

Tripādapuruṣaścaiva Tripādūrdhvastathaiva Ca |
Tryambakaśca Mahāvīryo Yogavīryaviśāradaḥ || 84

Vijayī Vinayī Jetā Vītarāgī Virājitaḥ |
Rudro Raudro Mahābhīmaḥ Prājñamukhyaḥ Sadāśuciḥ || 85

Antarjyotiranantātmā Pratyagātmā Nirantaraḥ |
Arūpaścātmarūpaśca Sarvabhāvavinirvṛtaḥ || 86

Antaḥ Śūnyo Bahiḥ Śūnyaḥ Śūnyātmā Śūnyabhāvanaḥ |
Antaḥpūrṇo Bahiḥpūrṇaḥ Pūrṇātmā Pūrṇabhāvanaḥ || 87

Antastyāgī Bahistyāgī Tyāgātmā Sarvayogavān |
Antaryāgī Bahiryāgī Sarvayogaparāyaṇaḥ || 88

Antarbhogī Bahirbhogī Sarvabhogaviduttamaḥ |
Antarniṣṭho Bahirniṣṭhaḥ Sarvaniṣṭhāmayastathā || 89

Bāhyāntaravimuktaśca Bāhyāntaravivarjitaḥ |
Śāntaḥ Śuddho Viśuddhaśca Nirvāṇaḥ Prakṛteḥ Paraḥ || 100

Akālaḥ Kālanemī Ca Kālakālo Janeśvaraḥ |
Kālātmā Kālakartā Ca Kālajñaḥ Kālanāśanaḥ || 101

Kaivalyapadadātā Ca Kaivalyasukhadāyakaḥ |
Kaivalyakalanādhāro Nirbharo Harṣavardhanaḥ || 102

Hṛdayastho Hṛṣīkeśo Govindo Garbhavarjitaḥ |
Sakalāgamapūjyaśca Nigamo Nigamāśrayaḥ || 103

Parāśaktiḥ Parākīrtiḥ Parāvṛttirnidhismṛtiḥ |
Parāvidyā Parākṣāntirvibhaktiryuktasadgatiḥ || 104

Svaprakāśaḥ Prakāśātmā Parasaṃvedanātmakaḥ |
Svasevyaḥ Svavidāṃ Svātmā Svasaṃvedyo'naghaḥ Kṣamī || 105

Svānusandhānaśīlātmā Svānusandhānagocaraḥ |
Svānusandhānaśūnyātmā Svānusandhānāśrayastathā || 106

Svabodhadarpaṇo'bhaṅgaḥ Kandarpakulanāśanaḥ |
Brahmacārī Brahmavettā Brāhmaṇo Brahmavittamaḥ || 107

Tattvabodhaḥ Sudhāvarṣaḥ Pāvanaḥ Pāpapāvakaḥ |
Brahmasūtravidheyātmā Brahmasūtrārdhanirṇayaḥ || 108

Ātyantiko Mahākalpaḥ Saṅkalpāvartanāśanaḥ |
Ādhivyādhiharaścaiva Saṃśayārṇavaśoṣakaḥ || 109

Tattvātmajñānasandeśo Mahānubhavabhāvitaḥ |
Ātmānubhavasampannaḥ Svānubhāvasukhāśrayaḥ || 110

Acintyaśca Bṛhadbhānuḥ Pramadotkarṣanāśanaḥ |
Aniketapraśāntātmā Śūnyavāso Jagadvapuḥ || 111

Cidgatiścinmayaścakrī Māyācakrapravartakaḥ |
Sarvavarṇavidārambhī Sarvārambhaparāyaṇaḥ || 112

Purāṇaḥ Pravaro Dātā Sundaraḥ Kanakāṅgadī |
Anisūyātmajo Dattaḥ Sarvajñaḥ Sarvakāmadaḥ || 113

Kāmajitkāmapālaśca Kāmī Kāmapradāgamaḥ |
Kāmavānkāmapoṣaśca Sarvakāmanivartakaḥ || 114

Sarvakarmaphalotpattiḥ Sarvakāmaphalapradaḥ |
Sarvakarmaphalaiḥ Pūjyaḥ Sarvakarmaphalāśrayaḥ || 115

Viśvakarmā Kṛtātmā Ca Kṛtajñaḥ Sarvasākṣikaḥ |
Sarvārambhaparityāgī Jaḍonmattapiśācavān || 116

Bhikṣurbhikṣākaraścaiva Bhaikṣāhārī Nirāśramī |
Akūlaścānukūlaśca Vikalo Hyakalastathā || 117

Jaṭilo Vanacārī Ca Daṇḍī Muṇḍī Ca Gaṇḍavān |
Dehadharmavihīnātmā Hyekākī Saṅgavarjitaḥ || 118

Āśramyanāśramārambho'nācārī Karmavarjitaḥ |
Asandehī Ca Sandehī Na Kiñcinna Ca Kiñcanaḥ || 119

Nṛdehī Dehaśūnyaśca Nābhāvī Bhāvanirgataḥ |
Nābrahmaca Parabrahma Svayameva Nirākulaḥ || 120

Anaghaścāguruścaiva Nāthanāthottamo Guruḥ |
Dvibhujaḥ Prākṛtaścaiva Janakaśca Pitāmahaḥ || 121

Anātmā Na Ca Nānātmā Nītirnītimatāṃ Varaḥ |
Sahajaḥ Sadṛśaḥ Siddhaścaikaścinmātra Eva Ca || 122

Na Kartāpi Ca Kartā Ca Bhoktā Bhogavivarjitaḥ |
Turīyasturīyātītaḥ Svacchaḥ Sarvamayastathā || 123

Sarvādhiṣṭhānarūpaśca Sarvadhyeyavivarjitaḥ |
Sarvalokanivāsātmā Sakalottamavanditaḥ || 124

Dehabhṛddehakṛccaiva Dehātmā Dehabhāvanaḥ |
Dehī Dehavibhaktaśca Dehabhāvaprakāśanaḥ || 125

Layastho Layaviccaiva Layābhāvaśca Bodhavān |
Layātīto Layasyānto Layabhāvanivāraṇaḥ || 126

Vimukhaḥ Pramukhaścaiva Pratyaṅmukhavadācarī |
Viśvabhugviśvadhṛgviśvo Viśvakṣemakarastatjā || 127

Avikṣipto'pramādī Ca Pararddhiḥ Paramārthadṛk |
Svānubhāvavihīnaśca Svānubhāvaprakāśanaḥ || 128

Nirindriyaśca Nirbuddhirnirābhāso Nirākṛtaḥ |
Nirahaṅkāraścarūpātmā Nirvapuḥ Sakalāśrayaḥ || 129

Śokaduḥkhaharaścaiva Bhogamokṣaphalapradaḥ |
Suprasannastathā Sūkṣmaḥ Śabdabrahmārthasaṅgrahaḥ || 130

Āgamāpāyaśūnyaśca Sthānadaśca Satāṅgatiḥ |
Akṛtaḥ Sukṛtaścaiva Kṛtakarmā Vinirvṛtaḥ || 131

Bhedatrayavaraścaiva Dehatrayavinirgataḥ |
Sarvakāmamayaścaiva Sarvakāmanivartakaḥ || 132

Siddheśvaro'jaraḥ Pañcabāṇadarpahutāśanaḥ |
Caturakṣarabījātmā Svabhūścitkīrtibhūṣaṇaḥ || 133

Agādhabuddhirakṣubdhaścandrasūryāgnilocanaḥ |
Yamadaṃṣṭro'tisaṃhartā Paramānandasāgaraḥ || 134

Līlāviśvambharo Bhānurbhairavo Bhīmalocanaḥ |
Brahmacaryāmbaraḥ Kālastvacalaścalanāntakaḥ || 135

Ādidevo Jagadyonirvāsavārivimardanaḥ |
Vikarmakarmakarmajño'nanyagamako'gamaḥ || 136

Abaddhakarmaśūnyaśca Kāmarāgakulakṣayaḥ |
Yogāndhakāramathanaḥ Padmajanmādivanditaḥ || 137

Bhaktakāmo'grajaścakrī Bhāvanirbhāvabhāvakaḥ |
Bhedāntako Mahānagryo Nigūho Gocarāntakaḥ || 138

Kālāgniśamanaḥ Śaṅkhacakrapadmagadādharaḥ |
Dīpto Dīnapatiḥ Śāstā Svacchando Muktidāyakaḥ || 139

Vyomadharmāmbaro Bhettā Bhasmadhārī Dharādharaḥ |
Dharmagupto'nvayātmā Ca Vyatirekārthanirṇayaḥ || 140

Ekānekaguṇābhāsābhāsanirbhāsavarjitaḥ |
Bhāvābhāvasvabhāvātmā Bhāvābhāvavibhāvavit || 141

Yogihṛdayaviśrāmo'nantavidyāvivardhanaḥ |
Vighnāntakastrikālajñastattvātmā Jñānasāgaraḥ || 142

Phalaśrutiḥ |

Nāmarūpātmakaṃ Caiva Avāṅmānasa Gocaraṃ |
Sarvaṃ Dattātmakaṃ Viśvaṃ Bhāvābhāvodbhavātmakam || 143

Iti Śrī Paramaṃ Divyaṃ Pavitraṃ Pāpanāśanam |
Dattātreyasahasrākhyaṃ Nāmastotraṃ Kṛtaṃ Mayā || 144

Atītānāgataṃ Caiva Vartamānaṃ Tadhaiva Ca |
Tadvidurye Paṭhaṃ Tyetat Guhyādguhyataraṃ Param || 145

Śṛtvedaṃ Paramaṃ Puṇyaṃ Martyo Hyamṛtamaśnute |
Sahasranāmakaṃ Stotraṃ Śraddhayā Parayā Bhuvi || 146

Idaṃ Stotramupāśritya Martyaścātmani Saṃsthitaḥ |
Paraṃsthānamavāpnoti Śaṅkaraṃ Prakṛte Param || 147

Ekaikamakṣaraṃ Puṃsāṃ Maṇimādyaṣṭasiddhidam |
Sarvapāpaharaṃ Caiva Brahmanirvāṇadāyakam || 148

Śivaṃ Pūrṇaṃ Paraṃ Caiva Nityaṃ Śuddhaṃ Nirañjanam |
Nidhānaṃ Paramaṃ Divyaṃ Dattātreyaṃ Jagadgurum || 149

Nirīhaṃ Pratimāśūnyaṃ Satvagaṃ Gaganopamam |
Viśuddhamakṣaraṃ Pūrṇaṃ Dattātreyaṃ Jagadgurum || 150

Avācyaṃ Praṇavātītaṃ Niṣprapañcaṃ Nirākalam |
Satyaṃ Siddhaṃ Mano'gamyaṃ Dattātreyaṃ Jagadgurum || 151

Kāraṇaṃ Kāraṇānāṃ Ca Nāmarūpavivarjitam |
Paramaṃ Paramānandaṃ Dattātreyaṃ Jagadguram || 152

Śāśvataṃ Sahajaṃ Śāntaṃ Pavitraṃ Ca Guṇātigam |
Satyaṃ Sanātanaṃ Sūkṣmaṃ Dattātreyaṃ Jagadguram || 153

Nirākāraṃ Nirābhāsaṃ Niṣkalaṅkaṃ Nirāmayam |
Nirālambaṃ Nijānandaṃ Dattātreyaṃ Jagadguram || 154

Deśakālārthanirmuktaṃ Deśakālasamāśrayam |
Parāparavinirmuktaṃ Dattātreyaṃ Jagadguram || 155

Nigīśvaraṃ Nirvikāraṃ Nirmalajñānarūpiṇam |
Guṇādanyamahaṃ Vande Dattātreyaṃ Jagadguram || 156

Ya Idaṃ Paṭhate Nityaṃ Pāṭhayedvāsamāhita |
Sarvānkāmānavāpnoti Dattātreyo Prasādataḥ || 157

Itīdaṃ Dattasāhasraṃ Sāyaṃ Prātaḥ Paṭhettu Yaḥ |
Sa Ihāmutra Labhate Nirvāṇaṃ Paramaṃ Sukham || 158

Guruvāre Dattabhakto Bhaktibhāvasamanvitaḥ |
Paṭhetsadaiva To Hyetatsa Labheccintitaṃ Dhruvam || 159

Iti Śrī Brahmāṇḍa Purāṇe Anukūlāgame Sanatkumāra
Brahmarṣi Saṃvāde Śrī Dattātreya Sahasranāma Stotraṃ
Saṃpūrṇam ||

श्री दत्तात्रेय सहस्रनाम स्तोत्रम् ॥

निखिलागमतत्त्वज्ञ ब्रह्मज्ञानपरायण । वदास्माकं मुक्त्युपायं सूत सर्वोपकारकम् ॥ १

सर्वदेवेषु को देवः सद्यो मोक्षप्रदो भवेत् ।
को मनुर्वा भवेत्तस्य सद्यः प्रीतिकरो ध्रुवम् ॥ २

सूत उवाच –

निगमागमतत्त्वज्ञो ह्यवधूतश्चिदम्बरः । भक्तवात्सल्यप्रवणो दत्त एव हि केवलः ॥ ३

सदा प्रसन्नवदनो भक्तचिन्तैकतत्परः ।
तस्य नामान्यनन्तानि वर्तन्तेऽथाप्यदः परम् ॥ ४

दत्तस्य नामसाहस्रं तस्य प्रीतिविवर्धनम् । यस्त्विदं पठते नित्यं दत्तात्रेयैकमानसः ॥ ५

मुच्यते सर्वपापेभ्यः स सस्द्यो नात्र संशयः ।
अन्ते तद्धाम संयाति पुनरावृत्तिदुर्लभम् ॥ ६

अस्य श्रीमद्दत्तात्रेयसहस्रनामस्तोत्रमन्त्रस्य अवधूत ऋषिः ।
अनुष्टुप्छन्दः । दिगम्बरो देवता । ॐ बीजम् । ह्रीं शक्तिः ।
क्रौं कीलकम् । श्रीदत्तात्रेयप्रीत्यर्थे जपे विनियोगः ॥

ध्यानम् ।

दिगम्बरं भस्मविलेपिताङ्गं बोधात्मकं मुक्तिकरं पर्सन्नम्।
निर्मानसं श्यामतनुं भजेऽहं दत्तात्रेयं ब्रह्मसमाधियुक्तम् ॥

सहस्रनाम स्तोत्रम् ।

दत्तात्रेयो महोयोगी योगेशश्चामरप्रभुम् । मुनिर्दिगम्बरो बालो मायामुक्तो मदापहः ॥ १

अवधूतो महानाथः शङ्करोऽमरवल्लभः । महादेवश्चादिदेवः पुराणप्रभुरीश्वरः ॥ २

सत्त्वकृत्सत्त्वभृद्भावः सत्त्वात्मा सत्त्वसागरः ।
सत्त्ववित्सत्त्वसाक्षी च सत्त्वसाध्योऽमराधिपः ॥ ३

भूतकृद्भूतभृच्चैव भूतात्मा भूतसम्भवः। भूतभावो भवो भूतवित्तथा भूतकारणः ॥ ४

भूतसाक्षी प्रभूतिश्च भूतानां परमा गतिः।
भूतसङ्गविहीनात्मा भूतात्मा भूतशङ्करः ॥ ५

भूतनाथो महानाथश्चादिनाथो महेश्वरः। सर्वभूतनिवासात्मा भूतसन्तापनाशनः ॥ ६

सर्वात्मा सर्वभृत्सर्वः सर्वज्ञः सर्वनिर्णयः।
सर्वसाक्षी बृहद्भानुः सर्ववित्सर्वमङ्गलः ॥ ७

शान्तः सत्यः समः पूर्णो ह्येकाकी कमलापतिः।
रामो रामप्रियश्चैव विरामो रामकारणम् ॥ ८

शुद्धात्मा पावनोऽनन्तः प्रतीतः परमार्थभृत्।
हंससाक्षी विभुश्चैव प्रभुः प्रलय इत्यपि ॥ ९

सिद्धात्मा परमात्मा च सिद्धानां परमा गतिः।
सिद्धिसिद्धस्तथा साध्यः साधनो ह्युत्तमस्तथा ॥ १०

सुलक्षणः सुमेधावी विद्यावान्विगतान्तरः।
विज्वरश्च महाबाहुर्बहुलानन्दवर्धनः ॥ ११

अव्यक्तपुरुषः प्राज्ञः परज्ञः परमार्थदृक्।
परापरविनिर्मुक्तो युक्तस्तत्त्वप्रकाशवान् ॥ १२

दयावान्भगवान्भावी भावात्मा भावकारणः।
भवसन्तापनाशश्च पुष्पवान्पण्डितो बुधः ॥ १३

प्रत्यक्षवस्तुर्विश्वात्मा प्रत्यग्ब्रह्म सनातनः।
प्रमाणविगतश्चैव प्रत्याहारनियोजकः ॥ १४

प्रणवः प्रणवातीतः प्रमुखः प्रलयात्मकः।
मृत्युञ्जयो विविक्तात्मा शङ्करात्मा परो वपुः ॥ १५

परमस्तनुविज्ञेयः परमात्मनि संस्थितः। प्रबोधकलनाधारः प्रभावप्रवरोत्तमः ॥ १६

चिदम्बरश्चिद्विलासश्चिदाकाशश्चिदुत्तमः।
चित्तचैतन्यचित्तात्मा देवानां परमा गतिः ॥ १७

अचेत्यश्चेतनाधारश्चेतनाचित्तविक्रमः ।
चित्तात्मा चेतनारूपो लसत्पङ्कजलोचनः ॥ १८

परब्रह्म परं ज्योतिः परं धाम परन्तपः । परं सूत्रं परं तन्त्रं पवित्रं परमोहवान् ॥ १९

क्षेत्रज्ञः क्षेत्रगः क्षेत्रः क्षेत्राधारः पुरञ्जनः ।
क्षेत्रशून्यो लोकसाक्षी क्षेत्रवान्बहुनायकः ॥ २०

योगेन्दो योगपूज्यश्च योग आत्मविदां शुचिः ।
योगमायाधरः स्थाणुरचलः कमलापतिः ॥ २१

योगेशो योगनिर्माता योगज्ञानप्रकाशनः ।
योगपालो लोकपालः संसारतमनाशनः ॥ २२

गुह्यो गुह्यतमो गुप्तो मुक्तो युक्तः सनातनः।
गहनो गगनाकारो गम्भीरो गणनायकः ॥ २३

गोविन्दो गोपतिर्गोप्ता गोभागो भावसंस्थितः ।
गोसाक्षी गोतमारिश्च गान्धारो गगनाकृतिः ॥ २४

योगयुक्तो भोगयुक्तः शङ्कामुक्तसमाधिमान्।
सहजः सकलेशानः कार्तवीर्यवरप्रदः ॥ २५

सरजा विरजाः पुंसो पावनः पापनाशनः ।
पुमान् परावरविनिर्मुक्तः परञ्ज्योतिः पुरातनः ॥ २६

नानाज्योतिरनेकात्मा स्वयञ्ज्योतिः सदाशिवः ।
दिव्यज्योतिर्मयश्चैव सत्यविज्ञानभास्करः ॥ २७

नित्यशुद्धः परः पूर्णः प्रकाशः प्रकटोद्भवः । प्रमादविगतश्चैव परेशः परविक्रमः ॥ २८

योगी योगो योगपश्च योगाभ्यासप्रकाशनः ।
योक्ता मोक्ता विधाता च त्राता पाता निरायुध्यः ॥ २९

नित्यमुक्तो नित्ययुक्तः सत्यः सत्यपराक्रमः ।
सत्त्वशुद्धिकरः सत्त्वस्तथा सत्त्वम्भृतां गतिः ॥ ३०

श्रीधरः श्रीवपुः श्रीमान् श्रीनिवासोऽमरार्चितः।
श्रीनिधिः श्रीपतिः श्रेष्ठः श्रेयस्कश्चरमाश्रयः॥ ३१

त्यागी त्यागार्थसम्पन्नस्त्यागात्मा त्यागविग्रहः।
त्यागलक्षणसिद्धात्मा त्यागज्ञस्त्यागकारणः॥ ३२

भोगो भोक्ता तथा भोग्यो भोगसाधनकारणः।
भोगी भोगार्थसम्पन्नो भोगज्ञानप्रकाशनः॥ ३३

केवलः केशवः कृष्णः कंवासाः कमलालयः।
कमलासनपूज्यश्च हरिरज्ञानखण्डनः॥ ३४

महात्मा महदादिश्च महेशोत्तमवन्दितः।
मनोबुद्धिविहीनात्मा मानात्मा मानवाधिपः॥ ३५

भुवनेशो विभूतिश्च धृतिर्मेधा स्मृतिर्दया।
दुःखदावानलो बुद्धः प्रबुद्धः परमेश्वरः॥ ३६

कामहा क्रोधहा चैव दम्भदर्पमदापहः। अज्ञानपतिमिरारिश्च भवारिर्भुवनेश्वरः॥ ३७

रूपकुद्रूपभृद्रूपी रूपात्मा रूपकारणः।
रूपज्ञो रूपसाक्षी च नामरूपो गुणान्तकः॥ ३८

अप्रमेयः प्रमेयश्च प्रमाणं प्रणवाश्रयः।
प्रमाणरहितोऽचिन्त्यश्चेतनाविगतोऽजरः॥ ३९

अक्षरोऽक्षरमुक्तश्च विज्वरो ज्वरनाशनः।
विशिष्टो वित्तशास्त्री च दृष्टो दृष्टान्तवर्जितः॥ ४०

गुणेशो गुणकायश्च गुणात्मा गणभावनः।
अनन्तगुणसम्पन्नो गुणगर्भो गुणाधिपः॥ ४१

गणेशो गुणनाथश्च गुणात्मा गणभावनः।
गणबन्धुर्विवेकात्मा गुणयुक्तः पराक्रमी॥ ४२

अतर्क्यः क्रतुरग्निश्च कृतज्ञः सफलाश्रयः।
यज्ञश्च यज्ञफल्दो यज्ञ इज्योऽमरोत्तमः॥ ४३

हिरण्यगर्भः श्रीगर्भः खगर्भः कुणपेश्वरः |
मायागर्भो लोकगर्भः स्वयम्भूर्भुवनान्तकः ॥ ४४

निष्पापो निबिडो नन्दी बोधी बोधसमाश्रयः |
बोधात्मा बोधनात्मा च भेदवैतण्डखण्डनः ॥ ४५

स्वाभाव्यो भावनिर्मुक्तो व्यक्तोऽव्यक्तसमाश्रयः |
नित्यतृप्तो निराभासो निर्वाणः शरणः सुहृत् ॥ ४६

गुह्येशो गुणगम्भीरो गुणदोषनिवारणः| गुणसङ्गविहीनश्च योगारेर्दर्पनाशनः ॥ ४७

आनन्दः परमानन्दः स्वानन्दसुखवर्धनः |
सत्यानन्दश्चिदानन्दः सर्वानन्दपरायणः ॥ ४८

सद्रूपः सहजः सत्यः स्वानन्दः सुमनोहरः |
सर्वः सर्वान्तरश्चैव पूर्वात्पूर्वतरस्तथा ॥ ४९

खमयः खपरः खादिः खम्ब्रह्म खतनुः खगः |
खवासाः खविहीनश्च खनिधिः खपराश्रयः ॥ ५०

अनन्तश्चादिरूपश्च सूर्यमण्डलमध्यगः |
अमोघः परमामोघः परोक्षः वरदः कविः ॥ ५१

विश्वचक्षु र्विश्वसाक्षी विश्वबाहुर्धनेश्वरः |
धनञ्जयो महातेजास्तेजिष्ठस्तैजसः सुखी ॥ ५२

ज्योतिर्ज्योतिर्मयो जेता ज्योतिषां ज्योतिरात्मकः |
ज्योतिषामपि ज्योतिश्च जनको जनमोहनः ॥ ५३

जितेन्द्रियो जितक्रोधो जितात्मा जितमानसः |
जितसङ्गो जितप्राणो जितसंसारवासनः ॥ ५४

निर्वासनो निरालम्बो निर्योगक्षेमवर्जितः |
निरीहो निरहङ्कारो निराशीर्निरुपाधिकः ॥ ५५

नित्यबोधो विविक्तात्मा विशुद्धोत्तमगौरवः |
विद्यार्थी परमार्थी च श्रद्धार्थी साधनात्मकः ॥ ५६

प्रत्याहारी निराहारी सर्वाहारपरायणः ।
नित्यशुद्धो निराकाङ्क्षी पारायणपरायणः ॥ ५७

अणोरणुतरः सूक्ष्मः स्थूलः स्थूलतरस्तथा।
एकस्तथाऽनेकरूपो विश्वरूपः सनातनः ॥ ५८

नैकरूपो विरूपात्मा नैकबोधमयोऽपि च ।
नैकनाममयश्चैव नैकविद्याविवर्धनः ॥ ५९

एकश्चैकान्तिकश्चैव नानाभावविवर्जितः ।
एकाक्षरस्तथा बीजः पूर्णबिम्बः सनातनः ॥ ६०

मन्त्रवीर्यो मन्त्रबीजः शास्त्रवीर्यो जगत्पतिः ।
नानावीर्यधरश्चैव शक्रेशः पृथिवीपतिः ॥ ६१

प्राणेशः प्राणदः प्राणः प्राणायामपरायणः ।
प्राणपञ्चकनिर्मुक्तः कोशपञ्चकवर्जितः ॥ ६२

निश्चलो निष्कलोऽसङ्गो निष्प्रपञ्चो निरामयः ।
निराधारो निराकारो निर्विकारो निरञ्जनः ॥ ६३

निष्प्रतीतो निराभासो निरासक्तो निराकुलः ।
निष्ठासर्वगतश्चैव निरारम्भो निराश्रयः ॥ ६४
निरन्तरः सत्त्वगोप्ता शान्तो दान्तो महामुनिः ।
निःशब्दः सुकृतः स्वस्थः सत्यवादी सुरेश्वरः ॥ ६५

ज्ञानदो ज्ञानविज्ञानी ज्ञानात्माऽऽनन्दपूरितः ।
ज्ञानयज्ञविदां दक्षो ज्ञानाग्निर्ज्वलनो बुधः ॥ ६६

दयावान्भवरोगारिश्चिकित्साचरमागतिः ।
चन्द्रमण्डलमध्यस्थश्चन्द्रकोटिसुशीतलः ॥ ६७

यन्तकृत्परमो यन्त्री यन्त्रारूढपराजितः । यन्त्रविद्यन्त्रवासश्च यन्त्राधारो धराधरः ॥ ६८

तत्त्वज्ञस्तत्त्वभूतात्मा महत्तत्त्वप्रकाशनः ।
तत्त्वसङ्ख्यानयोगज्ञः साङ्ख्यशास्त्रप्रवर्तकः ॥ ६९

अनन्तविक्रमो देवो माधवश्च धनेश्वरः |
साधुः साधुवरिष्ठात्मा सावधानोऽमरोत्तमः ॥ ७०

निःसङ्कल्पो निराधारो दुर्धरो ह्यात्मवित्पतिः |
आरोग्यसुखदश्चैव प्रवरो वासवस्तथा ॥ ७१

परेशः परमोदारः प्रत्यक्चैतन्यदुर्गमः | दुराधर्षो दुरावासो दूरत्वपरिनाशनः ॥ ७२

वेदविद्वेदकृद्वेदो वेदात्मा विमलाशयः | विविक्तसेवी च संसारश्रमनाशनस्तथा ॥ ७३

ब्रह्मयोनिर्बृहद्योनिर्विश्वयोनिर्विदेहवान् |
विशालाक्षो विश्वनाथो हाटकाङ्गदभूषणः ॥ ७४

अबाध्यो जगदाराध्यो जगदार्जवपालनः |
जनवान्धनवान्धर्मी धर्मगो धर्मवर्धनः ॥ ७५

अमृतः शाश्वतः साध्यः सिद्धिदः सुमनोहरः |
खलुब्रह्मखलुस्थानो मुनीनां परमा गतिः ॥ ७६

उपद्रष्टा तथा श्रेष्ठः शुचिर्भूतो ह्यनामयः | वेदसिद्धान्तवेद्यश्च मानसाह्लादवर्धनः ॥ ७७

देहदन्यो गुणादन्यो लोकादन्यो विवेकवित् |
दुष्टस्वप्नहरश्चैव गुरुर्गुरुवरोत्तमः ॥ ७८

कर्मी कर्मविनिर्मुक्तः संन्यासी साधकेश्वरः |
सर्वभावविहीनश्च तृष्णासङ्गनिवारकः ॥ ७९

त्यागी त्यागवपुस्त्यागस्त्यागदानविवर्जितः |
त्यागकारणत्यागात्मा सद्गुरुः सुखदायकः ॥ ८०

दक्षो दक्षादिवन्द्यश्च ज्ञानवादप्रवर्तकः |
शब्दब्रह्ममयात्मा च शब्दब्रह्मप्रकाशवान् ॥ ८१

ग्रसिष्णुः प्रभविष्णुश्च सहिष्णुर्विगतान्तरः |
विद्वत्तमो महावन्द्यो विशालोत्तमवाङ्मुनिः ॥ ८२

ब्रह्मविद्ब्रह्मभावश्च ब्रह्मर्षिर्ब्राह्मणप्रियः |

ब्रह्म ब्रह्मप्रकाशात्मा ब्रह्मविद्याप्रकाशनः ॥ ८३

अत्रिवंशप्रभूतात्मा तापसोत्तमवन्दितः ।
आत्मवासी विधेयात्मा ह्यत्रिवंशविवर्धनः ॥ ८४

प्रवर्तनो निवृत्तात्मा प्रलयोदकसन्निभः ।
नारायणो महागर्भो भार्गवप्रियकृत्तमः ॥ ८५

सङ्कल्पदुःखदलनः संसारतमनाशनः ।
त्रिविक्रमस्त्रिधाकारस्त्रिमूर्तिस्त्रिगुणात्मकः ॥ ८६

भेदत्रयहरश्चैव तापत्रयनिवारकः । दोषत्रयविभेदी च संशयार्णवखण्डनः ॥ ८७

असंशयस्त्वसम्मूढो ह्यवादी राजनन्दितः ।
राजयोगी महायोगी स्वभावगलितस्तथा ॥ ८८

पुण्यश्लोकः पवित्राङ्घ्रिर्ध्यानयोगपरायणः ।
ध्यानस्थो ध्यानगम्यश्च विधेयात्मा पुरातनः ॥ ८९

अविज्ञेयो ह्यन्तरात्मा मुख्यबिम्बसनातनः ।
जीवसञ्जीवनो जीवश्चिद्विलासश्चिदाश्रयः ॥ ९०

महेन्द्रोऽमरमान्यश्च योगेन्द्रो योगवित्तमः ।
योगधर्मस्तथा योगस्तत्त्वस्तत्त्वविनिश्चयः ॥ ९१

नैकबाहुरनन्तात्मा नैकनामपराक्रमः । नैकाक्षी नैकपादश्च नाथनाथोत्तमोत्तमः ॥ ९२

सहस्रशीर्षा पुरुषः सहस्राक्षः सहस्रपात् । सहस्ररूपदृक्चैव सहस्रारमयोद्भवः ॥ ९३

त्रिपादपुरुषश्चैव त्रिपादूर्ध्वस्तथैव च । त्र्यम्बकश्च महावीर्यो योगवीर्यविशारदः ॥ ९४

विजयी विनयी जेता वीतरागी विराजितः ।
रुद्रो रौद्रो महाभीमः प्राज्ञमुख्यः सदाशुचिः ॥ ९५

अन्तर्ज्योतिरनन्तात्मा प्रत्यगात्मा निरन्तरः । अरूपश्चात्मरूपश्च सर्वभावविनिर्वृतः ॥

अन्तः शून्यो बहिः शून्यः शून्यात्मा शून्यभावनः ।
अन्तःपूर्णो बहिःपूर्णः पूर्णात्मा पूर्णभावनः ॥ ९७

अन्तस्त्यागी बहिस्त्यागी त्यागात्मा सर्वयोगवान् ।
अन्तर्यागी बहिर्यागी सर्वयोगपरायणः ॥ ९८

अन्तर्भोगी बहिर्भोगी सर्वभोगविदुत्तमः ।
अन्तर्निष्ठो बहिर्निष्ठः सर्वनिष्ठामयस्तथा ॥ ९९

बाह्यान्तरविमुक्तश्च बाह्यान्तरविवर्जितः ।
शान्तः शुद्धो विशुद्धश्च निर्वाणः प्रकृतेः परः ॥ १००

अकालः कालनेमी च कालकालो जनेश्वरः ।
कालात्मा कालकर्ता च कालज्ञः कालनाशनः ॥ १०१

कैवल्यपददाता च कैवल्यसुखदायकः ।
कैवल्यकलनाधारो निर्भरो हर्षवर्धनः ॥ १०२

हृदयस्थो हृषीकेशो गोविन्दो गर्भवर्जितः ।
सकलागमपूज्यश्च निगमो निगमाश्रयः ॥ १०३

पराशक्तिः पराकीर्तिः परावृत्तिर्निधिस्मृतिः ।
पराविद्या पराक्षान्तिर्विभक्तिर्युक्तसद्गतिः ॥ १०४

स्वप्रकाशः प्रकाशात्मा परसंवेदनात्मकः ।
स्वसेव्यः स्वविदां स्वात्मा स्वसंवेद्योऽनघः क्षमी ॥ १०५

स्वानुसन्धानशीलात्मा स्वानुसन्धानगोचरः ।
स्वानुसन्धानशून्यात्मा स्वानुसन्धानाश्रयस्तथा ॥ १०६

स्वबोधदर्पणोऽभङ्गः कन्दर्पकुलनाशनः ।
ब्रह्मचारी ब्रह्मवेत्ता ब्राह्मणो ब्रह्मवित्तमः ॥ १०७

तत्त्वबोधः सुधावर्षः पावनः पापपावकः । ब्रह्मसूत्रविधेयात्मा ब्रह्मसूत्रार्धनिर्णयः ॥

आत्यन्तिको महाकल्पः सङ्कल्पावर्तनाशनः ।
आधिव्याधिहरश्चैव संशयार्णवशोषकः ॥ १०९

तत्त्वात्मज्ञानसन्देशो महानुभवभावितः ।
आत्मानुभवसम्पन्नः स्वानुभावसुखाश्रयः ॥ ११०

अचिन्त्यश्च बृहद्भानुः प्रमदोत्कर्षनाशनः ।
अनिकेतप्रशान्तात्मा शून्यवासो जगद्वपुः ॥ १११

चिद्गतिश्चिन्मयश्चक्री मायाचक्रप्रवर्तकः ।
सर्ववर्णविदारम्भी सर्वारम्भपरायणः ॥ ११२

पुराणः प्रवरो दाता सुन्दरः कनकाङ्गदी ।
अनिसूयात्मजो दत्तः सर्वज्ञः सर्वकामदः ॥ ११३

कामजित्कामपालश्च कामी कामप्रदागमः ।
कामवान्कामपोषश्च सर्वकामनिवर्तकः ॥ ११४

सर्वकर्मफलोत्पत्तिः सर्वकामफलप्रदः ।
सर्वकर्मफलैः पूज्यः सर्वकर्मफलाश्रयः ॥ ११५

विश्वकर्मा कृतात्मा च कृतज्ञः सर्वसाक्षिकः ।
सर्वारम्भपरित्यागी जडोन्मत्तपिशाचवान् ॥ ११६

भिक्षुर्भिक्षाकरश्चैव भैक्षाहारी निराश्रमी ।
अकूलश्चानुकूलश्च विकलो ह्यकलस्तथा ॥ ११७

जटिलो वनचारी च दण्डी मुण्डी च गण्डवान् ।
देहधर्मविहीनात्मा ह्येकाकी सङ्गवर्जितः ॥ ११८

आश्रम्यनाश्रमारम्भोऽनाचारी कर्मवर्जितः ।
असन्देही च सन्देही न किञ्चिन्न च किञ्चनः ॥ ११९

नृदेही देहशून्यश्च नाभावी भावनिर्गतः । नाब्रह्मच परब्रह्म स्वयमेव निराकुलः ॥ १२०

अनघश्चागुरुश्चैव नाथनाथोत्तमो गुरुः । द्विभुजः प्राकृतश्चैव जनकश्च पितामहः ॥ १२१

अनात्मा न च नानात्मा नीतिर्नीतिमतां वरः ।
सहजः सदृशः सिद्धश्चैकश्चिन्मात्र एव च ॥ १२२

न कर्तापि च कर्ता च भोक्ता भोगविवर्जितः ।
तुरीयस्तुरीयातीतः स्वच्छः सर्वमयस्तथा ॥ १२३

सर्वाधिष्ठानरूपश्च सर्वध्येयविवर्जितः ।
सर्वलोकनिवासात्मा सकलोत्तमवन्दितः ॥ १२४

देहभृद्देहकृच्चैव देहात्मा देहभावनः । देही देहविभक्तश्च देहभावप्रकाशनः ॥ १२५

लयस्थो लयविच्चैव लयाभावश्च बोधवान् ।
लयातीतो लयस्यान्तो लयभावनिवारणः ॥ १२६

विमुखः प्रमुखश्चैव प्रत्यङ्मुखवदाचरी ।
विश्वभुग्विश्वधृग्विश्वो विश्वक्षेमकरस्तत्जा ॥ १२७

अविक्षिप्तोऽप्रमादी च परर्द्धिः परमार्थदृक् ।
स्वानुभावविहीनश्च स्वानुभावप्रकाशनः ॥ १२८

निरिन्द्रियश्च निर्बुद्धिर्निराभासो निराकृतः ।
निरहङ्कारश्चरूपात्मा निर्वपुः सकलाश्रयः ॥ १२९

शोकदुःखहरश्चैव भोगमोक्षफलप्रदः ।
सुप्रसन्नस्तथा सूक्ष्मः शब्दब्रह्मार्थसङ्ग्रहः ॥ १३०

आगमापायशून्यश्च स्थानदश्च सताङ्गतिः ।
अकृतः सुकृतश्चैव कृतकर्मा विनिर्वृतः ॥ १३१

भेदत्रयवरश्चैव देहत्रयविनिर्गतः । सर्वकाममयश्चैव सर्वकामनिवर्तकः ॥ १३२

सिद्धेश्वरोऽजरः पञ्चबाणदर्पहुताशनः ।
चतुरक्षरबीजात्मा स्वभूश्चित्कीर्तिभूषणः ॥ १३३

अगाधबुद्धिरक्षुब्धश्चन्द्रसूर्याग्निलोचनः। यमदंष्ट्रोऽतिसंहर्ता परमानन्दसागरः ॥ १३४

लीलाविश्वम्भरो भानुर्भैरवो भीमलोचनः ।
ब्रह्मचर्याम्बरः कालस्त्वचलश्चलनान्तकः ॥ १३५

आदिदेवो जगद्योनिर्वासवारिविमर्दनः । विकर्मकर्मकर्मज्ञोऽनन्यगमकोऽगमः ॥ १३६

अबद्धकर्मशून्यश्च कामरागकुलक्षयः ।
योगान्धकारमथनः पद्मजन्मादिवन्दितः ॥ १३७

भक्तकामोऽग्रजश्चक्री भावनिर्भावभावकः ।
भेदान्तको महानग्र्यो निगूहो गोचरान्तकः ॥ १३८

कालाग्निशमनः शङ्खचक्रपद्मगदाधरः ।
दीप्तो दीनपतिः शास्ता स्वच्छन्दो मुक्तिदायकः ॥ १३९

व्योमधर्माम्बरो भेत्ता भस्मधारी धराधरः ।
धर्मगुप्तोऽन्वयात्मा च व्यतिरेकार्थनिर्णयः ॥ १४०

एकानेकगुणाभासाभासनिर्भासवर्जितः ।
भावाभावस्वभावात्मा भावाभावविभाववित् ॥ १४१

योगिहृदयविश्रामोऽनन्तविद्याविवर्धनः ।
विघ्नान्तकस्त्रिकालज्ञस्तत्त्वात्मा ज्ञानसागरः ॥ १४२

फलश्रुतिः ।

नामरूपात्मकं चैव अवाङ्मनस गोचरं ।
सर्वं दत्तात्मकं विश्वं भावाभावोद्भवात्मकम् ॥ १४३

इति श्री परमं दिव्यं पवित्रं पापनाशनम्।
दत्तात्रेयसहस्राख्यं नामस्तोत्रं कृतं मया ॥ १४४

अतीतानागतं चैव वर्तमानं तथैव च ।
तद्विदुर्ये पठं त्येतत् गुह्याद्गु ह्यतरं परम् ॥ १४५

शृत्वेदं परमं पुण्यं मर्त्यो ह्यमृतमश्नुते।
सहस्रनामकं स्तोत्रं श्रद्धया परया भुवि ॥ १४६

इदं स्तोत्रमुपाश्रित्य मर्त्यश्चात्मनि संस्थितः।
परंस्थानमवाप्नोति शङ्करं प्रकृते परम् ॥ १४७

एकैकमक्षरं पुंसां मणिमाद्यष्टसिद्धिदम्। सर्वपापहरं चैव ब्रह्मनिर्वाणदायकम् ॥ १४८

शिवं पूर्णं परं चैव नित्यं शुद्धं निरञ्जनम्।
निधानं परमं दिव्यं दत्तात्रेयं जगद्गु रुम् ॥ १४९

निरीहं प्रतिमाशून्यं सत्वगं गगनोपमम्। विशुद्धमक्षरं पूर्णं दत्तात्रेयं जगद्गुरुम् ॥ १५०

अवाच्यं प्रणवातीतं निष्प्रपञ्चं निराकलम्।
सत्यं सिद्धं मनोऽगम्यं दत्तात्रेयं जगद्गुरुम् ॥ १५१

कारणं कारणानां च नामरूपविवर्जितम्। परमं परमानन्दं दत्तात्रेयं जगद्गुरुम् ॥ १५२

शाश्वतं सहजं शान्तं पवित्रं च गुणातिगम्।
सत्यं सनातनं सूक्ष्मं दत्तात्रेयं जगद्गुरुम् ॥ १५३

निराकारं निराभासं निष्कलङ्कं निरामयम्।
निरालम्बं निजानन्दं दत्तात्रेयं जगद्गुरुम् ॥ १५४

देशकालार्थनिर्मुक्तं देशकालसमाश्रयम्।
परापरविनिर्मुक्तं दत्तात्रेयं जगद्गुरुम् ॥ १५५

निगीश्वरं निर्विकारं निर्मलज्ञानरूपिणम्। गुणादन्यमहं वन्दे दत्तात्रेयं जगद्गुरुम् ॥ १५६

य इदं पठते नित्यं पाठयेद्वासमाहित।
सर्वान्कामानवाप्नोति दत्तात्रेयो प्रसादतः ॥ १५७

इतीदं दत्तसाहस्रं सायं प्रातः पठेत्तु यः।
स इहामुत्र लभते निर्वाणं परमं सुखम् ॥ १५८

गुरुवारे दत्तभक्तो भक्तिभावसमन्वितः।
पठेत्सदैव तो ह्येतत्स लभेच्चिन्तितं ध्रुवम् ॥ १५९

इति श्री ब्रह्माण्डपुराणे अनुकूलागमे सनत्कुमारब्रह्मऋषि संवादे श्री दत्तात्रेय सहस्रनाम स्तोत्रं संपूर्णम् ॥

Dattatreya
Sahasranama
Stotram

Śrīmad Dattātreya Sahasra Nāmāvalī

श्रीमद् दत्तात्रेयसहस्रनामावली

1.	*Oṃ Śrī Dattātreyāya Namaḥ* |	ॐ श्री दत्तात्रेयाय नमः |
2.	*Oṃ Mahāyogine Namaḥ* |	ॐ महायोगिने नमः |
3.	*Oṃ Yogeśāya Namaḥ* |	ॐ योगेशाय नमः |
4.	*Oṃ Amaraprabhave Namaḥ* |	ॐ अमरप्रभवे नमः |
5.	*Oṃ Munaye Namaḥ* |	ॐ मुनये नमः |
6.	*Oṃ Digambarāya Namaḥ* |	ॐ दिगम्बराय नमः |
7.	*Oṃ Bālāya Namaḥ* |	ॐ बालाय नमः |
8.	*Oṃ Māyāmuktāya Namaḥ* |	ॐ मायामुक्ताय नमः |
9.	*Oṃ Madāpahāya Namaḥ* |	ॐ मदापहाय नमः |
10.	*Oṃ Avadhūtāya Namaḥ* |	ॐ अवधूताय नमः |
11.	*Oṃ Mahānāthāya Namaḥ* |	ॐ महानाथाय नमः |
12.	*Oṃ Śaṅkarāya Namaḥ* |	ॐ शङ्कराय नमः |
13.	*Oṃ Amaravallabhāya Namaḥ* |	ॐ अमरवल्लभाय नमः
14.	*Oṃ Mahādevāya Namaḥ* |	ॐ महादेवाय नमः |
15.	*Oṃ Ādidevāya Namaḥ* |	ॐ आदिदेवाय नमः |
16.	*Oṃ Purāṇaprabhave Namaḥ* |	ॐ पुराणप्रभवे नमः |
17.	*Oṃ Īśvarāya Namaḥ* |	ॐ ईश्वराय नमः |
18.	*Oṃ Sattvakṛte Namaḥ* |	ॐ सत्त्वकृते नमः |
19.	*Oṃ Sattvabhṛte Namaḥ* |	ॐ सत्त्वभृते नमः |
20.	*Oṃ Bhāvāya Namaḥ* |	ॐ भावाय नमः |
21.	*Oṃ Sattvātmane Namaḥ* |	ॐ सत्त्वात्मने नमः |
22.	*Oṃ Sattvasāgarāya Namaḥ* |	ॐ सत्त्वसागराय नमः |
23.	*Oṃ Sattvavide Namaḥ* |	ॐ सत्त्वविदे नमः |
24.	*Oṃ Sattvasākṣiṇe Namaḥ* |	ॐ सत्त्वसाक्षिणे नमः |

25.	*Oṃ Sattvasādhyāya Namaḥ* |	ॐ सत्त्वसाध्याय नमः |
26.	*Oṃ Amarādhipāya Namaḥ* |	ॐ अमराधिपाय नमः |
27.	*Oṃ Bhūtakṛte Namaḥ* |	ॐ भूतकृते नमः |
28.	*Oṃ Bhūtabhṛte Namaḥ* |	ॐ भूतभृते नमः |
29.	*Oṃ Bhūtātmane Namaḥ* |	ॐ भूतात्मने नमः |
30.	*Oṃ Bhūtasambhavāya Namaḥ*|	ॐ भूतसम्भवाय नमः |
31.	*Oṃ Bhūtabhavāya Namaḥ* |	ॐ भूतभवाय नमः |
32.	*Oṃ Bhāvāya Namaḥ* |	ॐ भावाय नमः |
33.	*Oṃ Bhūtavide Namaḥ* |	ॐ भूतविदे नमः |
34.	*Oṃ Bhūtakāraṇāya Namaḥ* |	ॐ भूतकारणाय नमः |
35.	*Oṃ Bhūtasākṣiṇe Namaḥ* |	ॐ भूतसाक्षिणे नमः |
36.	*Oṃ Prabhūtaye Namaḥ* |	ॐ प्रभूतये नमः |
37.	*Oṃ Bhūtānāṃ Paramaṃ Gataye Namaḥ* |	ॐ भूतानां परमं गतये नमः |
38.	*Oṃ Bhūtasaṅgavihīnātmane Namaḥ* |	ॐ भूतसङ्गविहीनात्मने नमः |
39.	*Oṃ Bhūtātmane Namaḥ* |	ॐ भूतात्मने नमः |
40.	*Oṃ Bhūtaśaṅkarāya Namaḥ* |	ॐ भूतशङ्कराय नमः |
41.	*Oṃ Bhūtanāthāya Namaḥ* |	ॐ भूतनाथाय नमः |
42.	*Oṃ Bhūtamahānāthāya Namaḥ* |	ॐ भूतमहानाथाय नमः |
43.	*Oṃ Bhūtādināthāya Namaḥ* |	ॐ भूतादिनाथाय नमः |
44.	*Oṃ Maheśvarāya Namaḥ* |	ॐ महेश्वराय नमः |
45.	*Oṃ Sarvabhūtanivāsātmane Namaḥ* |	ॐ सर्वभूतनिवासात्मने नमः |
46.	*Oṃ Bhūtasantāpanāśanāya Namaḥ* |	ॐ भूतसन्तापनाशनाय नमः |
47.	*Oṃ Sarvātmane Namaḥ* |	ॐ सर्वात्मने नमः |
48.	*Oṃ Sarvabhṛte Namaḥ* |	ॐ सर्वभृते नमः |
49.	*Oṃ Sarvāya Namaḥ* |	ॐ सर्वाय नमः |

50.	*Oṃ Sarvajñāya Namaḥ* |	ॐ सर्वज्ञाय नमः ।
51.	*Oṃ Sarvanirṇayāya Namaḥ* |	ॐ सर्वनिर्णयाय नमः ।
52.	*Oṃ Sarvasākṣiṇe Namaḥ* |	ॐ सर्वसाक्षिणे नमः ।
53.	*Oṃ Bṛhadbhānave Namaḥ* |	ॐ बृहद्भानवे नमः ।
54.	*Oṃ Sarvavide Namaḥ* |	ॐ सर्वविदे नमः ।
55.	*Oṃ Sarvamaṅgalāya Namaḥ* |	ॐ सर्वमङ्गलाय नमः ।
56.	*Oṃ Śāntāya Namaḥ* |	ॐ शान्ताय नमः ।
57.	*Oṃ Satyāya Namaḥ* |	ॐ सत्याय नमः ।
58.	*Oṃ Śamāya Namaḥ* |	ॐ शमाय नमः ।
59.	*Oṃ Samāya Namaḥ* |	ॐ समाय नमः ।
60.	*Oṃ Ekākine Namaḥ* |	ॐ एकाकिने नमः ।
61.	*Oṃ Kamalāpataye Namaḥ* |	ॐ कमलापतये नमः ।
62.	*Oṃ Rāmāya Namaḥ* |	ॐ रामाय नमः ।
63.	*Oṃ Rāmapriyāya Namaḥ* |	ॐ रामप्रियाय नमः ।
64.	*Oṃ Virāmāya Namaḥ* |	ॐ विरामाय नमः ।
65.	*Oṃ Rāmakāraṇāya Namaḥ* |	ॐ रामकारणाय नमः ।
66.	*Oṃ Śuddhātmane Namaḥ* |	ॐ शुद्धात्मने नमः ।
67.	*Oṃ Pavanāya Namaḥ* |	ॐ पवनाय नमः ।
68.	*Oṃ Anantāya Namaḥ* |	ॐ अनन्ताय नमः ।
69.	*Oṃ Pratītāya Namaḥ* |	ॐ प्रतीताय नमः ।
70.	*Oṃ Paramārthabhṛte Namaḥ* |	ॐ परमार्थभृते नमः ।
71.	*Oṃ Haṃsasākṣiṇe Namaḥ* |	ॐ हंससाक्षिणे नमः ।
72.	*Oṃ Vibhave Namaḥ* |	ॐ विभवे नमः ।
73.	*Oṃ Prabhave Namaḥ* |	ॐ प्रभवे नमः ।
74.	*Oṃ Pralayāya Namaḥ* |	ॐ प्रलयाय नमः ।
75.	*Oṃ Siddhātmane Namaḥ* |	ॐ सिद्धात्मने नमः ।
76.	*Oṃ Paramātmane Namaḥ* |	ॐ परमात्मने नमः ।
77.	*Oṃ Siddhānāṃ Paramagataye Namaḥ* |	ॐ सिद्धानां परमगतये नमः ।

78.	*Oṃ Siddhisiddhaye Namaḥ* |	ॐ सिद्धिसिद्धये नमः |
79.	*Oṃ Sādhyāya Namaḥ* |	ॐ साध्याय नमः |
80.	*Oṃ Sādhanāya Namaḥ* |	ॐ साधनाय नमः |
81.	*Oṃ Uttamāya Namaḥ* |	ॐ उत्तमाय नमः |
82.	*Oṃ Sulakṣaṇāya Namaḥ* |	ॐ सुलक्षणाय नमः |
83.	*Oṃ Sumedhāvine Namaḥ* |	ॐ सुमेधाविने नमः |
84.	*Oṃ Vidyavate Namaḥ* |	ॐ विद्यवते नमः |
85.	*Oṃ Vigatāntarāya Namaḥ* |	ॐ विगतान्तराय नमः |
86.	*Oṃ Vijvarāya Namaḥ* |	ॐ विज्वराय नमः |
87.	*Oṃ Mahābāhave Namaḥ* |	ॐ महाबाहवे नमः |
88.	*Oṃ Bahulānandavardhanāya Namaḥ* |	ॐ बहुलानन्दवर्धनाय नमः |
89.	*Oṃ Avyaktapuruṣāya Namaḥ* |	ॐ अव्यक्तपुरुषाय नमः |
90.	*Oṃ Prajñāya Namaḥ* |	ॐ प्रज्ञाय नमः |
91.	*Oṃ Parajñāya Namaḥ* |	ॐ परज्ञाय नमः |
92.	*Oṃ Paramārthadṛśe Namaḥ* |	ॐ परमार्थदृशे नमः |
93.	*Oṃ Parāparavinirmuktāya Namaḥ* |	ॐ परापरविनिर्मुक्ताय नमः |
94.	*Oṃ Yuktāya Namaḥ* |	ॐ युक्ताय नमः |
95.	*Oṃ Tattvaprakāśavate Namaḥ* |	ॐ तत्त्वप्रकाशवते नमः |
96.	*Oṃ Dayāvate Namaḥ* |	ॐ दयावते नमः |
97.	*Oṃ Bhagavate Namaḥ* |	ॐ भगवते नमः |
98.	*Oṃ Bhāvine Namaḥ* |	ॐ भाविने नमः |
99.	*Oṃ Bhāvātmane Namaḥ* |	ॐ भावात्मने नमः |
100.	*Oṃ Bhāvakāraṇāya Namaḥ* |	ॐ भावकारणाय नमः |
101.	*Oṃ Bhavasantāpanāśanāya Namaḥ* |	ॐ भवसन्तापनाशनाय नमः |
102.	*Oṃ Puṣpavate Namaḥ* |	ॐ पुष्पवते नमः |
103.	*Oṃ Paṇḍitāya Namaḥ* |	ॐ पण्डिताय नमः |
104.	*Oṃ Buddhāya Namaḥ* |	ॐ बुद्धाय नमः |

105.	*Oṃ Pratyakṣavastave Namaḥ* |	ॐ प्रत्यक्षवस्तवे नमः |
106.	*Oṃ Viśvātmane Namaḥ* |	ॐ विश्वात्मने नमः |
107.	*Oṃ Pratyagbrahmasanātanāya Namaḥ* |	ॐ प्रत्यग्ब्रह्मसनातनाय नमः |
108.	*Oṃ Pramāṇavigatāya Namaḥ* |	ॐ प्रमाणविगताय नमः |
109.	*Oṃ Pratyāhāraṇī Yojakāya Namaḥ* |	ॐ प्रत्याहारणी योजकाय नमः |
110.	*Oṃ Praṇavāya Namaḥ* |	ॐ प्रणवाय नमः |
111.	*Oṃ Praṇavātītāya Namaḥ* |	ॐ प्रणवातीताय नमः |
112.	*Oṃ Pramukhāya Namaḥ* |	ॐ प्रमुखाय नमः |
113.	*Oṃ Pralayātmakāya Namaḥ* |	ॐ प्रलयात्मकाय नमः |
114.	*Oṃ Mṛtyuñjayāya Namaḥ* |	ॐ मृत्युञ्जयाय नमः |
115.	*Oṃ Viviktātmane Namaḥ* |	ॐ विविक्तात्मने नमः |
116.	*Oṃ Śaṅkarātmane Namaḥ* |	ॐ शङ्करात्मने नमः |
117.	*Oṃ Parasmaivapuṣe Namaḥ* |	ॐ परस्मैवपुषे नमः |
118.	*Oṃ Paramāya Namaḥ* |	ॐ परमाय नमः |
119.	*Oṃ Tanuvijñeyāya Namaḥ* |	ॐ तनुविज्ञेयाय नमः |
120.	*Oṃ Paramātmanisaṃsthitāya Namaḥ* |	ॐ परमात्मनिसंस्थिताय नमः |
121.	*Oṃ Prabodhakalanādhārāya Namaḥ* |	ॐ प्रबोधकलनाधाराय नमः |
122.	*Oṃ Prabhāva Pravarottamāya Namaḥ* |	ॐ प्रभाव प्रवरोत्तमाय नमः |
123.	*Oṃ Cidambarāya Namaḥ* |	ॐ चिदम्बराय नमः |
124.	*Oṃ Cidvilāsāya Namaḥ* |	ॐ चिद्विलासाय नमः |
125.	*Oṃ Cidākāśāya Namaḥ* |	ॐ चिदाकाशाय नमः |
126.	*Oṃ Ciduttamāya Namaḥ* |	ॐ चिदुत्तमाय नमः |
127.	*Oṃ Citta Caitanya Cittātmane Namaḥ* |	ॐ चित्त चैतन्य चित्तात्मने नमः |

128.	*Oṃ Devānāṃ Paramāgataye Namaḥ* |	ॐ देवानां परमागतये नमः |
129.	*Oṃ Acetyāya Namaḥ* |	ॐ अचेत्याय नमः |
130.	*Oṃ Cetanādhārāya Namaḥ* |	ॐ चेतनाधाराय नमः |
131.	*Oṃ Cetanācittavikramāya Namaḥ* |	ॐ चेतनाचित्तविक्रमाय नमः |
132.	*Oṃ Cittātmane Namaḥ* |	ॐ चित्तात्मने नमः |
133.	*Oṃ Cetanārūpāya Namaḥ* |	ॐ चेतनारूपाय नमः |
134.	*Oṃ Lasatpaṅkajalocanāya Namaḥ* |	ॐ लसत्पङ्कजलोचनाय नमः |
135.	*Oṃ Parabrahmaṇe Namaḥ* |	ॐ परब्रह्मणे नमः |
136.	*Oṃ Parañjyotiye Namaḥ* |	ॐ परञ्ज्योतिये नमः |
137.	*Oṃ Parandhāmne Namaḥ* |	ॐ परन्धाम्ने नमः |
138.	*Oṃ Parantapase Namaḥ* |	ॐ परन्तपसे नमः |
139.	*Oṃ Paraṃsūtrāya Namaḥ* |	ॐ परंसूत्राय नमः |
140.	*Oṃ Paratantrāya Namaḥ* |	ॐ परतन्त्राय नमः |
141.	*Oṃ Pavitrāya Namaḥ* |	ॐ पवित्राय नमः |
142.	*Oṃ Paramohavate Namaḥ* |	ॐ परमोहवते नमः |
143.	*Oṃ Kṣetrajñāya Namaḥ* |	ॐ क्षेत्रज्ञाय नमः |
144.	*Oṃ Kṣetragāya Namaḥ* |	ॐ क्षेत्रगाय नमः |
145.	*Oṃ Kṣetrāya Namaḥ* |	ॐ क्षेत्राय नमः |
146.	*Oṃ Kṣetrādhārāya Namaḥ* |	ॐ क्षेत्राधाराय नमः |
147.	*Oṃ Purāñjyanāya Namaḥ* |	ॐ पुराञ्ज्यनाय नमः |
148.	*Oṃ Kṣetraśūnyāya Namaḥ* |	ॐ क्षेत्रशून्याय नमः |
149.	*Oṃ Lokasākṣiṇe Namaḥ* |	ॐ लोकसाक्षिणे नमः |
150.	*Oṃ Kṣetravate Namaḥ* |	ॐ क्षेत्रवते नमः |
151.	*Oṃ Bahunāyakāya Namaḥ* |	ॐ बहुनायकाय नमः |
152.	*Oṃ Yogīndrāya Namaḥ* |	ॐ योगीन्द्राय नमः |
153.	*Oṃ Yogapūjyāya Namaḥ* |	ॐ योगपूज्याय नमः |
154.	*Oṃ Yogyāya Namaḥ* |	ॐ योग्याय नमः |

155.	*Oṃ Ātmavidaṃśucaye Namaḥ* |	ॐ आत्मविदंशुचये नमः |
156.	*Oṃ Yogamāyādharāya Namaḥ* |	ॐ योगमायाधराय नमः |
157.	*Oṃ Sthānave Namaḥ* |	ॐ स्थानवे नमः |
158.	*Oṃ Acalāya Namaḥ* |	ॐ अचलाय नमः |
159.	*Oṃ Kamalāpataye Namaḥ* |	ॐ कमलापतये नमः |
160.	*Oṃ Yogeśāya Namaḥ* |	ॐ योगेशाय नमः |
161.	*Oṃ Yoganimantre Namaḥ* |	ॐ योगनिमन्त्रे नमः |
162.	*Oṃ Yogajñānaprakāśakāya Namaḥ* |	ॐ योगज्ञानप्रकाशकाय नमः |
163.	*Oṃ Yogapālāya Namaḥ* |	ॐ योगपालाय नमः |
164.	*Oṃ Lokapālāya Namaḥ* |	ॐ लोकपालाय नमः |
165.	*Oṃ Saṃsāratamonāśanāya Namaḥ* |	ॐ संसारतमोनाशनाय नमः |
166.	*Oṃ Guhyāya Namaḥ* |	ॐ गुह्याय नमः |
167.	*Oṃ Guhyatamāya Namaḥ* |	ॐ गुह्यतमाय नमः |
168.	*Oṃ Guptaye Namaḥ* |	ॐ गुप्तये नमः |
169.	*Oṃ Muktāya Namaḥ* |	ॐ मुक्ताय नमः |
170.	*Oṃ Yuktāya Namaḥ* |	ॐ युक्ताय नमः |
171.	*Oṃ Sanātanāya Namaḥ* |	ॐ सनातनाय नमः |
172.	*Oṃ Gahanāya Namaḥ* |	ॐ गहनाय नमः |
173.	*Oṃ Gaganākārāya Namaḥ* |	ॐ गगनाकाराय नमः |
174.	*Oṃ Gambhīrāya Namaḥ* |	ॐ गम्भीराय नमः |
175.	*Oṃ Gaṇanāyakāya Namaḥ* |	ॐ गणनायकाय नमः |
176.	*Oṃ Govindāya Namaḥ* |	ॐ गोविन्दाय नमः |
177.	*Oṃ Gopataye Namaḥ* |	ॐ गोपतये नमः |
178.	*Oṃ Goptre Namaḥ* |	ॐ गोप्त्रे नमः |
179.	*Oṃ Gobhāgāya Namaḥ* |	ॐ गोभागाय नमः |
180.	*Oṃ Bhāvasaṃsthitāya Namaḥ* |	ॐ भावसंस्थिताय नमः |
181.	*Oṃ Gosākṣiṇe Namaḥ* |	ॐ गोसाक्षिणे नमः |

182.	*Oṃ Gotamāraye Namaḥ* |	ॐ गोतमारये नमः |
183.	*Oṃ Gāndhārāya Namaḥ* |	ॐ गान्धाराय नमः |
184.	*Oṃ Gaganākṛtaye Namaḥ* |	ॐ गगनाकृतये नमः |
185.	*Oṃ Yogayuktāya Namaḥ* |	ॐ योगयुक्ताय नमः |
186.	*Oṃ Bhogayuktāya Namaḥ* |	ॐ भोगयुक्ताय नमः |
187.	*Oṃ Śaṅkāmukta Samādhimate Namaḥ* |	ॐ शङ्कामुक्त समाधिमते नमः |
188.	*Oṃ Sahajāya Namaḥ* |	ॐ सहजाय नमः |
189.	*Oṃ Sakaleśanāya Namaḥ* |	ॐ सकलेशनाय नमः |
190.	*Oṃ Kārtavīryavarapradāya Namaḥ* |	ॐ कार्तवीर्यवरप्रदाय नमः |
191.	*Oṃ Sarajase Namaḥ* |	ॐ सरजसे नमः |
192.	*Oṃ Virajase Namaḥ* |	ॐ विरजसे नमः |
193.	*Oṃ Puṃse Namaḥ* |	ॐ पुंसे नमः |
194.	*Oṃ Pāvanāya Namaḥ* |	ॐ पावनाय नमः |
195.	*Oṃ Pāpanāśanāya Namaḥ* |	ॐ पापनाशनाय नमः |
196.	*Oṃ Parāvaravinirmuktāya Namaḥ* |	ॐ परावरविनिर्मुक्ताय नमः |
197.	*Oṃ Parañjyotiye Namaḥ* |	ॐ परञ्ज्योतिये नमः |
198.	*Oṃ Purātanāya Namaḥ* |	ॐ पुरातनाय नमः |
199.	*Oṃ Nānājyotiṣe Namaḥ* |	ॐ नानाज्योतिषे नमः |
200.	*Oṃ Anekātmane Namaḥ* |	ॐ अनेकात्मने नमः |
201.	*Oṃ Svayañjyotiṣe* |	ॐ स्वयञ्ज्योतिषे |
202.	*Oṃ Sadāśivāya Namaḥ* |	ॐ सदाशिवाय नमः |
203.	*Oṃ Divyajyotirmayāya Namaḥ* |	ॐ दिव्यज्योतिर्मयाय नमः |
204.	*Oṃ Satyavijñānabhāskarāya Namaḥ* |	ॐ सत्यविज्ञानभास्कराय नमः |
205.	*Oṃ Nityaśuddhāya Namaḥ* |	ॐ नित्यशुद्धाय नमः |

206.	*Oṃ Parāya Namaḥ* |	ॐ पराय नमः |
207.	*Oṃ Pūrṇāya Namaḥ* |	ॐ पूर्णाय नमः |
208.	*Oṃ Prakāśāya Namaḥ* |	ॐ प्रकाशाय नमः |
209.	*Oṃ Prakaṭodbhavāya Namaḥ* |	ॐ प्रकटोद्भवाय नमः |
210.	*Oṃ Pramādavigatāya Namaḥ* |	ॐ प्रमादविगताय नमः |
211.	*Oṃ Pareśāya Namaḥ* |	ॐ परेशाय नमः |
212.	*Oṃ Paravikramāya Namaḥ* |	ॐ परविक्रमाय नमः |
213.	*Oṃ Yogine Namaḥ* |	ॐ योगिने नमः |
214.	*Oṃ Yogāya Namaḥ* |	ॐ योगाय नमः |
215.	*Oṃ Yogapāya Namaḥ* |	ॐ योगपाय नमः |
216.	*Oṃ Yogābhyāsaprakāśanāya Namaḥ* |	ॐ योगाभ्यासप्रकाशनाय नमः |
217.	*Oṃ Yoktre Namaḥ* |	ॐ योक्त्रे नमः |
218.	*Oṃ Moktre Namaḥ* |	ॐ मोक्त्रे नमः |
219.	*Oṃ Vidhātre Namaḥ* |	ॐ विधात्रे नमः |
220.	*Oṃ Trātre Namaḥ* |	ॐ त्रात्रे नमः |
221.	*Oṃ Pātre Namaḥ* |	ॐ पात्रे नमः |
222.	*Oṃ Nirāyudhāya Namaḥ* |	ॐ निरायुधाय नमः |
223.	*Oṃ Nityamuktāya Namaḥ* |	ॐ नित्यमुक्ताय नमः |
224.	*Oṃ Nityayuktāya Namaḥ* |	ॐ नित्ययुक्ताय नमः |
225.	*Oṃ Satyāya Namaḥ* |	ॐ सत्याय नमः |
226.	*Oṃ Satyaparākramāya Namaḥ* |	ॐ सत्यपराक्रमाय नमः |
227.	*Oṃ Sattvaśuddhikarāya Namaḥ* |	ॐ सत्त्वशुद्धिकराय नमः
228.	*Oṃ Sattvāya Namaḥ* |	ॐ सत्त्वाय नमः |
229.	*Oṃ Sattvabhṛtāṅgataye Namaḥ* |	ॐ सत्त्वभृताङ्गतये नमः
230.	*Oṃ Śrīdharāya Namaḥ* |	ॐ श्रीधराय नमः |
231.	*Oṃ Śrīvapuṣe Namaḥ* |	ॐ श्रीवपुषे नमः |
232.	*Oṃ Śrīmate Namaḥ* |	ॐ श्रीमते नमः |
233.	*Oṃ Śrīnivāsāya Namaḥ* |	ॐ श्रीनिवासाय नमः |

234.	*Oṃ Amarārcitāya Namaḥ* |	ॐ अमरार्चिताय नमः |
235.	*Oṃ Śrīnidhaye Namaḥ* |	ॐ श्रीनिधये नमः |
236.	*Oṃ Śrīpataye Namaḥ* |	ॐ श्रीपतये नमः |
237.	*Oṃ Śreṣṭhāya Namaḥ* |	ॐ श्रेष्ठाय नमः |
238.	*Oṃ Śreyaskāya Namaḥ* |	ॐ श्रेयस्काय नमः |
239.	*Oṃ Caramāśrayāya Namaḥ* |	ॐ चरमाश्रयाय नमः |
240.	*Oṃ Tyāgine Namaḥ* |	ॐ त्यागिने नमः |
241.	*Oṃ Tyāgājyasampannāya Namaḥ* |	ॐ त्यागाज्यसम्पन्नाय नमः |
242.	*Oṃ Tyāgātmane Namaḥ* |	ॐ त्यागात्मने नमः |
243.	*Oṃ Tyāgavigrahāya Namaḥ* |	ॐ त्यागविग्रहाय नमः |
244.	*Oṃ Tyāgalakṣaṇasiddhātmane Namaḥ* |	ॐ त्यागलक्षणसिद्धात्मने नमः|
245.	*Oṃ Tyāgajñāya Namaḥ* |	ॐ त्यागज्ञाय नमः |
246.	*Oṃ Tyāgakāraṇāya Namaḥ* |	ॐ त्यागकारणाय नमः |
247.	*Oṃ Bhogāya Namaḥ* |	ॐ भोगाय नमः |
248.	*Oṃ Bhoktre Namaḥ* |	ॐ भोक्त्रे नमः |
249.	*Oṃ Bhogyāya Namaḥ* |	ॐ भोग्याय नमः |
250.	*Oṃ Bhogasādhanakāraṇāya Namaḥ* |	ॐ भोगसाधनकारणाय नमः |
251.	*Oṃ Bhogine Namaḥ* |	ॐ भोगिने नमः |
252.	*Oṃ Bhogārthasampannāya Namaḥ*	ॐ भोगार्थसम्पन्नाय नमः
253.	*Oṃ Bhogajñānaprakāśanāya Namaḥ* |	ॐ भोगज्ञानप्रकाशनाय नमः |
254.	*Oṃ Kevalāya Namaḥ* |	ॐ केवलाय नमः |
255.	*Oṃ Keśavāya Namaḥ* |	ॐ केशवाय नमः |
256.	*Oṃ Kṛṣṇāya Namaḥ* |	ॐ कृष्णाय नमः |
257.	*Oṃ Kaṃvāsase Namaḥ* |	ॐ कंवाससे नमः |
258.	*Oṃ Kamalālayāya Namaḥ* |	ॐ कमलालयाय नमः |

259.	*Oṃ Kamalāsanapūjyāya Namaḥ* |	ॐ कमलासनपूज्याय नमः |
260.	*Oṃ Haraye Namaḥ* |	ॐ हरये नमः |
261.	*Oṃ Ajñānakhaṇḍanāya Namaḥ* |	ॐ अज्ञानखण्डनाय नमः
262.	*Oṃ Mahātmane Namaḥ* |	ॐ महात्मने नमः |
263.	*Oṃ Mahadādaye Namaḥ* |	ॐ महदादये नमः |
264.	*Oṃ Maheśottamavanditā Namaḥ* |	ॐ महेशोत्तमवन्दिता नमः
265.	*Oṃ Manovṛddhivihīnātmane Namaḥ* |	ॐ मनोवृद्धिविहीनात्मने नमः |
266.	*Oṃ Mānātmane Namaḥ* |	ॐ मानात्मने नमः |
267.	*Oṃ Mānavādhipāya Namaḥ* |	ॐ मानवाधिपाय नमः |
268.	*Oṃ Bhuvaneśāya Namaḥ* |	ॐ भुवनेशाय नमः |
269.	*Oṃ Vibhūtaye Namaḥ* |	ॐ विभूतये नमः |
270.	*Oṃ Dhṛtaye Namaḥ* |	ॐ धृतये नमः |
271.	*Oṃ Medhāye Namaḥ* |	ॐ मेधाये नमः |
272.	*Oṃ Smṛtaye Namaḥ* |	ॐ स्मृतये नमः |
273.	*Oṃ Dayāye Namaḥ* |	ॐ दयाये नमः |
274.	*Oṃ Duḥkhadāvānalāya Namaḥ* |	ॐ दुःखदावानलाय नमः
275.	*Oṃ Buddhāya Namaḥ* |	ॐ बुद्धाय नमः |
276.	*Oṃ Prabuddhāya Namaḥ* |	ॐ प्रबुद्धाय नमः |
277.	*Oṃ Parameśvarāya Namaḥ* |	ॐ परमेश्वराय नमः |
278.	*Oṃ Kāmaghnāya Namaḥ* |	ॐ कामघ्नाय नमः |
279.	*Oṃ Krodhaghnāya Namaḥ* |	ॐ क्रोधघ्नाय नमः |
280.	*Oṃ Dambhadarpamadāpahāya Namaḥ* |	ॐ दम्भदर्पमदापहाय नमः |
281.	*Oṃ Ajñānatimirāraye Namaḥ* |	ॐ अज्ञानतिमिरारये नमः|
282.	*Oṃ Bhavāraye Namaḥ* |	ॐ भवारये नमः|
283.	*Oṃ Bhuvaneśvarāya Namaḥ* |	ॐ भुवनेश्वराय नमः |
284.	*Oṃ Rūpakṛte Namaḥ* |	ॐ रूपकृते नमः |

285.	*Oṃ Rūpabhṛte Namaḥ* |	ॐ रूपभृते नमः |
286.	*Oṃ Rūpiṇe Namaḥ* |	ॐ रूपिणे नमः |
287.	*Oṃ Rūpātmane Namaḥ* |	ॐ रूपात्मने नमः |
288.	*Oṃ Rūpakāraṇāya Namaḥ* |	ॐ रूपकारणाय नमः |
289.	*Oṃ Rūpajñāya Namaḥ* |	ॐ रूपज्ञाय नमः |
290.	*Oṃ Rūpasākṣiṇe Namaḥ* |	ॐ रूपसाक्षिणे नमः |
291.	*Oṃ Nāmarūpāya Namaḥ* |	ॐ नामरूपाय नमः |
292.	*Oṃ Guṇāntakāya Namaḥ* |	ॐ गुणान्तकाय नमः |
293.	*Oṃ Aprameyāya Namaḥ* |	ॐ अप्रमेयाय नमः |
294.	*Oṃ Prameyāya Namaḥ* |	ॐ प्रमेयाय नमः |
295.	*Oṃ Pramāṇāya Namaḥ* |	ॐ प्रमाणाय नमः |
296.	*Oṃ Praṇavāśrayāya Namaḥ* |	ॐ प्रणवाश्रयाय नमः |
297.	*Oṃ Pramāṇarahitāya Namaḥ* |	ॐ प्रमाणरहिताय नमः |
298.	*Oṃ Acintyāya Namaḥ* |	ॐ अचिन्त्याय नमः |
299.	*Oṃ Cetanāvigatāya Namaḥ* |	ॐ चेतनाविगताय नमः |
300.	*Oṃ Ajarāya Namaḥ* |	ॐ अजराय नमः |
301.	*Oṃ Akṣarāya Namaḥ* |	ॐ अक्षराय नमः |
302.	*Oṃ Akṣaramuktāya Namaḥ* |	ॐ अक्षरमुक्ताय नमः |
303.	*Oṃ Vijvarāya Namaḥ* |	ॐ विज्वराय नमः |
304.	*Oṃ Jvaranāśanāya Namaḥ* |	ॐ ज्वरनाशनाय नमः |
305.	*Oṃ Viśiṣṭāya Namaḥ* |	ॐ विशिष्टाय नमः |
306.	*Oṃ Vittaśāstriṇe Namaḥ* |	ॐ वित्तशास्त्रिणे नमः |
307.	*Oṃ Dṛṣṭāya Namaḥ* |	ॐ दृष्टाय नमः |
308.	*Oṃ Dṛṣṭāntavarjitāya Namaḥ* |	ॐ दृष्टान्तवर्जिताय नमः
309.	*Oṃ Guṇeśāya Namaḥ* |	ॐ गुणेशाय नमः |
310.	*Oṃ Guṇakāyāya Namaḥ* |	ॐ गुणकायाय नमः |
311.	*Oṃ Guṇātmane Namaḥ* |	ॐ गुणात्मने नमः |
312.	*Oṃ Guṇabhāvanāya Namaḥ* |	ॐ गुणभावनाय नमः |

313.	*Oṃ Anantaguṇasampannāya Namaḥ* |	ॐ अनन्तगुणसम्पन्नाय नमः ।
314.	*Oṃ Guṇagarbhāya Namaḥ* |	ॐ गुणगर्भाय नमः ।
315.	*Oṃ Guṇādhipāya Namaḥ* |	ॐ गुणाधिपाय नमः ।
316.	*Oṃ Guṇeśāya Namaḥ* |	ॐ गुणेशाय नमः ।
317.	*Oṃ Guṇanāthāya Namaḥ* |	ॐ गुणनाथाय नमः ।
318.	*Oṃ Guṇātmane Namaḥ* |	ॐ गुणात्मने नमः ।
319.	*Oṃ Guṇabhāvanāya Namaḥ* |	ॐ गुणभावनाय नमः ।
320.	*Oṃ Guṇabandhave Namaḥ* |	ॐ गुणबन्धवे नमः ।
321.	*Oṃ Vivekātmane Namaḥ* |	ॐ विवेकात्मने नमः ।
322.	*Oṃ Guṇayuktāya Namaḥ* |	ॐ गुणयुक्ताय नमः ।
323.	*Oṃ Parākramiṇe Namaḥ* |	ॐ पराक्रमिणे नमः ।
324.	*Oṃ Atarkāya Namaḥ* |	ॐ अतर्काय नमः ।
325.	*Oṃ Ākṛtave Namaḥ* |	ॐ आकृतवे नमः ।
326.	*Oṃ Agnaye Namaḥ* |	ॐ अग्नये नमः ।
327.	*Oṃ Kṛtajñāya Namaḥ* |	ॐ कृतज्ञाय नमः ।
328.	*Oṃ Saphalāśrayāya Namaḥ* |	ॐ सफलाश्रयाय नमः ।
329.	*Oṃ Yajñāya Namaḥ* |	ॐ यज्ञाय नमः ।
330.	*Oṃ Yajñaphaladātre Namaḥ* |	ॐ यज्ञफलदात्रे नमः ।
331.	*Oṃ Yajñātmane Namaḥ* |	ॐ यज्ञात्मने नमः ।
332.	*Oṃ Ījanāya Namaḥ* |	ॐ ईजनाय नमः ।
333.	*Oṃ Amarottamāya Namaḥ* |	ॐ अमरोत्तमाय नमः ।
334.	*Oṃ Hiraṇyagarbhāya Namaḥ* |	ॐ हिरण्यगर्भाय नमः ।
335.	*Oṃ Śrīgarbhāya Namaḥ* |	ॐ श्रीगर्भाय नमः ।
336.	*Oṃ Svagarbhāya Namaḥ* |	ॐ स्वगर्भाय नमः ।
337.	*Oṃ Kuṇapeśvarāya Namaḥ* |	ॐ कुणपेश्वराय नमः ।
338.	*Oṃ Māyogarbhāya Namaḥ* |	ॐ मायोगर्भाय नमः ।
339.	*Oṃ Lokagarbhāya Namaḥ* |	ॐ लोकगर्भाय नमः ।
340.	*Oṃ Svayambhuve Namaḥ* |	ॐ स्वयम्भुवे नमः ।

341.	*Oṃ Bhuvanāntakāya Namaḥ* |	ॐ भुवनान्तकाय नमः |
342.	*Oṃ Niṣpāpāya Namaḥ* |	ॐ निष्पापाय नमः |
343.	*Oṃ Nibiḍāya Namaḥ* |	ॐ निबिडाय नमः |
344.	*Oṃ Nandine Namaḥ* |	ॐ नन्दिने नमः |
345.	*Oṃ Bodhine Namaḥ* |	ॐ बोधिने नमः |
346.	*Oṃ Bodhasamāśrayāya Namaḥ* |	ॐ बोधसमाश्रयाय नमः |
347.	*Oṃ Bodhātmane Namaḥ* |	ॐ बोधात्मने नमः |
348.	*Oṃ Bodhanātmane Namaḥ* |	ॐ बोधनात्मने नमः |
349.	*Oṃ Bhedavaitaṇḍakhaṇḍanāya Namaḥ* |	ॐ भेदवैतण्डखण्डनाय नमः |
350.	*Oṃ Svabhāvyāya Namaḥ* |	ॐ स्वभाव्याय नमः |
351.	*Oṃ Bhāvavimuktāya Namaḥ* |	ॐ भावविमुक्ताय नमः |
352.	*Oṃ Vyaktāya Namaḥ* |	ॐ व्यक्ताय नमः |
353.	*Oṃ Avyaktasamāśrayāya Namaḥ* |	ॐ अव्यक्तसमाश्रयाय नमः |
354.	*Oṃ Nityatṛptāya Namaḥ* |	ॐ नित्यतृप्ताय नमः |
355.	*Oṃ Nirābhāsāya Namaḥ* |	ॐ निराभासाय नमः |
356.	*Oṃ Nirvāṇāya Namaḥ* |	ॐ निर्वाणाय नमः |
357.	*Oṃ Śaraṇāya Namaḥ* |	ॐ शरणाय नमः |
358.	*Oṃ Suhṛde Namaḥ* |	ॐ सुहृदे नमः |
359.	*Oṃ Guhyeśāya Namaḥ* |	ॐ गुह्येशाय नमः |
360.	*Oṃ Guṇagambhīrāya Namaḥ* |	ॐ गुणगम्भीराय नमः |
361.	*Oṃ Guṇadośanivāraṇāya Namaḥ* |	ॐ गुणदोशनिवारणाय नमः |
362.	*Oṃ Guṇasaṅgavihīnāya Namaḥ* |	ॐ गुणसङ्गविहीनाय नमः |
363.	*Oṃ Yogārerdarpanāśanāya Namaḥ* |	ॐ योगारेर्दर्पनाशनाय नमः |
364.	*Oṃ Ānandāya Namaḥ* |	ॐ आनन्दाय नमः |
365.	*Oṃ Paramānandāya Namaḥ* |	ॐ परमानन्दाय नमः |

366.	*Oṃ Svānandasukhavardhanāya Namaḥ* |	ॐ स्वानन्दसुखवर्धनाय नमः |
367.	*Oṃ Satyānandāya Namaḥ* |	ॐ सत्यानन्दाय नमः |
368.	*Oṃ Cidānandāya Namaḥ* |	ॐ चिदानन्दाय नमः |
369.	*Oṃ Sarvānandaparāyaṇāya Namaḥ* |	ॐ सर्वानन्दपरायणाय नमः |
370.	*Oṃ Sadrūpāya Namaḥ* |	ॐ सद्रूपाय नमः |
371.	*Oṃ Sahajāya Namaḥ* |	ॐ सहजाय नमः |
372.	*Oṃ Satyāya Namaḥ* |	ॐ सत्याय नमः |
373.	*Oṃ Svānandāya Namaḥ* |	ॐ स्वानन्दाय नमः |
374.	*Oṃ Sumanoharāya Namaḥ* |	ॐ सुमनोहराय नमः |
375.	*Oṃ Sarvāya Namaḥ* |	ॐ सर्वाय नमः |
376.	*Oṃ Sarvāntarāya Namaḥ* |	ॐ सर्वान्तराय नमः |
377.	*Oṃ Pūrvātpūrvāntarāya Namaḥ* |	ॐ पूर्वात्पूर्वान्तराय नमः |
378.	*Oṃ Svamayāya Namaḥ* |	ॐ स्वमयाय नमः |
379.	*Oṃ Svaparāya Namaḥ* |	ॐ स्वपराय नमः |
380.	*Oṃ Svādaye Namaḥ* |	ॐ स्वादये नमः |
381.	*Oṃ Svambrahmaṇe Namaḥ* |	ॐ स्वम्ब्रह्मणे नमः |
382.	*Oṃ Svatanave Namaḥ* |	ॐ स्वतनवे नमः |
383.	*Oṃ Svagāya Namaḥ* |	ॐ स्वगाय नमः |
384.	*Oṃ Svavāsase Namaḥ* |	ॐ स्ववाससे नमः |
385.	*Oṃ Svavihīnāya Namaḥ* |	ॐ स्वविहीनाय नमः |
386.	*Oṃ Svanidhaye Namaḥ* |	ॐ स्वनिधये नमः |
387.	*Oṃ Svaparākṣayāya Namaḥ* |	ॐ स्वपराक्षयाय नमः |
388.	*Oṃ Anantāya Namaḥ* |	ॐ अनन्ताय नमः |
389.	*Oṃ Ādirūpāya Namaḥ* |	ॐ आदिरूपाय नमः |
390.	*Oṃ Sūryamaṇḍalamadhyagāya Namaḥ* |	ॐ सूर्यमण्डलमध्यगाय नमः |
391.	*Oṃ Amoghāya Namaḥ* |	ॐ अमोघाय नमः |

392.	*Oṃ Paramāmoghāya Namaḥ* |	ॐ परमामोघाय नमः |
393.	*Oṃ Pareśāya Namaḥ* |	ॐ परेशाय नमः |
394.	*Oṃ Parādāya Namaḥ* |	ॐ परादाय नमः |
395.	*Oṃ Kavaye Namaḥ* |	ॐ कवये नमः |
396.	*Oṃ Viśvacakṣuṣe Namaḥ* |	ॐ विश्वचक्षुषे नमः |
397.	*Oṃ Viśvasākṣiṇe Namaḥ* |	ॐ विश्वसाक्षिणे नमः |
398.	*Oṃ Viśvabāhave Namaḥ* |	ॐ विश्वबाहवे नमः |
399.	*Oṃ Dhaneśvarāya Namaḥ* |	ॐ धनेश्वराय नमः |
400.	*Oṃ Dhanañjayāya Namaḥ* |	ॐ धनञ्जयाय नमः |
401.	*Oṃ Mahātejase Namaḥ* |	ॐ महातेजसे नमः |
402.	*Oṃ Tejiṣṭhāya Namaḥ* |	ॐ तेजिष्ठाय नमः |
403.	*Oṃ Tejasāya Namaḥ* |	ॐ तेजसाय नमः |
404.	*Oṃ Sukhine Namaḥ* |	ॐ सुखिने नमः |
405.	*Oṃ Jyotiṣe Namaḥ* |	ॐ ज्योतिषे नमः |
406.	*Oṃ Jyotirmayāya Namaḥ* |	ॐ ज्योतिर्मयाय नमः |
407.	*Oṃ Jetre Namaḥ* |	ॐ जेत्रे नमः |
408.	*Oṃ Jyotiṣāṃ Jyotirātmakāya Namaḥ* |	ॐ ज्योतिषां ज्योतिरात्मकाय नमः |
409.	*Oṃ Jyotiṣāmapi Jyotiṣe Namaḥ* |	ॐ ज्योतिषामपि ज्योतिषे नमः |
410.	*Oṃ Janakāya Namaḥ* |	ॐ जनकाय नमः |
411.	*Oṃ Janamohanāya Namaḥ* |	ॐ जनमोहनाय नमः |
412.	*Oṃ Jitendriyāya Namaḥ* |	ॐ जितेन्द्रियाय नमः |
413.	*Oṃ Jitakrodhāya Namaḥ* |	ॐ जितक्रोधाय नमः |
414.	*Oṃ Jitātmane Namaḥ* |	ॐ जितात्मने नमः |
415.	*Oṃ Jitamānasāya Namaḥ* |	ॐ जितमानसाय नमः |
416.	*Oṃ Jitasaṅgāya Namaḥ* |	ॐ जितसङ्गाय नमः |
417.	*Oṃ Jitaprāṇāya Namaḥ* |	ॐ जितप्राणाय नमः |
418.	*Oṃ Jitasaṃsāra Namaḥ* |	ॐ जितसंसार नमः |
419.	*Oṃ Nirvāsanāya Namaḥ* |	ॐ निर्वासनाय नमः |

420.	*Oṃ Nirālambāya Namaḥ* |	ॐ निरालम्बाय नमः ।
421.	*Oṃ Niryogakṣemavarjitāya Namaḥ* |	ॐ निर्योगक्षेमवर्जिताय नमः ।
422.	*Oṃ Nirīhāya Namaḥ* |	ॐ निरीहाय नमः ।
423.	*Oṃ Nirahaṅkārāya Namaḥ* |	ॐ निरहङ्काराय नमः ।
424.	*Oṃ Nirāśīnirupādhikāya Namaḥ* |	ॐ निराशीनिरुपाधिकाय नमः ।
425.	*Oṃ Nirlābodhyāya Namaḥ* |	ॐ निर्लाबोध्याय नमः ।
426.	*Oṃ Viviktātmane Namaḥ* |	ॐ विविक्तात्मने नमः ।
427.	*Oṃ Viśuddhottama Gauravāya Namaḥ* |	ॐ विशुद्धोत्तम गौरवाय नमः ।
428.	*Oṃ Vidyārthine Namaḥ* |	ॐ विद्यार्थिने नमः ।
429.	*Oṃ Paramārthine Namaḥ* |	ॐ परमार्थिने नमः ।
430.	*Oṃ Śraddhārthine Namaḥ* |	ॐ श्रद्धार्थिने नमः ।
431.	*Oṃ Sādhanātmakāya Namaḥ* |	ॐ साधनात्मकाय नमः ।
432.	*Oṃ Pratyāhāriṇe Namaḥ* |	ॐ प्रत्याहारिणे नमः ।
433.	*Oṃ Nirāhāriṇe Namaḥ* |	ॐ निराहारिणे नमः ।
434.	*Oṃ Sarvāhāraparāyaṇāya Namaḥ* |	ॐ सर्वाहारपरायणाय नमः ।
435.	*Oṃ Nityaśuddhāya Namaḥ* |	ॐ नित्यशुद्धाय नमः ।
436.	*Oṃ Nirākāṅkṣiṇe Namaḥ* |	ॐ निराकाङ्क्षिणे नमः ।
437.	*Oṃ Pārāyaṇaparāyaṇāya Namaḥ* |	ॐ पारायणपरायणाय नमः ।
438.	*Oṃ Aṇornutarayā Namaḥ* |	ॐ अणोर्नुतरया नमः ।
439.	*Oṃ Sūkṣmāya Namaḥ* |	ॐ सूक्ष्माय नमः ।
440.	*Oṃ Sthūlāya Namaḥ* |	ॐ स्थूलाय नमः ।
441.	*Oṃ Sthūlatarāya Namaḥ* |	ॐ स्थूलतराय नमः ।
442.	*Oṃ Ekāya Namaḥ* |	ॐ एकाय नमः ।
443.	*Oṃ Anekarūpāya Namaḥ* |	ॐ अनेकरूपाय नमः ।

444.	*Oṃ Viśvarūpāya Namaḥ* |	ॐ विश्वरूपाय नमः |
445.	*Oṃ Sanātanāya Namaḥ* |	ॐ सनातनाय नमः |
446.	*Oṃ Naikarūpāya Namaḥ* |	ॐ नैकरूपाय नमः |
447.	*Oṃ Nirūpātmane Namaḥ* |	ॐ निरूपात्मने नमः |
448.	*Oṃ Naikabodhamayāya Namaḥ* |	ॐ नैकबोधमयाय नमः |
449.	*Oṃ Naikanāmamayāya Namaḥ* |	ॐ नैकनाममयाय नमः |
450.	*Oṃ Naikavidyāvivardhanāya Namaḥ* |	ॐ नैकविद्याविवर्धनाय नमः |
451.	*Oṃ Ekāya Namaḥ* |	ॐ एकाय नमः |
452.	*Oṃ Ekāntikāya Namaḥ* |	ॐ एकान्तिकाय नमः |
453.	*Oṃ Nānābhāvavivarjitāya Namaḥ* |	ॐ नानाभावविवर्जिताय नमः |
454.	*Oṃ Ekākṣarāya Namaḥ* |	ॐ एकाक्षराय नमः |
455.	*Oṃ Bījāya Namaḥ* |	ॐ बीजाय नमः |
456.	*Oṃ Pūrṇabimbāya Namaḥ* |	ॐ पूर्णबिम्बाय नमः |
457.	*Oṃ Sanātanāya Namaḥ* |	ॐ सनातनाय नमः |
458.	*Oṃ Mantravīryāya Namaḥ* |	ॐ मन्त्रवीर्याय नमः |
459.	*Oṃ Mantrabījāya Namaḥ* |	ॐ मन्त्रबीजाय नमः |
460.	*Oṃ Śāstravīryāya Namaḥ* |	ॐ शास्त्रवीर्याय नमः |
461.	*Oṃ Jagatpataye Namaḥ* |	ॐ जगत्पतये नमः |
462.	*Oṃ Nānāvīryadharāya Namaḥ* |	ॐ नानावीर्यधराय नमः |
463.	*Oṃ Śaktreśāya Namaḥ* |	ॐ शक्त्रेशाय नमः |
464.	*Oṃ Pṛthivīpataye Namaḥ* |	ॐ पृथिवीपतये नमः |
465.	*Oṃ Prāṇeśāya Namaḥ* |	ॐ प्राणेशाय नमः |
466.	*Oṃ Prāṇadāya Namaḥ* |	ॐ प्राणदाय नमः |
467.	*Oṃ Prāṇāya Namaḥ* |	ॐ प्राणाय नमः |
468.	*Oṃ Prāṇāyāmaparāyaṇāya Namaḥ* |	ॐ प्राणायामपरायणाय नमः |
469.	*Oṃ Praṇapañcakanirmuktāya Namaḥ* |	ॐ प्रणपञ्चकनिर्मुक्ताय नमः |

470.	*Oṃ Kośapañcakavarjitāya Namaḥ* |	ॐ कोशपञ्चकवर्जिताय नमः |
471.	*Oṃ Niścalāya Namaḥ* |	ॐ निश्चलाय नमः |
472.	*Oṃ Niṣkalāya Namaḥ* |	ॐ निष्कलाय नमः |
473.	*Oṃ Asaṅgāya Namaḥ* |	ॐ असङ्गाय नमः |
474.	*Oṃ Niṣprapañcāya Namaḥ* |	ॐ निष्प्रपञ्चाय नमः |
475.	*Oṃ Nirāmayāya Namaḥ* |	ॐ निरामयाय नमः |
476.	*Oṃ Nirādhārāya Namaḥ* |	ॐ निराधाराय नमः |
477.	*Oṃ Nirākārāya Namaḥ* |	ॐ निराकाराय नमः |
478.	*Oṃ Nirvikāryāya Namaḥ* |	ॐ निर्विकार्याय नमः |
479.	*Oṃ Nirañjanāya Namaḥ* |	ॐ निरञ्जनाय नमः |
480.	*Oṃ Niṣpratītāya Namaḥ* |	ॐ निष्प्रतीताय नमः |
481.	*Oṃ Nirābhāsāya Namaḥ* |	ॐ निराभासाय नमः |
482.	*Oṃ Nirāsaktāya Namaḥ* |	ॐ निरासक्ताय नमः |
483.	*Oṃ Nirākulāya Namaḥ* |	ॐ निराकुलाय नमः |
484.	*Oṃ Niṣṭhāsarvagatāya Namaḥ* |	ॐ निष्ठासर्वगताय नमः |
485.	*Oṃ Nirārambhāya Namaḥ* |	ॐ निरारम्भाय नमः |
486.	*Oṃ Nirāśrayāya Namaḥ* |	ॐ निराश्रयाय नमः |
487.	*Oṃ Nirantarāya Namaḥ* |	ॐ निरन्तराय नमः |
488.	*Oṃ Sattvagoptre Namaḥ* |	ॐ सत्त्वगोप्त्रे नमः |
489.	*Oṃ Śāntāya Namaḥ* |	ॐ शान्ताय नमः |
490.	*Oṃ Dāntāya Namaḥ* |	ॐ दान्ताय नमः |
491.	*Oṃ Mahāmunaye Namaḥ* |	ॐ महामुनये नमः |
492.	*Oṃ Niḥśabdāya Namaḥ* |	ॐ निःशब्दाय नमः |
493.	*Oṃ Sukṛtāya Namaḥ* |	ॐ सुकृताय नमः |
494.	*Oṃ Svasthāya Namaḥ* |	ॐ स्वस्थाय नमः |
495.	*Oṃ Satyavādine Namaḥ* |	ॐ सत्यवादिने नमः |
496.	*Oṃ Sureśvarāya Namaḥ* |	ॐ सुरेश्वराय नमः |
497.	*Oṃ Jñānadāya Namaḥ* |	ॐ ज्ञानदाय नमः |

498.	*Oṃ Jñānavijñānine Namaḥ* |	ॐ ज्ञानविज्ञानिने नमः |
499.	*Oṃ Jñānātmane Namaḥ* |	ॐ ज्ञानात्मने नमः |
500.	*Oṃ Ānandapūretāya Namaḥ* |	ॐ आनन्दपूरेताय नमः |
501.	*Oṃ Jñānayajñavidāṃ Dakṣāya Namaḥ* |	ॐ ज्ञानयज्ञविदां दक्षाय नमः |
502.	*Oṃ Jñānāgnaye Namaḥ* |	ॐ ज्ञानाग्नये नमः |
503.	*Oṃ Jvalanāya Namaḥ* |	ॐ ज्वलनाय नमः |
504.	*Oṃ Budhāya Namaḥ* |	ॐ बुधाय नमः |
505.	*Oṃ Dayāvate Namaḥ* |	ॐ दयावते नमः |
506.	*Oṃ Bhavarogāraye Namaḥ* |	ॐ भवरोगारये नमः |
507.	*Oṃ Cikitsā Caramāgalāye Namaḥ* |	ॐ चिकित्सा चरमा गलाये नमः |
508.	*Oṃ Candramaṇḍala Madhyasthāya Namaḥ* |	ॐ चन्द्रमण्डल मध्यस्थाय नमः |
509.	*Oṃ Candrakoṭisuśīlālaye Namaḥ* |	ॐ चन्द्रकोटिसुशीलालये नमः |
510.	*Oṃ Yantrakṛte Namaḥ* |	ॐ यन्त्रकृते नमः |
511.	*Oṃ Paramāya Namaḥ* |	ॐ परमाय नमः |
512.	*Oṃ Yantriṇe Namaḥ* |	ॐ यन्त्रिणे नमः |
513.	*Oṃ Yantrārūḍhāparājitāya Namaḥ* |	ॐ यन्त्रारूढापराजिताय नमः |
514.	*Oṃ Yantravide Namaḥ* |	ॐ यन्त्रविदे नमः |
515.	*Oṃ Yantravāsāya Namaḥ* |	ॐ यन्त्रवासाय नमः |
516.	*Oṃ Yantrādhārāya Namaḥ* |	ॐ यन्त्राधाराय नमः |
517.	*Oṃ Dharādhārāya Namaḥ* |	ॐ धराधाराय नमः |
518.	*Oṃ Tattvajñāya Namaḥ* |	ॐ तत्त्वज्ञाय नमः |
519.	*Oṃ Tattvabhūtātmane Namaḥ* |	ॐ तत्त्वभूतात्मने नमः |
520.	*Oṃ Mahattattvaprakāśanāya Namaḥ* |	ॐ महत्तत्त्वप्रकाशनाय नमः |

521.	*Oṃ Tattvasaṅkhyānayogajñāya Namaḥ |*	ॐ तत्त्व सङ्ख्यान योगज्ञाय नमः ।
522.	*Oṃ Sāṅkhyaśāstrapravartakāya Namaḥ |*	ॐ साङ्ख्य शास्त्र प्रवर्तकाय नमः ।
523.	*Oṃ Ananta Vikramāya Namaḥ |*	ॐ अनन्त विक्रमाय नमः ।
524.	*Oṃ Devāya Namaḥ |*	ॐ देवाय नमः ।
525.	*Oṃ Mādhavāya Namaḥ |*	ॐ माधवाय नमः ।
526.	*Oṃ Dhaneśvarāya Namaḥ |*	ॐ धनेश्वराय नमः।
527.	*Oṃ Sādhave Namaḥ |*	ॐ साधवे नमः।
528.	*Oṃ Sādhu Variṣṭhātmane Namaḥ |*	ॐ साधु वरिष्ठात्मने नमः।
529.	*Oṃ Sāvadhānāya Namaḥ |*	ॐ सावधानाय नमः ।
530.	*Oṃ Amarottamāya Namaḥ |*	ॐ अमरोत्तमाय नमः ।
531.	*Oṃ Niḥsaṅkalpāya Namaḥ |*	ॐ निःसङ्कल्पाय नमः ।
532.	*Oṃ Nirādhārāya Namaḥ |*	ॐ निराधाराय नमः ।
533.	*Oṃ Durdharāya Namaḥ |*	ॐ दुर्धराय नमः ।
534.	*Oṃ Ātmavide Namaḥ |*	ॐ आत्मविदे नमः ।
535.	*Oṃ Pataye Namaḥ |*	ॐ पतये नमः ।
536.	*Oṃ Ārogyasukhadāya Namaḥ |*	ॐ आरोग्यसुखदाय नमः।
537.	*Oṃ Pravarāya Namaḥ |*	ॐ प्रवराय नमः।
538.	*Oṃ Vāsavāya Namaḥ |*	ॐ वासवाय नमः ।
539.	*Oṃ Pareśāya Namaḥ |*	ॐ परेशाय नमः।
540.	*Oṃ Paramodārāya Namaḥ |*	ॐ परमोदाराय नमः।
541.	*Oṃ Pratyakcaitanya Durgamāya Namaḥ |*	ॐ प्रत्यक्चैतन्य दुर्गमाय नमः ।
542.	*Oṃ Durādharṣāya Namaḥ |*	ॐ दुराधर्षाय नमः ।
543.	*Oṃ Durāvāsāya Namaḥ |*	ॐ दुरावासाय नमः ।

544.	*Oṃ Dūratvaparināśanāya Namaḥ* |	ॐ दूरत्वपरिनाशनाय नमः |
545.	*Oṃ Vedavide Namaḥ* |	ॐ वेदविदे नमः |
546.	*Oṃ Vedakṛte Namaḥ* |	ॐ वेदकृते नमः |
547.	*Oṃ Vedāya Namaḥ* |	ॐ वेदाय नमः |
548.	*Oṃ Vedātmane Namaḥ* |	ॐ वेदात्मने नमः |
549.	*Oṃ Vimalāśayāya Namaḥ* |	ॐ विमलाशयाय नमः |
550.	*Oṃ Viviktasevine Namaḥ* |	ॐ विविक्तसेविने नमः |
551.	*Oṃ Saṃsāraśramanāśanāya Namaḥ* |	ॐ संसारश्रमनाशनाय नमः |
552.	*Oṃ Brahmayonaye Namaḥ* |	ॐ ब्रह्मयोनये नमः |
553.	*Oṃ Bṛhadyonaye Namaḥ* |	ॐ बृहद्योनये नमः |
554.	*Oṃ Viśvayonaye Namaḥ* |	ॐ विश्वयोनये नमः |
555.	*Oṃ Videhavate Namaḥ* |	ॐ विदेहवते नमः |
556.	*Oṃ Viśālākṣāya Namaḥ* |	ॐ विशालाक्षाय नमः |
557.	*Oṃ Viśvanāthāya Namaḥ* |	ॐ विश्वनाथाय नमः |
558.	*Oṃ Hāṭakāṅgadabhūṣaṇāya Namaḥ* |	ॐ हाटकाङ्गदभूषणाय नमः |
559.	*Oṃ Abādhyāya Namaḥ* |	ॐ अबाध्याय नमः |
560.	*Oṃ Jagadārādhyāya Namaḥ* |	ॐ जगदाराध्याय नमः |
561.	*Oṃ Jagadākhilapālanāya Namaḥ* |	ॐ जगदाखिलपालनाय नमः |
562.	*Oṃ Janavate Namaḥ* |	ॐ जनवते नमः |
563.	*Oṃ Dhanavate Namaḥ* |	ॐ धनवते नमः |
564.	*Oṃ Dharmiṇe Namaḥ* |	ॐ धर्मिणे नमः |
565.	*Oṃ Dharmagāya Namaḥ* |	ॐ धर्मगाय नमः |
566.	*Oṃ Dharmavardhanāya Namaḥ* |	ॐ धर्मवर्धनाय नमः |
567.	*Oṃ Amṛtāya Namaḥ* |	ॐ अमृताय नमः |
568.	*Oṃ Śāśvatāya Namaḥ* |	ॐ शाश्वताय नमः |
569.	*Oṃ Sādhyāya Namaḥ* |	ॐ साध्याय नमः |

570.	*Oṃ Siddhidāya Namaḥ* |	ॐ सिद्धिदाय नमः ।
571.	*Oṃ Sumanoharāya Namaḥ* |	ॐ सुमनोहराय नमः ।
572.	*Oṃ Khalubrahma Khalusthānāya Namaḥ* |	ॐ खलुब्रह्म खलुस्थानाय नमः ।
573.	*Oṃ Munīnāṃ Paramāgataye Namaḥ* |	ॐ मुनीनां परमागतये नमः ।
574.	*Oṃ Upadṛṣṭe Namaḥ* |	ॐ उपदृष्टे नमः ।
575.	*Oṃ Śreṣṭhāya Namaḥ* |	ॐ श्रेष्ठाय नमः ।
576.	*Oṃ Śucirbhūtāya Namaḥ* |	ॐ शुचिर्भूताय नमः ।
577.	*Oṃ Anāmayāya Namaḥ* |	ॐ अनामयाय नमः ।
578.	*Oṃ Vedasiddhāntavedyāya Namaḥ* |	ॐ वेदसिद्धान्तवेद्याय नमः ।
579.	*Oṃ Mānasāhlādavardhanāya Namaḥ* |	ॐ मानसाह्लादवर्धनाय नमः ।
580.	*Oṃ Dehādanyāya Namaḥ* |	ॐ देहादन्याय नमः ।
581.	*Oṃ Guṇādanyāya Namaḥ* |	ॐ गुणादन्याय नमः ।
582.	*Oṃ Lokādanyāya Namaḥ* |	ॐ लोकादन्याय नमः ।
583.	*Oṃ Vivekavide Namaḥ* |	ॐ विवेकविदे नमः ।
584.	*Oṃ Duṣṭasvapnaharāya Namaḥ* |	ॐ दुष्टस्वप्नहराय नमः ।
585.	*Oṃ Gurave Namaḥ* |	ॐ गुरवे नमः ।
586.	*Oṃ Guruvarottamāya Namaḥ* |	ॐ गुरुवरोत्तमाय नमः ।
587.	*Oṃ Karmiṇe Namaḥ* |	ॐ कर्मिणे नमः ।
588.	*Oṃ Karmavinirmuktāya Namaḥ* |	ॐ कर्मविनिर्मुक्ताय नमः
589.	*Oṃ Saṃnyāsine Namaḥ* |	ॐ संन्यासिने नमः ।
590.	*Oṃ Sādhakeśvarāya Namaḥ* |	ॐ साधकेश्वराय नमः ।
591.	*Oṃ Sarvabhāvavihināya Namaḥ* |	ॐ सर्वभावविहिनाय नमः
592.	*Oṃ Tṛṣṇāsaṅganivāraṇāya Namaḥ* |	ॐ तृष्णासङ्गनिवारणाय नमः ।
593.	*Oṃ Tyāgine Namaḥ* |	ॐ त्यागिने नमः ।
594.	*Oṃ Tyagavapuṣe Namaḥ* |	ॐ त्यगवपुषे नमः ।

595.	Oṃ Tyāgāya Namaḥ |	ॐ त्यागाय नमः |
596.	Oṃ Tyāgadānavivarjitāya Namaḥ |	ॐ त्यागदानविवर्जिताय नमः |
597.	Oṃ Tyāgakāraṇatyāgātmane Namaḥ |	ॐ त्यागकारणत्यागात्मने नमः |
598.	Oṃ Sadgurave Namaḥ |	ॐ सद्गुरवे नमः |
599.	Oṃ Sukhadāyakāya Namaḥ |	ॐ सुखदायकाय नमः |
600.	Oṃ Dakṣāya Namaḥ |	ॐ दक्षाय नमः |
601.	Oṃ Dakṣādi Vandyāya Namaḥ |	ॐ दक्षादि वन्द्याय नमः |
602.	Oṃ Jñānavādapravatakāya Namaḥ |	ॐ ज्ञानवादप्रवतकाय नमः |
603.	Oṃ Śabdabrahmamayātmane Namaḥ |	ॐ शब्दब्रह्ममयात्मने नमः |
604.	Oṃ Śabdabrahmaprakāśavate Namaḥ |	ॐ शब्दब्रह्मप्रकाशवते नमः |
605.	Oṃ Grasiṣṇave Namaḥ |	ॐ ग्रसिष्णवे नमः |
606.	Oṃ Prabhaviṣṇave Namaḥ |	ॐ प्रभविष्णवे नमः |
607.	Oṃ Sahiṣṇave Namaḥ |	ॐ सहिष्णवे नमः |
608.	Oṃ Vigatāntarāya Namaḥ |	ॐ विगतान्तराय नमः |
609.	Oṃ Vidvattamāya Namaḥ |	ॐ विद्वत्तमाय नमः |
610.	Oṃ Mahāvandyāya Namaḥ |	ॐ महावन्द्याय नमः |
611.	Oṃ Viśālottama Vāṅmunaye Namaḥ |	ॐ विशालोत्तम वाङ्मुनये नमः |
612.	Oṃ Brahmavide Namaḥ |	ॐ ब्रह्मविदे नमः |
613.	Oṃ Brahmabhāvāya Namaḥ |	ॐ ब्रह्मभावाय नमः |
614.	Oṃ Brahmarṣaye Namaḥ |	ॐ ब्रह्मऋषये नमः |
615.	Oṃ Brāhmaṇapriyāya Namaḥ |	ॐ ब्राह्मणप्रियाय नमः |
616.	Oṃ Brahmaṇe Namaḥ |	ॐ ब्रह्मणे नमः |
617.	Oṃ Brahmaprakāśātmane Namaḥ |	ॐ ब्रह्मप्रकाशात्मने नमः|

618.	*Oṃ Brahmavidyāprakāśanāya Namaḥ |*	ॐ ब्रह्मविद्याप्रकाशनाय नमः ।
619.	*Oṃ Atrivaṃśaprabhūtātmane Namaḥ |*	ॐ अत्रिवंशप्रभूतात्मने नमः ।
620.	*Oṃ Tāpasottam Vanditāya Namaḥ |*	ॐ तापसोत्तम् वन्दिताय नमः ।
621.	*Oṃ Ātmavāsine Namaḥ |*	ॐ आत्मवासिने नमः ।
622.	*Oṃ Vidheyātmane Namaḥ |*	ॐ विधेयात्मने नमः ।
623.	*Oṃ Atrivaṃśavivardhanāya Namaḥ |*	ॐ अत्रिवंशविवर्धनाय नमः ।
624.	*Oṃ Pravartanāya Namaḥ |*	ॐ प्रवर्तनाय नमः ।
625.	*Oṃ Nivṛttātmane Namaḥ |*	ॐ निवृत्तात्मने नमः ।
626.	*Oṃ Pralayodakasannibhāya Namaḥ |*	ॐ प्रलयोदकसन्निभाय नमः ।
627.	*Oṃ Nārāyaṇāya Namaḥ |*	ॐ नारायणाय नमः ।
628.	*Oṃ Mahāgarbhāya Namaḥ |*	ॐ महागर्भाय नमः ।
629.	*Oṃ Bhārgavapriyakṛttamāya Namaḥ |*	ॐ भार्गवप्रियकृत्तमाय नमः ।
630.	*Oṃ Saṅkalpaduḥkhadalanāya Namaḥ |*	ॐ सङ्कल्पदुःखदलनाय नमः ।
631.	*Oṃ Saṃsāratamanāśanāya Namaḥ |*	ॐ संसारतमनाशनाय नमः ।
632.	*Oṃ Trivikramāya Namaḥ |*	ॐ त्रिविक्रमाय नमः ।
633.	*Oṃ Tridhākārāya Namaḥ |*	ॐ त्रिधाकाराय नमः ।
634.	*Oṃ Trimūrtaye Namaḥ |*	ॐ त्रिमूर्तये नमः ।
635.	*Oṃ Triguṇātmakāya Namaḥ |*	ॐ त्रिगुणात्मकाय नमः ।
636.	*Oṃ Bhedatrayaharāya Namaḥ |*	ॐ भेदत्रयहराय नमः ।
637.	*Oṃ Tāpatrayanivārakāya Namaḥ |*	ॐ तापत्रयनिवारकाय नमः ।
638.	*Oṃ Doṣatrayavibhedine Namaḥ |*	ॐ दोषत्रयविभेदिने नमः

639.	*Oṃ Saṃśayārṇavakhaṇḍanāya Namaḥ* |	ॐ संशयार्णवखण्डनाय नमः ।
640.	*Oṃ Asaṃśayāya Namaḥ* |	ॐ असंशयाय नमः ।
641.	*Oṃ Asaṃmūḍhāya Namaḥ* |	ॐ असंमूढाय नमः ।
642.	*Oṃ Avādine Namaḥ* |	ॐ अवादिने नमः ।
643.	*Oṃ Rājavanditāya Namaḥ* |	ॐ राजवन्दिताय नमः ।
644.	*Oṃ Rājayogine Namaḥ* |	ॐ राजयोगिने नमः ।
645.	*Oṃ Mahāyogine Namaḥ* |	ॐ महायोगिने नमः ।
646.	*Oṃ Svabhāvagalitāya Namaḥ* |	ॐ स्वभावगलिताय नमः।
647.	*Oṃ Puṇyaślokāya Namaḥ* |	ॐ पुण्यश्लोकाय नमः ।
648.	*Oṃ Pavitrāṅghraye Namaḥ* |	ॐ पवित्राङ्घ्रये नमः ।
649.	*Oṃ Dhyānayogaparāyaṇāya Namaḥ* |	ॐ ध्यानयोगपरायणाय नमः ।
650.	*Oṃ Dhyānasthāya Namaḥ* |	ॐ ध्यानस्थाय नमः ।
651.	*Oṃ Dhyānagamyāya Namaḥ* |	ॐ ध्यानगम्याय नमः ।
652.	*Oṃ Vidheyātmane Namaḥ* |	ॐ विधेयात्मने नमः ।
653.	*Oṃ Purātanāya Namaḥ* |	ॐ पुरातनाय नमः ।
654.	*Oṃ Avijñeyāya Namaḥ* |	ॐ अविज्ञेयाय नमः ।
655.	*Oṃ Antarātmane Namaḥ* |	ॐ अन्तरात्मने नमः ।
656.	*Oṃ Mukhyabimbasanātanāya Namaḥ* |	ॐ मुख्यबिम्बसनातनाय नमः ।
657.	*Oṃ Jīvasañjīvanāya Namaḥ* |	ॐ जीवसञ्जीवनाय नमः
658.	*Oṃ Jīvāya Namaḥ* |	ॐ जीवाय नमः ।
659.	*Oṃ Cidvilāsāya Namaḥ* |	ॐ चिद्विलासाय नमः ।
660.	*Oṃ Cidāśrayāya Namaḥ* |	ॐ चिदाश्रयाय नमः ।
661.	*Oṃ Mahendrāya Namaḥ* |	ॐ महेन्द्राय नमः ।
662.	*Oṃ Amaramānyāya Namaḥ* |	ॐ अमरमान्याय नमः ।
663.	*Oṃ Yogīndrāya Namaḥ* |	ॐ योगीन्द्राय नमः ।
664.	*Oṃ Yogavidmayāya Namaḥ* |	ॐ योगविद्मयाय नमः ।

665.	*Oṃ Yogadharmāya Namaḥ* |	ॐ योगधर्माय नमः |
666.	*Oṃ Yogāya Namaḥ* |	ॐ योगाय नमः |
667.	*Oṃ Tattvāya Namaḥ* |	ॐ तत्त्वाय नमः |
668.	*Oṃ Tattvaviniścayāya Namaḥ* |	ॐ तत्त्वविनिश्चयाय नमः
669.	*Oṃ Naikabāhave Namaḥ* |	ॐ नैकबाहवे नमः |
670.	*Oṃ Anantātmane Namaḥ* |	ॐ अनन्तात्मने नमः |
671.	*Oṃ Naikanānāparākroṇāya Namaḥ* |	ॐ नैकनानापराक्रोणाय नमः |
672.	*Oṃ Naikākṣiṇe Namaḥ* |	ॐ नैकाक्षिणे नमः |
673.	*Oṃ Naikapādāya Namaḥ* |	ॐ नैकपादाय नमः |
674.	*Oṃ Nāthanāthāya Namaḥ* |	ॐ नाथनाथाय नमः |
675.	*Oṃ Uttamottamāya Namaḥ* |	ॐ उत्तमोत्तमाय नमः |
676.	*Oṃ Sahasraśīrṣiṇe Namaḥ* |	ॐ सहस्रशीर्षिणे नमः |
677.	*Oṃ Puruṣāya Namaḥ* |	ॐ पुरुषाय नमः |
678.	*Oṃ Sahasrākṣāya Namaḥ* |	ॐ सहस्राक्षाय नमः |
679.	*Oṃ Sahasrapade Namaḥ* |	ॐ सहस्रपदे नमः |
680.	*Oṃ Sahasrarūpadṛśe Namaḥ* |	ॐ सहस्ररूपदृशे नमः |
681.	*Oṃ Sahasrāmaya Udbhavāya Namaḥ* |	ॐ सहस्रामय उद्भवाय नमः |
682.	*Oṃ Tripāda Puruṣāya Namaḥ* |	ॐ त्रिपाद पुरुषाय नमः |
683.	*Oṃ Tripadordhvāya Namaḥ* |	ॐ त्रिपदोर्ध्वाय नमः |
684.	*Oṃ Tryayambakāya Namaḥ* |	ॐ त्र्यम्बकाय नमः |
685.	*Oṃ Mahāvīryāya Namaḥ* |	ॐ महावीर्याय नमः |
686.	*Oṃ Yogavīryaviśāradāya Namaḥ* |	ॐ योगवीर्यविशारदाय नमः |
687.	*Oṃ Vijayine Namaḥ* |	ॐ विजयिने नमः |
688.	*Oṃ Vinayine Namaḥ* |	ॐ विनयिने नमः |
689.	*Oṃ Jetre Namaḥ* |	ॐ जेत्रे नमः |
690.	*Oṃ Vītarāgiṇe Namaḥ* |	ॐ वीतरागिणे नमः |
691.	*Oṃ Virājitāya Namaḥ* |	ॐ विराजिताय नमः |

692.	*Oṃ Rudrāya Namaḥ* |	ॐ रुद्राय नमः |
693.	*Oṃ Raudrāya Namaḥ* |	ॐ रौद्राय नमः |
694.	*Oṃ Mahābhīmāya Namaḥ* |	ॐ महाभीमाय नमः |
695.	*Oṃ Prājñamukhyāya Namaḥ* |	ॐ प्राज्ञमुख्याय नमः |
696.	*Oṃ Sadāśucaye Namaḥ* |	ॐ सदाशुचये नमः |
697.	*Oṃ Antarjyotiṣe Namaḥ* |	ॐ अन्तर्ज्योतिषे नमः |
698.	*Oṃ Anantātmane Namaḥ* |	ॐ अनन्तात्मने नमः |
699.	*Oṃ Pratyagātmane Namaḥ* |	ॐ प्रत्यगात्मने नमः |
700.	*Oṃ Nirantarāya Namaḥ* |	ॐ निरन्तराय नमः |
701.	*Oṃ Arūpāya Namaḥ* |	ॐ अरूपाय नमः |
702.	*Oṃ Ātmarūpāya Namaḥ* |	ॐ आत्मरूपाय नमः |
703.	*Oṃ Sarvabhāvavinirvṛttāya Namaḥ* |	ॐ सर्वभावविनिर्वृत्ताय नमः |
704.	*Oṃ Antaḥśūnyāya Namaḥ* |	ॐ अन्तःशून्याय नमः |
705.	*Oṃ Bahiḥśūnyāya Namaḥ* |	ॐ बहिःशून्याय नमः |
706.	*Oṃ Śūnyātmane Namaḥ* |	ॐ शून्यात्मने नमः |
707.	*Oṃ Śūnyabhāvanāya Namaḥ* |	ॐ शून्यभावनाय नमः |
708.	*Oṃ Antaḥpūrṇāya Namaḥ* |	ॐ अन्तःपूर्णाय नमः |
709.	*Oṃ Bahiḥpūrṇāya Namaḥ* |	ॐ बहिःपूर्णाय नमः |
710.	*Oṃ Pūrṇātmane Namaḥ* |	ॐ पूर्णात्मने नमः |
711.	*Oṃ Pūrṇabhāvanāya Namaḥ* |	ॐ पूर्णभावनाय नमः |
712.	*Oṃ Antastyāgine Namaḥ* |	ॐ अन्तस्त्यागिने नमः |
713.	*Oṃ Bahistyāgine Namaḥ* |	ॐ बहिस्त्यागिने नमः |
714.	*Oṃ Tyāgātmane Namaḥ* |	ॐ त्यागात्मने नमः |
715.	*Oṃ Sarvayogavate Namaḥ* |	ॐ सर्वयोगवते नमः |
716.	*Oṃ Antaryogine Namaḥ* |	ॐ अन्तर्योगिने नमः |
717.	*Oṃ Bahiryogine Namaḥ* |	ॐ बहिर्योगिने नमः |
718.	*Oṃ Sarvayogaparāyaṇāya Namaḥ* |	ॐ सर्वयोगपरायणाय नमः |

719.	*Oṃ Antarbhogine Namaḥ |*	ॐ अन्तर्भोगिने नमः ।
720.	*Oṃ Bahirbhogine Namaḥ |*	ॐ बहिर्भोगिने नमः ।
721.	*Oṃ Sarvabhigaviduttamāya Namaḥ |*	ॐ सर्वभिगविदुत्तमाय नमः ।
722.	*Oṃ Antarniṣṭhāya Namaḥ |*	ॐ अन्तर्निष्ठाय नमः ।
723.	*Oṃ Bahirniṣṭhāya Namaḥ |*	ॐ बहिर्निष्ठाय नमः ।
724.	*Oṃ Sarvaniṣṭhāmayāya Namaḥ |*	ॐ सर्वनिष्ठामयाय नमः ।
725.	*Oṃ Bāhyāntaravimuktāya Namaḥ |*	ॐ बाह्यान्तरविमुक्ताय नमः ।
726.	*Oṃ Bāhyāntaravivarjitāya Namaḥ |*	ॐ बाह्यान्तरविवर्जिताय नमः ।
727.	*Oṃ Śāntāya Namaḥ |*	ॐ शान्ताय नमः ।
728.	*Oṃ Śuddhāya Namaḥ |*	ॐ शुद्धाय नमः ।
729.	*Oṃ Viśuddhāya Namaḥ |*	ॐ विशुद्धाय नमः ।
730.	*Oṃ Nirvāṇāya Namaḥ |*	ॐ निर्वाणाय नमः ।
731.	*Oṃ Prakṛtice Parāya Namaḥ |*	ॐ प्रकृतिचे पराय नमः ।
732.	*Oṃ Akālāya Namaḥ |*	ॐ अकालाय नमः ।
733.	*Oṃ Kālanemine Namaḥ |*	ॐ कालनेमिने नमः ।
734.	*Oṃ Kālakālāya Namaḥ |*	ॐ कालकालाय नमः ।
735.	*Oṃ Janeśvarāya Namaḥ |*	ॐ जनेश्वराय नमः ।
736.	*Oṃ Kālātmane Namaḥ |*	ॐ कालात्मने नमः ।
737.	*Oṃ Kālakartre Namaḥ |*	ॐ कालकर्त्रे नमः ।
738.	*Oṃ Kālajñāya Namaḥ |*	ॐ कालज्ञाय नमः ।
739.	*Oṃ Kālanāśanāya Namaḥ |*	ॐ कालनाशनाय नमः ।
740.	*Oṃ Kaivalypadadātre Namaḥ |*	ॐ कैवल्यपददात्रे नमः ।
741.	*Oṃ Kaivalyasukhadāyakāya Namaḥ |*	ॐ कैवल्यसुखदायकाय नमः ।
742.	*Oṃ Kaivalyālayadharāya Namaḥ |*	ॐ कैवल्यालयधराय नमः ।

743.	*Oṃ Nirbharāya Namaḥ* |	ॐ निर्भराय नमः ।
744.	*Oṃ Harşavardhanāya Namaḥ* |	ॐ हर्षवर्धनाय नमः ।
745.	*Oṃ Hṛdayasthāya Namaḥ* |	ॐ हृदयस्थाय नमः ।
746.	*Oṃ Hṛṣikeṣāya Namaḥ* |	ॐ हृषिकेषाय नमः ।
747.	*Oṃ Govindāya Namaḥ* |	ॐ गोविन्दाय नमः ।
748.	*Oṃ Garbhavarjitāya Namaḥ* |	ॐ गर्भवर्जिताय नमः ।
749.	*Oṃ Sakalāgamapūjyāya Namaḥ* |	ॐ सकलागमपूज्याय नमः ।
750.	*Oṃ Nigamāya Namaḥ* |	ॐ निगमाय नमः ।
751.	*Oṃ Nigamāśrayāya Namaḥ* |	ॐ निगमाश्रयाय नमः ।
752.	*Oṃ Parāśaktaye Namaḥ* |	ॐ पराशक्तये नमः ।
753.	*Oṃ Parākīrtaye Namaḥ* |	ॐ पराकीर्तये नमः ।
754.	*Oṃ Parāvṛttaye Namaḥ* |	ॐ परावृत्तये नमः ।
755.	*Oṃ Nidhismṛtaye Namaḥ* |	ॐ निधिस्मृतये नमः ।
756.	*Oṃ Parāvidyā Parākṣāntaye Namaḥ* |	ॐ पराविद्या पराक्षान्तये नमः ।
757.	*Oṃ Vibhaktaye Namaḥ* |	ॐ विभक्तये नमः ।
758.	*Oṃ Yuktasadgataye Namaḥ* |	ॐ युक्तसद्गतये नमः ।
759.	*Oṃ Svaprakāśāya Namaḥ* |	ॐ स्वप्रकाशाय नमः ।
760.	*Oṃ Prakāśātmane Namaḥ* |	ॐ प्रकाशात्मने नमः ।
761.	*Oṃ Parāsaṃvedanātmakāya Namaḥ* |	ॐ परासंवेदनात्मकाय नमः ।
762.	*Oṃ Svasevyāya Namaḥ* |	ॐ स्वसेव्याय नमः ।
763.	*Oṃ Svavidaṃ Svātmane Namaḥ* |	ॐ स्वविदं स्वात्मने नमः ।
764.	*Oṃ Svasaṃvedyāya Namaḥ* |	ॐ स्वसंवेद्याय नमः ।
765.	*Oṃ Anaghāya Namaḥ* |	ॐ अनघाय नमः ।
766.	*Oṃ Kṣamiṇe Namaḥ* |	ॐ क्षमिणे नमः ।

767.	*Oṃ Svānusandhāna Śīlātmane Namaḥ* |	ॐ स्वानुसन्धान शीलात्मने नमः |
768.	*Oṃ Svānusandhāna Gocarāya Namaḥ* |	ॐ स्वानुसन्धान गोचराय नमः |
769.	*Oṃ Svānusandhāna Śūnyātmane Namaḥ* |	ॐ स्वानुसन्धान शून्यात्मने नमः |
770.	*Oṃ Svanusandhānāśrayāya Namaḥ* |	ॐ स्वनुसन्धानाश्रयाय नमः |
771.	*Oṃ Svabodhadarpaṇāya Namaḥ* |	ॐ स्वबोधदर्पणाय नमः |
772.	*Oṃ Abhaṅgāya Namaḥ* |	ॐ अभङ्गाय नमः |
773.	*Oṃ Kandarpakulanāśanāya Namaḥ* |	ॐ कन्दर्पकुलनाशनाय नमः |
774.	*Oṃ Brahmacāriṇe Namaḥ* |	ॐ ब्रह्मचारिणे नमः |
775.	*Oṃ Brahmavetre Namaḥ* |	ॐ ब्रह्मवेत्रे नमः |
776.	*Oṃ Brāhmaṇāya Namaḥ* |	ॐ ब्राह्मणाय नमः |
777.	*Oṃ Brahmavittamāya Namaḥ* |	ॐ ब्रह्मवित्तमाय नमः |
778.	*Oṃ Tattvabodhāya Namaḥ* |	ॐ तत्त्वबोधाय नमः |
779.	*Oṃ Sudhāvarṣāya Namaḥ* |	ॐ सुधावर्षाय नमः |
780.	*Oṃ Pavanāya Namaḥ* |	ॐ पवनाय नमः |
781.	*Oṃ Pāpapāvakāya Namaḥ* |	ॐ पापपावकाय नमः |
782.	*Oṃ Brahmasūtravidheyātmane Namaḥ* |	ॐ ब्रह्मसूत्रविधेयात्मने नमः |
783.	*Oṃ Brahmasūtrārthanirṇayāya Namaḥ* |	ॐ ब्रह्मसूत्रार्थनिर्णयाय नमः |
784.	*Oṃ Atyantikāya Namaḥ* |	ॐ अत्यन्तिकाय नमः |
785.	*Oṃ Mahākalpāya Namaḥ* |	ॐ महाकल्पाय नमः |
786.	*Oṃ Saṅkalpāvarta Nāśanāya Namaḥ* |	ॐ सङ्कल्पावर्त नाशनाय नमः |

787.	*Oṃ Ādhivyādhiharāya Namaḥ* |	ॐ आधिव्याधिहराय नमः ।
788.	*Oṃ Saṃśayārṇava Śoṣakāya Namaḥ* |	ॐ संशयार्णव शोषकाय नमः ।
789.	*Oṃ Tattvātmajñānasandeśāya Namaḥ* |	ॐ तत्त्वात्मज्ञानसन्देशाय नमः ।
790.	*Oṃ Mahānubhāvabhāvitāya Namaḥ* |	ॐ महानुभावभाविताय नमः ।
791.	*Oṃ Ātmānubhavasampannāya Namaḥ* |	ॐ आत्मानुभवसम्पन्नाय नमः ।
792.	*Oṃ Svānubhavasukhāśrayāya Namaḥ* |	ॐ स्वानुभवसुखाश्रयाय नमः ।
793.	*Oṃ Acintyāya Namaḥ* |	ॐ अचिन्त्याय नमः ।
794.	*Oṃ Bṛhadbhānave Namaḥ* |	ॐ बृहद्भानवे नमः ।
795.	*Oṃ Pramadotkarṣanāśanāya Namaḥ* |	ॐ प्रमदोत्कर्षनाशनाय नमः ।
796.	*Oṃ Aniketa Praśāntātmane Namaḥ* |	ॐ अनिकेत प्रशान्तात्मने नमः ।
797.	*Oṃ Śūnyavāsāya Namaḥ* |	ॐ शून्यवासाय नमः ।
798.	*Oṃ Jagadvapuṣe Namaḥ* |	ॐ जगद्वपुषे नमः ।
799.	*Oṃ Cidgataye Namaḥ* |	ॐ चिद्गतये नमः ।
800.	*Oṃ Cinmayāya Namaḥ* |	ॐ चिन्मयाय नमः ।
801.	*Oṃ Cakriṇe* |	ॐ चक्रिणे ।
802.	*Oṃ Māyācakrapravartakāya Namaḥ* |	ॐ मायाचक्रप्रवर्तकाय नमः ।
803.	*Oṃ Sarvavarṇavidārambhiṇe Namaḥ* |	ॐ सर्ववर्णविदारम्भिणे नमः ।
804.	*Oṃ Sarvārambhaparāyaṇāya Namaḥ* |	ॐ सर्वारम्भपरायणाय नमः ।
805.	*Oṃ Purāṇāya Namaḥ* |	ॐ पुराणाय नमः ।

806.	*Oṃ Pravarāya Namaḥ* |	ॐ प्रवराय नमः ।
807.	*Oṃ Dātre Namaḥ* |	ॐ दात्रे नमः ।
808.	*Oṃ Sunarāya Namaḥ* |	ॐ सुनराय नमः ।
809.	*Oṃ Kanakāṅgadine Namaḥ* |	ॐ कनकाङ्गदिने नमः ।
810.	*Oṃ Anasūyātmajāya Namaḥ* |	ॐ अनसूयात्मजाय नमः।
811.	*Oṃ Dattāya Namaḥ* |	ॐ दत्ताय नमः ।
812.	*Oṃ Sarvajñāya Namaḥ* |	ॐ सर्वज्ञाय नमः ।
813.	*Oṃ Sarvakāmadāya Namaḥ* |	ॐ सर्वकामदाय नमः ।
814.	*Oṃ Kāmajite Namaḥ* |	ॐ कामजिते नमः ।
815.	*Oṃ Kāmapālāya Namaḥ* |	ॐ कामपालाय नमः ।
816.	*Oṃ Kāmine Namaḥ* |	ॐ कामिने नमः ।
817.	*Oṃ Kāmapradāgamāya Namaḥ* |	ॐ कामप्रदागमाय नमः ।
818.	*Oṃ Kāmavate Namaḥ* |	ॐ कामवते नमः ।
819.	*Oṃ Kāmapoṣāya Namaḥ* |	ॐ कामपोषाय नमः ।
820.	*Oṃ Sarvakāmanivartakāya Namaḥ* |	ॐ सर्वकामनिवर्तकाय नमः ।
821.	*Oṃ Sarvakāmaphalotpattaye Namaḥ* |	ॐ सर्वकामफलोत्पत्तये नमः ।
822.	*Oṃ Sarvakāmaphalapradāya Namaḥ* |	ॐ सर्वकामफलप्रदाय नमः ।
823.	*Oṃ Sarvakāmaphalaiḥ Pūjyāya Namaḥ* |	ॐ सर्वकामफलैः पूज्याय नमः ।
824.	*Oṃ Sarvakāmaphalāśrayāya Namaḥ* |	ॐ सर्वकामफलाश्रयाय नमः ।
825.	*Oṃ Viśvakarmaṇe Namaḥ* |	ॐ विश्वकर्मणे नमः ।
826.	*Oṃ Kṛtātmane Namaḥ* |	ॐ कृतात्मने नमः ।
827.	*Oṃ Kṛtajñāya Namaḥ* |	ॐ कृतज्ञाय नमः ।
828.	*Oṃ Sarvasākṣikāya Namaḥ* |	ॐ सर्वसाक्षिकाय नमः ।

829.	*Oṃ Sarvārambhaparityāgine Namaḥ* |	ॐ सर्वारम्भपरित्यागिने नमः |
830.	*Oṃ Jaḍonmattapiśācavate Namaḥ* |	ॐ जडोन्मत्तपिशाचवते नमः |
831.	*Oṃ Bhikṣave Namaḥ* |	ॐ भिक्षवे नमः |
832.	*Oṃ Bhikṣākarāya Namaḥ* |	ॐ भिक्षाकराय नमः |
833.	*Oṃ Bhīkṣṇāhāriṇe Namaḥ* |	ॐ भीक्ष्णाहारिणे नमः |
834.	*Oṃ Nirāśramaṇe Namaḥ* |	ॐ निराश्रमणे नमः |
835.	*Oṃ Akulāya Namaḥ* |	ॐ अकुलाय नमः |
836.	*Oṃ Anukūlāya Namaḥ* |	ॐ अनुकूलाय नमः|
837.	*Oṃ Vikalāya Namaḥ* |	ॐ विकलाय नमः |
838.	*Oṃ Akalāya Namaḥ* |	ॐ अकलाय नमः |
839.	*Oṃ Jaṭilāya Namaḥ* |	ॐ जटिलाय नमः |
840.	*Oṃ Vanacāriṇe Namaḥ* |	ॐ वनचारिणे नमः |
841.	*Oṃ Daṇḍine Namaḥ* |	ॐ दण्डिने नमः |
842.	*Oṃ Muṇḍine Namaḥ* |	ॐ मुण्डिने नमः |
843.	*Oṃ Gandhine Namaḥ* |	ॐ गन्धिने नमः |
844.	*Oṃ Dehadharmavihīnātmane Namaḥ* |	ॐ देहधर्मविहीनात्मने नमः |
845.	*Oṃ Ekākine Namaḥ* |	ॐ एकाकिने नमः |
846.	*Oṃ Saṅgavarjitāya Namaḥ* |	ॐ सङ्गवर्जिताय नमः |
847.	*Oṃ Āśramiṇe Namaḥ* |	ॐ आश्रमिणे नमः |
848.	*Oṃ Anāśramārambhāya Namaḥ* |	ॐ अनाश्रमारम्भाय नमः|
849.	*Oṃ Anācāriṇe Namaḥ* |	ॐ अनाचारिणे नमः |
850.	*Oṃ Karmavarjitāya Namaḥ* |	ॐ कर्मवर्जिताय नमः |
851.	*Oṃ Asandehine Namaḥ* |	ॐ असन्देहिने नमः |
852.	*Oṃ Sandehine Namaḥ* |	ॐ सन्देहिने नमः |

853.	*Oṃ Nakiñcanāya Namaḥ* |	ॐ नकिञ्चनाय नमः ।
854.	*Oṃ Nṛdehine Namaḥ* |	ॐ नृदेहिने नमः ।
855.	*Oṃ Dehaśūnyāya Namaḥ* |	ॐ देहशून्याय नमः ।
856.	*Oṃ Nābhāvine Namaḥ* |	ॐ नाभाविने नमः ।
857.	*Oṃ Bhāvanirgatāya Namaḥ* |	ॐ भावनिर्गताय नमः ।
858.	*Oṃ Nābrahmaṇe Namaḥ* |	ॐ नाब्रह्मणे नमः ।
859.	*Oṃ Parabrahmaṇe Namaḥ* |	ॐ परब्रह्मणे नमः ।
860.	*Oṃ Svayameva Nirākulāya Namaḥ* |	ॐ स्वयमेव निराकुलाय नमः ।
861.	*Oṃ Anaghāya Namaḥ* |	ॐ अनघाय नमः ।
862.	*Oṃ Agurave Namaḥ* |	ॐ अगुरवे नमः ।
863.	*Oṃ Nāthanāthottamāya Namaḥ* |	ॐ नाथनाथोत्तमाय नमः
864.	*Oṃ Gurave Namaḥ* |	ॐ गुरवे नमः ।
865.	*Oṃ Dvibhujāya Namaḥ* |	ॐ द्विभुजाय नमः ।
866.	*Oṃ Prākṛtāya Namaḥ* |	ॐ प्राकृताय नमः ।
867.	*Oṃ Janakāya Namaḥ* |	ॐ जनकाय नमः ।
868.	*Oṃ Pitāmahāya Namaḥ* |	ॐ पितामहाय नमः ।
869.	*Oṃ Anātmane Namaḥ* |	ॐ अनात्मने नमः ।
870.	*Oṃ Nacanānātmane Namaḥ* |	ॐ नचनानात्मने नमः ।
871.	*Oṃ Nītaye Namaḥ* |	ॐ नीतये नमः ।
872.	*Oṃ Nītimatāṃ Varāya Namaḥ* |	ॐ नीतिमतां वराय नमः
873.	*Oṃ Sahajāya Namaḥ* |	ॐ सहजाय नमः ।
874.	*Oṃ Sadṛśāya Namaḥ* |	ॐ सदृशाय नमः ।
875.	*Oṃ Siddhāya Namaḥ* |	ॐ सिद्धाय नमः ।
876.	*Oṃ Ekāya Namaḥ* |	ॐ एकाय नमः ।
877.	*Oṃ Cinmātrāya Namaḥ* |	ॐ चिन्मात्राय नमः ।
878.	*Oṃ Nakartre Namaḥ* |	ॐ नकर्त्रे नमः ।
879.	*Oṃ Kartre Namaḥ* |	ॐ कर्त्रे नमः ।
880.	*Oṃ Bhoktre Namaḥ* |	ॐ भोक्त्रे नमः ।

881.	*Oṃ Bhogavivarjitāya Namaḥ* |	ॐ भोगविवर्जिताय नमः |
882.	*Oṃ Turīyāya Namaḥ* |	ॐ तुरीयाय नमः |
883.	*Oṃ Turīyātītāya Namaḥ* |	ॐ तुरीयातीताय नमः |
884.	*Oṃ Svacchāya Namaḥ* |	ॐ स्वच्छाय नमः |
885.	*Oṃ Sarvamayāya Namaḥ* |	ॐ सर्वमयाय नमः |
886.	*Oṃ Sarvādhiṣṭhānarūpaya Namaḥ* |	ॐ सर्वाधिष्ठानरूपय नमः |
887.	*Oṃ Sarvadhyeyavivarjitāya Namaḥ* |	ॐ सर्वध्येयविवर्जिताय नमः |
888.	*Oṃ Sarvalokanivāsātmane Namaḥ* |	ॐ सर्वलोकनिवासात्मने नमः |
889.	*Oṃ Sakalottamavanditāya Namaḥ*	ॐ सकलोत्तमवन्दिताय नमः
890.	*Oṃ Dehabhṛte Namaḥ* |	ॐ देहभृते नमः |
891.	*Oṃ Dehakṛte Namaḥ* |	ॐ देहकृते नमः |
892.	*Oṃ Dehātmane Namaḥ* |	ॐ देहात्मने नमः |
893.	*Oṃ Dehabhāvanāya Namaḥ* |	ॐ देहभावनाय नमः |
894.	*Oṃ Dehine Namaḥ* |	ॐ देहिने नमः |
895.	*Oṃ Dehavibhaktāya Namaḥ* |	ॐ देहविभक्ताय नमः |
896.	*Oṃ Dehabhāvaprakāśanāya Namaḥ* |	ॐ देहभावप्रकाशनाय नमः |
897.	*Oṃ Layasthāya Namaḥ* |	ॐ लयस्थाय नमः |
898.	*Oṃ Layavide Namaḥ* |	ॐ लयविदे नमः |
899.	*Oṃ Layabhāvāya Namaḥ* |	ॐ लयभावाय नमः |
900.	*Oṃ Bodhavate Namaḥ* |	ॐ बोधवते नमः |
901.	*Oṃ Layātītāya Namaḥ* |	ॐ लयातीताय नमः |
902.	*Oṃ Layasyāntāya Namaḥ* |	ॐ लयस्यान्ताय नमः |
903.	*Oṃ Layabhāvanivāraṇāya Namaḥ*	ॐ लयभावनिवारणाय नमः
904.	*Oṃ Vimukhāya Namaḥ* |	ॐ विमुखाय नमः |
905.	*Oṃ Pramukhāya Namaḥ* |	ॐ प्रमुखाय नमः |

906.	*Oṃ Pratyaṅmukhavadācāriṇe Namaḥ* |	ॐ प्रत्यङ्मुखवदाचारिणे नमः |
907.	*Oṃ Viśvabhuje Namaḥ* |	ॐ विश्वभुजे नमः |
908.	*Oṃ Viśvaghṛṣe Namaḥ* |	ॐ विश्वघृषे नमः |
909.	*Oṃ Viśvāya Namaḥ* |	ॐ विश्वाय नमः |
910.	*Oṃ Viśvakṣemakarāya Namaḥ* |	ॐ विश्वक्षेमकराय नमः |
911.	*Oṃ Avikṣiptāya Namaḥ* |	ॐ अविक्षिप्ताय नमः |
912.	*Oṃ Apramādine Namaḥ* |	ॐ अप्रमादिने नमः |
913.	*Oṃ Parārdhaye Namaḥ* |	ॐ परार्धये नमः |
914.	*Oṃ Paramārthadṛśe Namaḥ* |	ॐ परमार्थदृशे नमः |
915.	*Oṃ Svānubhavavihīnāya Namaḥ* |	ॐ स्वानुभवविहीनाय नमः |
916.	*Oṃ Svānubhavaprakāśanāya Namaḥ* |	ॐ स्वानुभवप्रकाशनाय नमः |
917.	*Oṃ Nirindriyāya Namaḥ* |	ॐ निरिन्द्रियाय नमः |
918.	*Oṃ Nirbuddhaye Namaḥ* |	ॐ निर्बुद्धये नमः |
919.	*Oṃ Nirābhāsāya Namaḥ* |	ॐ निराभासाय नमः |
920.	*Oṃ Nirākṛtāya Namaḥ* |	ॐ निराकृताय नमः |
921.	*Oṃ Nirahaṅkārāya Namaḥ* |	ॐ निरहङ्काराय नमः |
922.	*Oṃ Rūpātmane Namaḥ* |	ॐ रूपात्मने नमः |
923.	*Oṃ Nirvapuṣe Namaḥ* |	ॐ निर्वपुषे नमः |
924.	*Oṃ Sakalāśrayāya Namaḥ* |	ॐ सकलाश्रयाय नमः |
925.	*Oṃ Śokaduḥkhaharāya Namaḥ* |	ॐ शोकदुःखहराय नमः |
926.	*Oṃ Bhogamokṣaphalapradāya Namaḥ* |	ॐ भोगमोक्षफलप्रदाय नमः |
927.	*Oṃ Suprasannāya Namaḥ* |	ॐ सुप्रसन्नाय नमः |
928.	*Oṃ Sūkṣmāya Namaḥ* |	ॐ सूक्ष्माय नमः |

929.	*Oṃ Śabdabrahmārthasaṃgṛhāya Namaḥ* |	ॐ शब्दब्रह्मार्थसंगृहाय नमः |
930.	*Oṃ Āgamāpāya Śūnyāya Namaḥ* |	ॐ आगमापाय शून्याय नमः|
931.	*Oṃ Sthānadāya Namaḥ* |	ॐ स्थानदाय नमः |
932.	*Oṃ Satāṅgataye Namaḥ* |	ॐ सताङ्गतये नमः |
933.	*Oṃ Ākṛtāya Namaḥ* |	ॐ आकृताय नमः |
934.	*Oṃ Sukṛtāya Namaḥ* |	ॐ सुकृताय नमः |
935.	*Oṃ Kṛtakarmavinirvṛtāya Namaḥ*	ॐ कृतकर्मविनिर्वृताय नमः
936.	*Oṃ Bhedatrayaharāya Namaḥ* |	ॐ भेदत्रयहराय नमः |
937.	*Oṃ Dehatrayavinirgatāya Namaḥ*|	ॐ देहत्रयविनिर्गताय नमः |
938.	*Oṃ Sarvakāmapradāya Namaḥ* |	ॐ सर्वकामप्रदाय नमः |
939.	*Oṃ Sarvakāmanivartakāya Namaḥ* |	ॐ सर्वकामनिवर्तकाय नमः |
940.	*Oṃ Siddheśvarāya Namaḥ* |	ॐ सिद्धेश्वराय नमः |
941.	*Oṃ Ajarāya Namaḥ* |	ॐ अजराय नमः |
942.	*Oṃ Pañcabāṇadarpahutāśanāya Namaḥ* |	ॐ पञ्चबाणदर्पहुताशनाय नमः |
943.	*Oṃ Caturākṣarabījātmane Namaḥ*	ॐ चतुराक्षरबीजात्मने नमः
944.	*Oṃ Svabhuve Namaḥ* |	ॐ स्वभुवे नमः |
945.	*Oṃ Citkīrtibhūṣaṇāya Namaḥ* |	ॐ चित्कीर्तिभूषणाय नमः |
946.	*Oṃ Agādhabuddhaye Namaḥ* |	ॐ अगाधबुद्धये नमः |
947.	*Oṃ Akṣubdhāya Namaḥ* |	ॐ अक्षुब्धाय नमः |
948.	*Oṃ Candrasūryāgnilocanāya Namaḥ* |	ॐ चन्द्रसूर्याग्निलोचनाय नमः |
949.	*Oṃ Yamadaṃṣṭrāya Namaḥ* |	ॐ यमदंष्ट्राय नमः |
950.	*Oṃ Atisaṃhartre Namaḥ* |	ॐ अतिसंहर्त्रे नमः |
951.	*Oṃ Paramānandasāgarāya Namaḥ* |	ॐ परमानन्दसागराय नमः |

952.	*Oṃ Līlāviśvambharāya Namaḥ |*	ॐ लीलाविश्वम्भराय नमः ।
953.	*Oṃ Bhānave Namaḥ |*	ॐ भानवे नमः ।
954.	*Oṃ Bhairavāya Namaḥ |*	ॐ भैरवाय नमः ।
955.	*Oṃ Bhīmalocanāya Namaḥ |*	ॐ भीमलोचनाय नमः ।
956.	*Oṃ Brahmacarmāmbarāya Namaḥ |*	ॐ ब्रह्मचर्माम्बराय नमः ।
957.	*Oṃ Kālāya Namaḥ |*	ॐ कालाय नमः ।
958.	*Oṃ Acalāya Namaḥ |*	ॐ अचलाय नमः ।
959.	*Oṃ Calanāntakāya Namaḥ |*	ॐ चलनान्तकाय नमः ।
960.	*Oṃ Ādidevāya Namaḥ |*	ॐ आदिदेवाय नमः ।
961.	*Oṃ Jagadyonaye Namaḥ |*	ॐ जगद्योनये नमः ।
962.	*Oṃ Vāsavāri Vimardanāya Namaḥ*	ॐ वासवारि विमर्दनाय नमः।
963.	*Oṃ Vikarmakarmakarmajñāya Namaḥ |*	ॐ विकर्मकर्मकर्मज्ञाय नमः ।
964.	*Oṃ Ananya Gamakāya Namaḥ |*	ॐ अनन्य गमकाय नमः ।
965.	*Oṃ Agamāya Namaḥ |*	ॐ अगमाय नमः ।
966.	*Oṃ Abaddhakarmaśūnyāya Namaḥ |*	ॐ अबद्धकर्मशून्याय नमः ।
967.	*Oṃ Kāmarāgakulakṣayāya Namaḥ*	ॐ कामरागकुलक्षयाय नमः।
968.	*Oṃ Yogāndhakāramathanāya Namaḥ |*	ॐ योगान्धकारमथनाय नमः ।
969.	*Oṃ Padmajanmādivanditāya Namaḥ |*	ॐ पद्मजन्मादिवन्दिताय नमः ।
970.	*Oṃ Bhaktakāmāya Namaḥ |*	ॐ भक्तकामाय नमः ।
971.	*Oṃ Agrajāya Namaḥ |*	ॐ अग्रजाय नमः ।
972.	*Oṃ Cakriṇe Namaḥ |*	ॐ चक्रिणे नमः ।
973.	*Oṃ Bhāvanirbhāvakāya Namaḥ |*	ॐ भावनिर्भावकाय नमः ।
974.	*Oṃ Bhedāṅkāya Namaḥ |*	ॐ भेदाङ्काय नमः ।
975.	*Oṃ Mahate Namaḥ |*	ॐ महते नमः ।

976.	*Oṃ Agragāya Namaḥ* |	ॐ अग्रगाय नमः ।
977.	*Oṃ Niguhāya Namaḥ* |	ॐ निगुहाय नमः ।
978.	*Oṃ Gocarāntakāya Namaḥ* |	ॐ गोचरान्तकाय नमः ।
979.	*Oṃ Kālāgniśamanāya Namaḥ* |	ॐ कालाग्निशमनाय नमः ।
980.	*Oṃ Śaṅkha Cakra Ppadma Gadādharāya Namaḥ* |	ॐ शङ्खचक्रपद्मगदाधराय नमः ।
981.	*Oṃ Dīptāya Namaḥ* |	ॐ दीप्ताय नमः ।
982.	*Oṃ Dīnapataye Namaḥ* |	ॐ दीनपतये नमः ।
983.	*Oṃ Śāstre Namaḥ* |	ॐ शास्त्रे नमः ।
984.	*Oṃ Svacchandāya Namaḥ* |	ॐ स्वच्छन्दाय नमः ।
985.	*Oṃ Muktidāyakāya Namaḥ* |	ॐ मुक्तिदायकाय नमः ।
986.	*Oṃ Vyomadharmāmbarāya Namaḥ* |	ॐ व्योमधर्माम्बराय नमः ।
987.	*Oṃ Bhettre Namaḥ* |	ॐ भेत्त्रे नमः ।
988.	*Oṃ Bhasmadhāriṇe Namaḥ* |	ॐ भस्मधारिणे नमः ।
989.	*Oṃ Dharādharāya Namaḥ* |	ॐ धराधराय नमः ।
990.	*Oṃ Dharmaguptāya Namaḥ* |	ॐ धर्मगुप्ताय नमः ।
991.	*Oṃ Anvayātmane Namaḥ* |	ॐ अन्वयात्मने नमः ।
992.	*Oṃ Vyatirekārthanirṇayāya Namaḥ* |	ॐ व्यतिरेकार्थनिर्णयाय नमः ।
993.	*Oṃ Ekoneka Guṇabhāsā Bhāsa Nirbhāsavarjitāya Namaḥ* |	ॐ एकोनेक गुणभासा भास निर्भासवर्जिताय नमः ।
994.	*Oṃ Bhāvābhāva Svabhāvātmane Namaḥ* |	ॐ भावाभाव स्वभावात्मने नमः ।
995.	*Oṃ Bhāvābhāva Vibhāvavide Namaḥ* |	ॐ भावाभाव विभावविदे नमः ।
996.	*Oṃ Yogīhṛdayaviśrāmāya Namaḥ*|	ॐ योगीहृदयविश्रामाय नमः।
997.	*Oṃ Anantavidyāvivardhanāya Namaḥ* |	ॐ अनन्तविद्याविवर्धनाय नमः ।

998.	*Oṃ Vighnāntakāya Namaḥ* |	ॐ विघ्नान्तकाय नमः |
999.	*Oṃ Trikālajñāya Namaḥ* |	ॐ त्रिकालज्ञाय नमः |
1000.	*Oṃ Tattvātmajñānasāgarāya Namaḥ* |	ॐ तत्त्वात्मज्ञानसागराय नमः |

Iti Śrīmad Dattātreya Sahasranāmāvalī Sampūrṇam ||

इति श्रीमद् दत्तात्रेय सहस्रनामावली सम्पूर्णम् ॥

About the Author

(http://Ramamurthy.jaagruti.co.in)

Dr. Ramamurthy is a versatile personality having experience and expertise in various areas of banking, related IT solutions, information security, IT audit, Vedas, Samskrutam and so on.

His thirst for continuous learning does not subside. Even at the age of late fifties, he did research on a unique topic "Information Technology and Samskrutam" and obtained Ph.D. – doctorate degree from University of Madras. He is into a project of developing a Samskrutam based compiler.

It is his passion to spread his knowledge and experience through conducting classes, training programs and writing books.

He has already published books as detailed below. Further books are in pipe-line.

#	Title	Remarks	Pages
		Indology Related	
1.	*Shrī Lalitā Sahasranāmam*	English Translation of Shrī *Bhāskararāya's Bhāśyam*	750
2.	Power of *Shrī Vidyā*	The Secrets Demystified – With Lucid English Rendering and Commentaries	80
3.	ஸ்ரீ வித்யையின் ஶக்தி	ஸ்ரீ வித்யா ரகசியங்கள்	100
4.	*Samatā* – समता	An Exposition of Similarities in *Lalitā Sahasranāma* with *Soundaryalaharī*, *Saptaśatī*, *Viśṇu Sahasranāma* and *Shrīmad Bhagavad Gīta*	172
5.	ஸமதா – समता	ஸ்ரீ லலிதா ஸஹஸ்ரநாமம் ஸௌந்தர்யலஹரீ, ஸப்தஶதீ, ஸ்ரீ விஷ்ணு ஸஹஸ்ரநாமம் மற்றும் ஸ்ரீமத் பகவத் கீதைகளில் ஒற்றுமையின் ஒரு வெளிப்பாடு	266
6.	*Advaita* In *Shākta*	Advaita Philosophy Discussed in Shakta Related Books	80
7.	*Shrī Lalitā Triśatī*	300 Divine Names of The Celestial Mother – **English** Translation of *Shrī Ādhi Śaṅkara's Bhāśyam*	193
8.	ஸ்ரீ லலிதா த்ரிஶதி	300 Divine Names of The Celestial Mother – Tamil Translation of *Shrī Ādi Śaṅkara's Bhāśyam*	234

#	Title	Remarks	Pages
9.	Secrets of *Mahāśakti*	Chandi Demystified	78
10.	*Daśa Mahā Vidyā*	Ten Cosmic Forms of The Divine Mother	60
11.	ஸ்ரீ வித்யா பேதங்கள்	ஸ்ரீவித்யா உபாசனையின் படிகள் - கோவை ஶதச் சண்டீ மலர்	51
12.	*Shrīvidya* Variances	Variances In Srividya Upasana	50
13.	ஸ்ரீ தேவீ ஸ்துதிகள்	பல முக்கிய அம்பாள் ஸ்தோத்ரங்கள்	133
14.	Śrī Devī Stutis – श्रीदेवी स्तुति:	Various Important Stotras of Sri Devi	223
15.	ஷண்மத மந்த்ரங்கள்	பொள்ளாச்சி ஸ்ரீ ஸஹஸ்ரசண்டீ மஹாயாக நினைவு மலர்	145
16.	*Śanmata Mantras* – षण्मत मन्त्रा:	Important Mantras Relating to Gods of Six Religions	87
17.	தேவதா மந்த்ரங்கள்	அக்கரைப்பட்டி ஸஹஸ்ரசண்டீ மஹாயாக நினைவு மலர்	32
18.	ஆதி ஶங்கரரும் ஷண்மதமும்	ஷண்மதங்களைப் பற்றிய ஒரு அறிமுகம்	32
19.	ஸ்ரீ ஷண்மத தேவதா அர்ச்சனை	ஸ்ரீ மஹா கும்பாபிஷேக மலர்	64
20.	*Vaidhīka* Wedding	Typical Wedding Process in English	56
21.	வைதீகத் திருமணம்	Typical Wedding Process in Tamil	57
22.	ஸ்ரீகுரு பாத பூஜா விதானம்	சித்தகிரி ஸஹஸ்ரசண்டீ மலர்	44
23.	குரு வார வழிபாடு		70
24.	ஸ்ரீவித்யா ஷடாம்னாய மந்த்ரங்கள்	சித்தகிரி ஸஹஸ்ரசண்டீ மலர்	60
25.	*Ekatā*	Oneness Among Shiva, *Viṣṇu* and Shakti	277
26.	ஏகதா - एकता	ஶிவபெருமான், விஷ்ணு மற்றும் ஶக்திக்குள் ஒற்றுமை	370
27.	*Vedas* – An Analytical Perspective	A Description of Veda, Vedanta, Vedanga, Jyotisha, Shastra, Etc.	240
28.	வேதங்கள் - ஒரு பகுப்பாய்வு	A Description of Veda, Vedanta, Vedanga, Jyotisha, Shastra, Etc.	280
29.	பரமாச்சார்யாள் நோக்கில் ஸ்ரீ லலிதாம்பிகா	The Explanation Given by Paramacharya on Some of The Names in Lalitā *Sahasranāma*	175
30.	*Ṣaṇṇavati Tarpaṇa*	Repaying Debts to Ancestors	42
31.	ஷண்ணவதி தர்பணம்	முன்னோர் கடன் தீர்த்தல்	48
32.	*Shrī Mahā Pratyangirā Devī*	Holy Divine Mother in Ferocious Form	41
33.	ஸ்ரீ மஹா ப்ரத்யங்கிரா தேவீ	தெய்வீக அன்னையின் பயங்கர வடிவம்	51
34.	*Śrī Chakra Navāvarṇam*	Marvels of *Śrī Chakra*	115
35.	ஸ்ரீ சக்ர நவாவர்ணம்	ஸ்ரீ சக்ரத்தின் அதிசயங்கள்	130

#	Title	Remarks	Pages
36.	அம்பிகையின் (திரு) அவதாரங்கள்	ஸ்ரீ தேவியின் பல்வேறு அவதாரங்கள்	142
37.	Incarnations of Holy Mother	Different Incarnations of *Śrī Devī*	140
38.	ஸ்ரீ பிரணவானந்தர் - ஒரு சரிதம்	ஒரு அரிய ஸ்வாமிகளின் திவ்ய சரிதம்	121
39.	ஸன்யாஸம் - ஓர் அலசல்	ஹிந்து மத ஸன்யாஸ பேதங்கள் - ஒரு பகுப்பாய்வு	140
40.	Asceticism – An Analysis	A Study of Hindu *Sanyasam*	140
41.	ஶாந்தமும் ப்ரணவமும்	(ஸ்ரீ ஶாந்தானந்தரும் ஸ்ரீ ப்ரணவானந்தரும்) குரு சிஷ்யருக்கு உபதேசங்கள்	120
42.	ஸ்ரீ ஸஹஸ்ராக்ஷரீ வித்யா	2020 சாதுர்மாஸ்ய மலர்	84
43.	*Shakta Upanishats*	*Upanishats* About *Sri Devi*	385
44.	ஶாக்த உபநிஷதங்கள்	*Upanishats* About *Sri Devi*	400
45.	ஸ்ரீ **தேவீ கீதை**	Sri Devi Geeta	194
46.	*Śrī Devī Gīta*	Sri Devi Geeta	180
47.	*Śrī Gāyatrī Sahasranāmam*	1,000 Divine Names of *Śrī Gāyatrī Mātā*	392
48.	ஸ்ரீ **காயத்ரி** ஸஹஸ்ரநாமம்	ஸ்ரீ **காயத்ரி** மாதாவின் 1,000 திவ்ய நாமங்கள்	450
49.	ஸ்ரீ ஸௌந்தர்யலஹரீ - ஒரு உள் அறிவு	ஒரு உள்-அறிவு	250
50.	*Śrī Soundaryalaharī* – an Insight	An Insight	200
51.	ஸ்ரீ ஶிவானந்த^{3}லஹரீ- ஒரு உள் அறிவு	ஒரு உள்-அறிவு	176
52.	*Śrī Śivānandalaharī* – an Insight	An Insight	129
53.	*Śrī Vārāhī Devī*	Holy Divine Mother with A Hog Face	96
54.	ஸ்ரீ வாராஹீ தேவீ	பன்றி முகத்துடன் கூடிய புனிதத் தெய்வீக அன்னை	106
55.	Śrī Vijaya Bhairavar	A Terrifying, Sacred, Divine Form of Lord Shiva	164
56.	ஸ்ரீ விஜய பை$_4$ரவர்	ஶிவபெருமானின் ஒரு திகிலூட்டும் புனித தெய்வீக உருவம்	188
57.	ஸ்ரீ ப$_4$த்$_3$ர காளீ	ஸ்ரீ தேவியின் ஒரு திகிலூட்டும் புனித தெய்வீக உருவம் – 1st Devi of Dasha Maha Vidya	226
58.	*Śrī Bhadra Kālī*	A Startling, Sacred and Divine Form of *Śrī Devī* – 1st Devi of Dasha Maha Vidya	224
59.	திதி^{2} நித்யா தே^{3}விகள்	16 *Tithi Nitya Devis*	230
60.	*Tithi Nityā Devis*	16 *Tithi Nitya Devis*	186
61.	ஸ்ரீ தாரா – நீல ஸரஸ்வதீ	2nd Devi of Dasha Maha Vidya	182
62.	*Śrī Tārā Devī* – Blue *Saraswatī*	2nd Devi of Dasha Maha Vidya	174
63.	*Śrī Tripura Sundarī Devī*	3rd Devi of Dasha Maha Vidya	182
64.	ஸ்ரீ த்ரிபுர ஸுந்தரீ தேவீ	3rd Devi of Dasha Maha Vidya	192

#	Title	Remarks	Pages
65.	*Śrī Bhuvaneshwari Devī*	4th Devi of Dasha Maha Vidya	137
66.	ஸ்ரீ புவனேஸ்வரீ தேவீ	4th Devi of Dasha Maha Vidya	151
67.	*Śrī Tripura Bhairavi Devi*	5th Devi of Dasha Maha Vidya	132
68.	ஸ்ரீ த்ரிபுர பைரவீதேவீ	5th Devi of Dasha Maha Vidya	146
69.	*Śrī Kamalātmikā Devi*	6th Devi of Dasha Maha Vidya	138
70.	ஸ்ரீ சின்ன மஸ்தா தேவீ	6th Devi of Dasha Maha Vidya	164
71.	*Śrī Dhūmāvatī Devī*	7th Devi of Dasha Maha Vidya	141
72.	ஸ்ரீ தூமாவதீ தேவீ	7th Devi of Dasha Maha Vidya	166
73.	*Śrī Bhagalāmukhī Devī*	8th Devi of Dasha Maha Vidya	158
74.	ஸ்ரீ பகலாமுகீ தேவீ	8th Devi of Dasha Maha Vidya	186
75.	*Śrī Mātangī Devī*	9th Devi of Dasha Maha Vidya	145
76.	ஸ்ரீ மாதங்கீ^{3} தே^{3}வீ	9th Devi of Dasha Maha Vidya	171
77.	*Śrī Kamalātmikā Devī*	10th Devi of Dasha Maha Vidya	170
78.	ஸ்ரீ கமலாத்மிகா தே^{3}வீ	10th Devi of Dasha Maha Vidya	226
79.	*Chaṇḍī Homa Vidhānam*	Process of Performing Chandi Homam	60
80.	சண்டி ஹோம விதானம்	Process of Performing Chandi Homam	80
81.	ஸ்ரீ ருத்^{3}ர ந்யாசம் & த்ரிஶதீ	300 Divine names of Lord Rudra and Japa Nyasam	224
82.	*Śrī Rudra Nyāsa & Triśatī*	300 Divine names of Lord Rudra and Japa Nyasam	160
83.	ஸ்ரீ ஸூர்ய ஸஹஸ்ர நாமம்	கருத்துக்களுடன் ஒரு விளக்கம்	404
84.	*Śrī Sūrya Sahasranāmam*	Explanation with Comments	320
85.	Kaliviḍambanam	An explanation	97
86.	கலிவிட^{3}ம்ப^{3}னம்	ஒரு விளக்கம்	100
87.	*Mūka Pancaśatī*	An Understanding	428
88.	மூக பஞ்ச ஶதி	ஒரு புரிதல்	577
89.	*Śrī Dattatreyar*	*Ādi Guru*	154
90.	ஸ்ரீ த^{3}த்தாத்ரேயர்	ஆதி^{3} கு^{3}ரு	174
91.	தெய்வீகத் தாயின் பத்து பிரபஞ்ச வடிவங்கள்	ஒருங்கிணைந்த த3ஶ மஹா வித்3யா	1,396
92.	Ten Cosmic Forms of the Divine Mother	Integrated *Daśa Mahā Vidyā*	1,402
93.	Ten Cosmic Forms of the Divine Mother – Volume 1	Integrated *Daśa Mahā Vidyā* – Volume 1	751
94.	Ten Cosmic Forms of the Divine Mother – Volume 1	Integrated *Daśa Mahā Vidyā* – Volume 2	678
95.	ஸ்ரீ த^{3}த்தாத்ரேய ஸஹஸ்ரநாம	பா^{4}ஷ்யம்	395
96.	*Śrī Dattatreya Sahasranāma*	*Bhāşyam*	310
	Applied Samskrutam Based		
97.	*Paribhāshā Stora–S*	An Exploration of *Lalitā Sahasranāmam*	96

Hari Om Tat Sat

*****

www.ingramcontent.com/pod-product-compliance
Lightning Source LLC
Chambersburg PA
CBHW011802160726
48282CB00035B/1231

* 9 7 8 9 3 3 4 3 9 5 6 5 5 *